10th
BLUE
BOOK®
Dolls & Values

by Jan Foulke

photographs
by Howard Foulke

Published by

Hobby
House
Press
TM

Hobby House Press, Inc.
Cumberland, Maryland 21502

Other Titles by Author:

Blue Book of Dolls & Values®
2nd Blue Book of Dolls & Values®
3rd Blue Book of Dolls & Values®
4th Blue Book of Dolls & Values®
5th Blue Book of Dolls & Values®
6th Blue Book of Dolls & Values®
7th Blue Book of Dolls & Values®
8th Blue Book of Dolls & Values®
9th Blue Book of Dolls & Values®
Focusing on Effanbee Composition Dolls
Focusing on Treasury of Mme. Alexander Dolls
Focusing on Gebrüder Heubach Dolls
Kestner: King of Dollmakers
Simon & Halbig Dolls: The Artful Aspect
Doll Classics
Focusing on Dolls

The registered trademarks, the trademarks and the copyrights appearing in this book belong to the company under whose name they appear, unless otherwise noted.

The doll prices given within this book are intended as value guides rather than arbitrarily set prices. Each doll price recorded here is actually a compilation. The retail prices in this book are recorded as accurately as possible but in the case of errors, typographical, clerical or otherwise, the author and publisher assume no liability nor responsibility for any loss incurred by users of this book.

TITLE PAGE: A 24in (61cm) French Bébé by Rabery & Delphieu. *Kay & Wayne Jensen Collection.*

COVER (left to right): Gebrüder Heubach 8556 character, *Richard Wright Antiques*; 12in (31cm) vinyl *Shirley Temple, H & J Foulke, Inc.*; Kämmer & Reinhardt character baby, *Mary Barnes Kelley Collection.*

Using This Book

Doll collecting continues to increase in popularity every year. The great number of collectors entering the field has given rise to additional as well as larger doll shows, more dealers in dolls, more books on dolls, thicker doll magazines and more doll conventions and seminars, as well as an overwhelming offering of new dolls by

Composition *Sabu* by Mollye's, all original. See page 330 for additional information. *Dolly Valk Collection.*

mass-production companies and individual artists. This explosion has also increased the demand for old dolls and caused prices to rise as more collectors vie for the same relatively static number of old dolls.

With the average old doll representing a purchase of at least several hundred dollars, today's collectors must be as well-informed as possible about the dolls they are considering as additions to their collections. Since the first *BLUE BOOK OF DOLLS & VALUES* published in 1974, our objectives have remained the same:

• To present a book which will help collectors to identify dolls and learn more about them.

• To provide retail prices as a guide for buyers and sellers of dolls.

Since every edition of the *BLUE BOOK* has sold more copies than the previous one, we can only conclude that these objectives are in line with the needs of doll lovers, collectors, dealers and appraisers who keep buying the latest editions of our book.

The dolls presented in this book are listed alphabetically by maker, material or the trade name of the individual doll. An extensive index has been provided to help in locating a specific doll. Of course, in a book this size, not every doll ever made can be discussed, but we have tried to include a broad spectrum of dolls which are available, desirable, interesting, popular and even some that are rare.

For each doll we have provided historical information, a description of the doll, a copy of the mark or label, the retail selling price and a photograph or picture reference to a previous edition of the *BLUE BOOK* as there is not enough space to show a photograph of each doll in each edition.

The price for a doll which is listed in this price guide is the retail value of a doll fulfilling all of the criteria discussed in the following chapter if it is purchased from a dealer.

In some cases the doll sizes given are the only ones known to have been made, but in the cases of most of the French and German bisque, china, papier-mâché and wood dolls, sizes priced are chosen at random and listed sizes must not be interpreted as definitive. Additionally regarding size, it is impossible to list every doll in every possible size, especially for dolls which range from 6 to 42 inches (15 to 106cm). The user will need to call a little common sense into play to interpolate a price for an unlisted size.

The historical information given for some of the dolls would have been much more difficult to compile were it not for the original research already published by Dorothy S., Elizabeth A. and Evelyn J. Coleman; Johana G. Anderton; and Jürgen and Marianne Cieslik.

The data for the retail prices was gathered during 1989 and 1990 from antique shops and shows, auctions, doll shops and shows, advertisements in collectors' periodicals, lists from doll dealers, and purchases and sales reported by both collectors and dealers. This information, along with our own valuations and judgments, was computed into the range of prices shown in this book. If we could not find a sufficient number of dolls to be sure of giving a reliable range, we marked those prices "**."

In setting a price for each doll, we use a range to allow for the variables of originality, quality and condition which must be reflected in the price. As collectors become more sophisticated in their purchases, fine examples of a doll, especially those which are all original or with period clothing, can bring a premium of up to 50% more than prices quoted for ordinary examples. Sometimes a doll will bring a premium price because it is particularly cute, sweet, pretty or visually appealing, making an outstanding presentation.

There is no way to factor this appeal into a price guide.

The international market has been an important factor in the rise of domestic doll prices during the past few years because of the low value of the American dollar compared with foreign currency. The international interest has added a whole new dimension to the American doll market as increasing awareness of antique dolls in Japan, Germany, France and Switzerland among other countries is causing a great exodus and depletion of our supply of antique dolls.

Of particular interest in the international arena are French bisque bébés (except Steiners), French fashion ladies, German bisque character children, German bisque babies by Kestner, Kämmer & Reinhardt, and Hertel, Schwab & Co., German bisque closed-mouth shoulder heads, German bisque "dolly" faces (particularly small sizes) by Kestner, Kämmer & Reinhardt, and Handwerck, Lenci dolls, Käthe Kruse dolls and German celluloid dolls. This interest has caused continued price increases in some of these categories.

Although this outward flow of dolls has occurred several times during the past 25 years with the fluctuating international monetary rate, it has never before occurred to such an alarming extent. The Japanese market has been developing for some time and it is unpredictable how long this surge in dolls will continue. In various other areas of the arts, the Japanese swell has come and gone, but it shows no signs of diminishing in the doll area as yet. In the meantime, those doll categories of special interest to the Japanese will continue to rise in price.

All prices given for antique dolls are for those of good quality and condition, but showing normal wear, and appropriately dressed in new or old clothing, unless other specifications are given in the description accompanying that particular doll. Bisque or china heads should not be

Georgene Novelties **Raggedy Ann** with desirable black outlined nose. See page 364 for additional information. *Nancy A. Smith Collection.*

cracked, broken or repaired, but may have slight making imperfections, such as speckling, surface lines, darkened mold lines and uneven coloring. Bodies may have repairs or be nicely repainted, but should be old and appropriate to the head. A doll with old dress, shoes and wig will generally be higher than quoted prices as these items are in scarce supply and can easily cost over $50 each if purchased separately.

Prices given for modern dolls are for those in overall very good to excellent condition with original hair and clothing, except as noted. Composition may be lightly crazed, but should be colorful. Hard plastic and vinyl must be perfect. A never-played-with doll in original box with labels would bring a premium price.

The users of this book must keep in mind that no price guide is the final word. It cannot provide the absolute answer of what to pay. It should be used only as an aid in purchasing a doll. The final decision must be yours, for only you are on the scene, actually examining the specific doll in question. No book can take the place of actual field experience. Doll popularity can cycle; prices can fluctuate; regional variations can occur. Before you buy, do a lot of looking. Ask questions. Most dealers and collectors are glad to talk about their dolls and pleased to share their information with you.

6

Acknowledgements

Many people are important in the preparation of a book of this type. For their encouragement and support, again I want to thank our friends, associates, customers, fellow dealers, acquaintances, fans and readers in the doll world who helped make possible this *10th BLUE BOOK OF DOLLS & VALUES*.

Those who allowed us to use photographs of their dolls or who provided special information for use in this edition are indispensable: Mary Barnes Kelley, Ruth West, Miriam Blankman, Roberta Roberts, Betty Harms, Joanna Ott, Vern & Cathy Kiefer, Esther Schwartz, Lesley and Norman Hurford, Ingrid Liebers, Yvonne Baird, Eleanora Miller, Nancy A. Smith, Dolly Valk, Carole Stoessel Zvonar, Kay & Wayne Jensen, Anne Helm, David Simpson, Pearl Morley, Janet Anderson, Edna Black, Jane Alton, Virginia Ann Heyerdahl, Sheila Needle, Pat Brown, Margaret Benike, Becky & Jay Lowe, Elizabeth McIntyre, Maxine Salaman, Jackie Kaner, Richard Wright, Richard Saxman, Jimmy & Faye Rodolfos, Judy Newell, Joe Jackson & Joel Pearson, Rosemary Dent, Zelda Cushner, Richard W. Withington, Inc., and H & J Foulke, Inc.

Also much appreciation to several collectors who shared their wonderful dolls, but wish their contribution to remain anonymous and to the Colemans who allowed some marks to be reproduced from their book, *The Collector's Encyclopedia of Dolls*.

Thanks to Gary Ruddell and the staff at Hobby House Press, Inc., particularly to my editor Donna H. Felger, not only for the nitty-gritty details, but also the wonderful comprehensive index.

And, of course, to Howard, for without his beautiful photographs there would be no book.

Jan Foulke
October 1990

30in (76cm) German china head of the 1860s with exceptional molding. See page 138 for additional information. *H & J Foulke, Inc.*

Investing in Dolls

With the price of the average old doll representing a purchase of at least several hundred dollars in today's doll market, the assembling of a doll collection becomes rather costly. Actually, very few people buy dolls strictly as an investment; most collectors buy a doll because they like it. It has appeal to them for some reason: perhaps as an object of artistic beauty, perhaps because it evokes some kind of sentiment, perhaps it fills some need that they feel or speaks to something inside them. It is this personal feeling toward the doll which makes it of value to the collector.

However, most collectors expect to at least break even when they eventually sell their dolls. Unfortunately, there is no guarantee that any particular doll will appreciate consistently year after year; however, the track record for old or antique dolls is fairly good. If you are thinking of the future sale of your collection, be wary of buying expensive new or reproduction dolls. They have no track record and little resale value. Collectible dolls of the last 30 years are a risky market. Alexander dolls are a case in point. After many years of doubling their value the minute they were carried from the toy store shelves, dolls of the 1960s and 1980s have slid in price so that many are now bringing only 25% of their previous cost.

Because most collectors have only limited funds for purchasing dolls, they must be sure they are spending their dollars to the best advantage. There are many factors to consider when buying a doll, and this chapter will give some suggestions about what to look for and what to consider. Probably the primary tenet is that if a collector is not particularly well-informed about the doll he is thinking of adding to his collection, he should not purchase it unless he has confidence in the person selling it to him.

11in (31cm) bisque head **Bye-Lo Baby** socket head on composition body. See page 125 for additional information. *H & J Foulke, Inc.*

MARKS

Fortunately for collectors, most of the antique bisque, some of the papier-mâché, cloth and other types of antique dolls are marked or labeled. Marks and labels give the buyer confidence because they identify the trade name, the maker, the country of origin, the style or mold number, or perhaps even the patent date.

Most composition and modern dolls are marked with the maker's name and sometimes also the trade name of the doll and the date. Some dolls have tags sewn on or into their clothing to identify them; many still retain original hang tags.

Of course, many dolls are unmarked, but after you have seen quite a few dolls, you begin to notice their individual characteristics, so that you can often determine what a doll possibly is. When you have had some experience buying dolls, you begin to recognize an unusual face or an especially fine quality doll. Then there should be no hesitation about buying a doll marked only with a mold number or no mark at all. The doll has to speak for itself, and the price must be based upon the collector's frame of doll reference. That is, one must relate the face and quality to those of a known doll maker and make price judgments from that point.

QUALITY

The mark does not tell all about a doll. Two examples from the same mold could look entirely different and carry vastly different prices because of the quality of the work done on the doll, which can vary from head to head, even with dolls made from the same mold by one firm. To command top price, a bisque doll should have lovely bisque, decoration, eyes and hair.

Hard plastic *Ginny* with painted lashes, tagged clothes, Ginny button. See page 398 for additional information. *Nancy A. Smith Collection.*

Before purchasing a doll, the collector should determine whether the example is the best available of that type. Even the molding of one head can be much sharper with more delineation of details such as dimples or locks of hair. The molding detail is especially important to notice when purchasing dolls with character faces or molded hair.

The quality of the bisque should be smooth; dolls with bisque which is pimply, peppered with tiny black specks, unevenly colored or has noticeable firing lines on the face would be second choices at a lower price. However, collectors must keep in mind porcelain factories sold many heads with small manufacturing defects as companies were in business for profit and were producing expendable play items, not works of art. Small manufacturing defects do not devalue a doll. It is perfectly acceptable to have light speckling, light surface lines, firing lines in inconspicuous places, darkened mold lines, a few black specks or cheek rubs. The absolutely perfect bisque head is a rarity.

Since doll heads are hand-painted, the artistry of the decoration should be examined. The tinting of the complexion should be subdued and even, not harsh and splotchy. Artistic skill should be evident in the portrayal of the expression on the face and in details, such as the lips, eyebrows and eyelashes and particularly the eyes which should show highlights and shading when they are painted. On a doll with molded hair, individual brush marks to give the hair a more realistic look would be a desirable detail.

If a doll has a wig, the hair should be appropriate if not old. Dynel or synthetic wigs are not appropriate for antique dolls; a human hair or good quality mohair wig should be used. If a doll has glass eyes, they should have natural color and threading in the irises to give a lifelike appearance.

If a doll does not meet all of these standards, it should be priced lower than

16in (41cm) German bisque dolly face by Simon & Halbig, mold 1249 Santa. See page 384 for additional information. *H & J Foulke, Inc.*

one that does. Furthermore, an especially fine example will bring a premium over an ordinary but nice model.

CONDITION

Another factor which is important when pricing a doll is the condition. A bisque doll with a crack on the face or extensive professional repair involving the face would sell for one-quarter or less than a doll with only normal wear. An inconspicuous hairline would decrease the value

somewhat but in a rare doll it would not be as great a detriment as in a common doll. As the so-called better dolls are becoming more difficult to find, a hairline is more acceptable to collectors if there is a price adjustment. The same is true for a doll which has a spectacular face — a hairline would be less important to price in that doll than in one with an ordinary face.

Sometimes a head will have a factory flaw which occurred in the making, such as a firing crack, scratch, piece of kiln debris, dark specks, small bubbles, a ridge not smoothed out or light surface lines. Since the factory was producing toys for a profit and not creating works of art, all heads with slight flaws were not discarded, especially if they were inconspicuous or could be covered. If these factory defects are not detracting, they have little or no affect on the value of the doll.

It is to be expected that an old doll will show some wear: perhaps there is a rub on the nose or cheek, a few small "wig pulls" or maybe a chipped earring hole; a Schoenhut doll or a Käthe Kruse may have some scuffs; an old papier-mâché may have a few age cracks; a china head may show wear on the hair; an old composition body may have scuffed toes or missing fingers. These are to be expected and do not necessarily affect the value of the doll. However, a doll in exceptional condition will bring more than "book price."

Unless an antique doll is rare or you particularly want that specific doll, do not pay top price for a doll which needs extensive work: restringing, setting eyes, repairing fingers, replacing body parts, new wig or dressing. All of these repairs add up to a considerable sum at the doll hospital, possibly making the total cost of the doll more than it is really worth.

Composition dolls in perfect condition are becoming harder to find. As their material is so susceptible to the atmosphere, their condition can deteriorate literally overnight. Even in excellent condition, a composition doll nearly always has some fine crazing or slight fading. It is very difficult to find a composition doll in mint condition and even harder to be sure that it will stay that way. However, in order for a composition doll to bring "book" price, there should be a minimum of crazing, very good coloring, original uncombed hair and original clothes in very good condition. Pay less for a doll which does not have original clothes and hair or one which may be all original but shows extensive play wear. Pay even less for one which has

heavy crazing and cracking or other damages. For composition dolls which are all original and unplayed with in original boxes with little or no crazing, allow a premium of about 50% over "book" price.

Hard plastic and vinyl dolls must be in excellent condition if they are at "book" price. The hair should be perfect in the original set; clothes should be completely original, fresh and unfaded. Skin tones should be natural with good cheek color. Add a premium of 25-50% for mint dolls never removed from their original boxes.

BODY

In order to command top price, an old doll must have the original or an appropriate old body in good condition. If a doll does not have the correct type of body, the buyer ends up not with a complete doll, but with parts which may not be worth as much as one whole doll. As dolls are becoming more difficult to find, more are turning up with "put together" bodies. Many dolls are now entering the market from old collections which were assembled years ago. Some of these contain dolls which were "put together" before there was much information available about correct heads and bodies. Therefore, the body should be checked to make sure it is appropriate to the head, and all parts of the body should be checked to make sure that they are appropriate to each other. A body which has mixed parts from several makers or types of bodies is not worth as much as one which has correct parts.

Minor damage or repair to an old body does not affect the value of an antique doll. An original body carefully repaired, recovered or even if necessary completely repainted is preferable to a new one. An antique head on a new body would be worth only the value of its parts, whatever the price of the head and new body, not the full price of an antique doll. It is just a rule of thumb that an antique head is worth about 40-50% of the price of the complete doll. A very rare head could be worth up to 80%.

If there is a choice of body types for the same bisque head, a good quality ball-jointed composition body is more desirable that a crudely made five-piece body or stick-type body with just pieces of turned wood for upper arms and legs. Collectors prefer jointed composition bodies over kid ones for dolly-faced dolls, and pay more for the same face on a composition body.

Occasionally, the body adds value to the doll. In the case of bisque heads, a small doll with a completely jointed body, a French fashion-type with a wood-jointed body, a *Tête Jumeau* head on an adult body or a character baby head on a jointed toddler-type body would all be higher in price because of their special bodies.

As for the later modern dolls, a composition doll on the wrong body or a body in poor condition which is cracked and peeling would have a greatly reduced value. The same is true of a vinyl doll with replaced parts, body stains or chewed-off fingers.

CLOTHING

It is becoming increasingly difficult to find dolls in old clothing because as the years go by, fabrics continue to deteriorate. Consequently, collectors are paying more than "book price" for an antique doll if it has appropriate old clothes, shoes and hair. Even faded, somewhat worn, or carefully mended original or appropriate old clothes are preferable to new ones. As collectors become more sophisticated and selective, they realize the value of old doll clothing and accessories. Some dealers are now specializing in these areas. Good old leather doll shoes will bring over $75 per pair; a lovely Victorian white-work doll dress can easily cost $75; an old dress for a French fashion lady $300. Good old doll wigs can bring from $25 to $250.

However, when the clothing must be replaced and appropriate old clothing can-

not be obtained, the new clothes should be authentically styled for the age of the doll and constructed in fabrics which would have been available when the doll was produced. There are many reference books and catalog reprints which show dolls in original clothing, and doll supply companies offer patterns for dressing old dolls.

To bring top price, a modern doll must have original clothes. It is usually fairly

13in (33cm) unmarked brown composition *Patsy*-type girl. See page 113 for additional information. *H & J Foulke, Inc.*

simple to determine whether or not the clothing is original and factory made. Some makers even placed tags in the doll's clothing. Replaced clothing greatly reduces the price of modern dolls. Without the original clothing, it is often impossible to identify a modern doll as so many were made using the same face mold.

TOTAL ORIGINALITY

Totally original dolls nowadays are becoming rare. It is often difficult to determine whether the head and body and all other parts of the doll, including wig, eyes and clothes, have always been together. Many parts of a doll could be changed and clothing and accessories could be added over the years. Many dolls labeled "all original" are simply wearing contemporary clothing and wigs. Some collectors and dealers are "embellishing" the more expensive dolls by taking original clothing and wigs from cheaper dolls to further enhance the value of the more costly ones. Dolls with trunks of clothing and in boxed sets are particularly vulnerable to this type of raiding. Collectors should examine such items carefully before they pay ultra

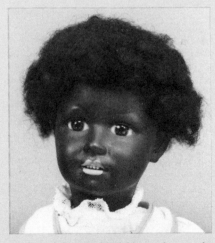

14in (36cm) German black bisque character by Simon & Halbig, mold 1368. See page 95 for additional information. *Private Collection.*

high prices for such ensembles. Of course, when these ensembles are genuine, they are the ultimate in doll collecting.

AGE

The oldest dolls do not necessarily command the highest prices. A lovely old china head with exquisite decoration and very unusual hairdo would bring a price of several thousand dollars, but not as much as a 20th century German bisque character child, one of which holds the current's world record doll price of nearly $170,000. Many desirable composition dolls of the 1930s and fairly recent but discontinued Alexander plastic dolls are selling at prices higher than older bisque dolls of 1890 to 1920. So in determining price, the age of the doll may or may not be significant.

SIZE

The size of a doll is usually taken into account when determining a price. Generally, the size and price for a certain doll are related: a smaller size is lower, a larger size is higher. However, there are a few exceptions on the small size. The 10in (25cm) #1 Jumeau, the 11in (28cm) *Shirley Temple,* the tiny German dolly-faced dolls on fully-jointed bodies and the 6in (9cm) *Wee Patsy* are examples of small dolls which bring higher prices than dolls in their series which may be larger.

AVAILABILITY

The price of a doll is directly related to its availability in most cases. The harder a doll is to find, the higher will be its price. Each year brings more new doll collectors than it brings newly discovered desirable old dolls; hence, the supply of old dolls is diminished. As long as the demand for certain antique and collectible dolls is greater than the supply, prices will rise. This explains the great increase in prices of less common dolls, such as the K & R and other German character children, early French dolls, early china heads and papier-mâchés, composition personality

12in (31cm) German bisque character baby by Armand Marseille, mold 560a. See page 321 for additional information. *H & J Foulke, Inc.*

dolls, Sasha dolls and some Alexander dolls which were made for only a limited period of time. Dolls which are fairly common, primarily the German dolly-faces and the later china head dolls which covered a long period of production, show a more gentle increase in price.

POPULARITY

There are fads in dolls just like in clothes, food and other aspects of life. Dolls which have recently risen in price because of their popularity are the early Jumeaus, small dolly-faces with jointed bodies, lady French fashion dolls, American cloth dolls, *Shirley Temples,* large composition babies, early *Barbie* dolls and the 8in (20cm) Alexander *Wendy* series dolls. Some dolls are popular enough to tempt collectors to pay prices higher than the availability factor warrants. Although *Shirley Temples,* Jumeaus, *Bye-Los, Hildas,* K & R 117, and some plastic Alexander dolls are not rare, the high prices they bring are due to their popularity.

DESIRABILITY

Some dolls may be very rare, but they do not bring a high price because they are not particularly desirable. There are not many collectors looking for them. Falling into this category are the dolls with shoulder heads made of rubber or rawhide. While an especially outstanding example will bring a high price, most examples bring very low prices in relationship to their rarity.

UNIQUENESS

Sometimes the uniqueness of a doll makes price determination very difficult. If a collector has never seen a doll exactly like it before, and it is not given in a price guide or even shown in any books, deciding what to pay can be a problem. In this case, the buyer has to use all of his available knowledge as a frame of reference in which to place the unknown doll. Perhaps a doll marked "A.M. 2000" or "S & H 1289" has been found, and the asking price is 25% higher than for the more commonly found numbers by that maker. Or perhaps a black *Kamkins* is offered for twice the price of a white one, or a French fashion lady with original wardrobe is offered at 60% more than a redressed one. In cases such as these, a collector must use his own judgment to determine what the doll is worth to him.

VISUAL APPEAL

Perhaps the most elusive aspect in pricing a doll is its visual appeal. Sometimes, particularly at auction, we have seen dolls bring well over their "book value" simply because of their look. Often this is nothing more than the handiwork of someone who had the ability to choose just the right wig, clothing and accessories to enhance the doll's visual appeal and make it look particularly cute, stunning, beautiful or otherwise especially outstanding.

Sometimes, though, the visual appeal comes from the face of the doll itself. It may be the way the teeth are put in, the placement of the eyes, the tinting on the face or the sharpness of the molding. Or it may not be any of these specific things; it may just be what some collectors refer to as the "presence" of the doll, an elusive undefinable quality which makes it just the best example known!

All-cloth doll by Rollinson. See page 368 for additional information. *Nancy A. Smith Collection.*

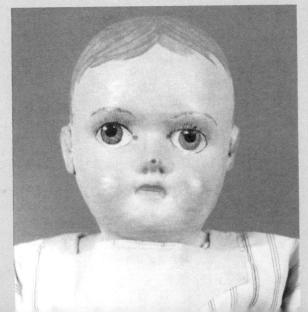

21in (53cm) German papier-mâché doll with flirting eyes. See page 339 for additional information. *Nancy A. Smith Collection.*

Selling A Doll

So many times we are asked by people, "How do I go about selling a doll?" that it seems a few paragraphs on the topic would be in order. The first logical step would be to look through the *BLUE BOOK* to identify the doll that you have and to ascertain a retail price. Work from there to decide what you might ask for your doll. It is very difficult for a private person to get a retail price for a doll.

Be realistic about the condition. If you have a marked 18in (46cm) *Shirley Temple* doll with combed hair, no clothing, faded face with crazing and a piece off of her nose, do not expect to get book price of $600 for her because that would be a retail price for an excellent doll, all original, in pristine unplayed-with condition if purchased from a dealer. Your very used doll is probably worth only $50 to $75 as it will have to be purchased by someone who would want to restore it.

If you have an antique doll with a perfect bisque head, but no wig, no clothes and unstrung, but having all of its body parts, you can probably expect to get about half its retail value depending upon how desirable that particular doll is. If your doll has perfect bisque head with original wig, clothing and shoes, you can probably get up to 75% of its retail value.

As to actually selling the doll, there are several possibilities. Possibly the easiest is to advertise in your local paper. You may not think there are any doll collectors in your area but there probably are. You might also check your local paper to see if anyone is advertising to purchase dolls; many dealers and collectors do so. Check the paper to find out about antique shows in your area. If anyone has dolls, ask if they would be interested in buying your doll. Also, you could inquire at antique shops in your area for dealers who specialize in dolls. You will probably get a higher price from a specialist than a general antique dealer as the former are more familiar with the market for specific dolls. A roster of doll specialists is available from The National Antique Doll Dealers Association, Inc., P.O. Box 143, Wellesley Hills, MA 02181.

You could consign your doll to an auction. If it is a common doll, it will probably do quite well at a local sale. If it is a more rare doll, consider sending it to one of the auction houses which specializes in selling dolls; most of them will accept one doll if it is a good one and they will probably get the best price for you. It would probably be worth your while to purchase a doll magazine (*Doll Reader®*, 900 Frederick St., Cumberland, MD 21502) in which you will find ads from auction houses, doll shows and leading dealers. You could advertise in doll magazines, but you might have to ship the doll and guarantee return privileges if the buyer does not like it.

If you cannot find your doll in the *BLUE BOOK*, it might be a good idea to have it professionally appraised. This will involve your paying a fee to have the doll evaluated. We provide this service and can be contacted through *Doll Reader* for which we write a regular column. Many museums and auction houses also appraise dolls.

17in (43cm) *Bébé Phenix* incised "*92." For further information see page 50. *Ruth West Antique Dolls*.

RIGHT: 21in (53cm) A 10 T Bébé. For further information see page 397. *Private Collection*.

ABOVE LEFT: 4½in (12cm) German all-bisque character incised "P 711." For further information see page 58. *H & J Foulke, Inc.*

ABOVE RIGHT: 3¼in (8cm) German all-bisque flapper with molded hat. For further information see page 61. *H & J Foulke, Inc.*

LEFT: German all-bisque nodders *Periwinkle* and *Scraps*. For further information see page 61. *H & J Foulke, Inc.*

3in (8cm) German all-bisque immobile children with all-bisque animals on a string. For further information see page 61. *H & J Foulke, Inc.*

German all-bisque immobile black family with adults 2¼in (6cm) tall. For further information see page 61. *H & J Foulke, Inc.*

Alt, Beck & Gottschalck #1304 boy with glass eyes. For further information see page 63. *H & J Foulke, Inc.*

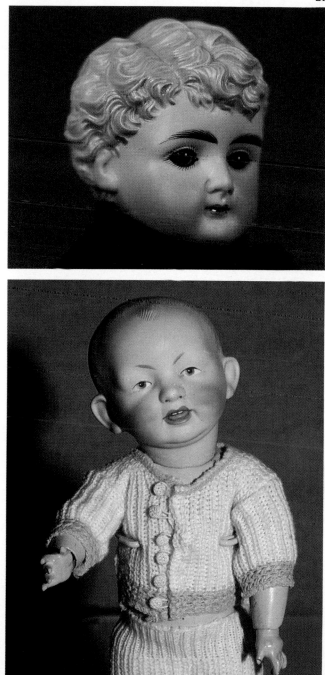

12in (31cm) Alt, Beck & Gottschalck #1322 character toddler. For further information see page 66. *Margaret Benike Collection.*

LEFT: 18in (46cm) Alt, Beck & Gottschalck #911 child, socket head on jointed composition body. For further information see page 64. *Maxine Salaman Collection.*

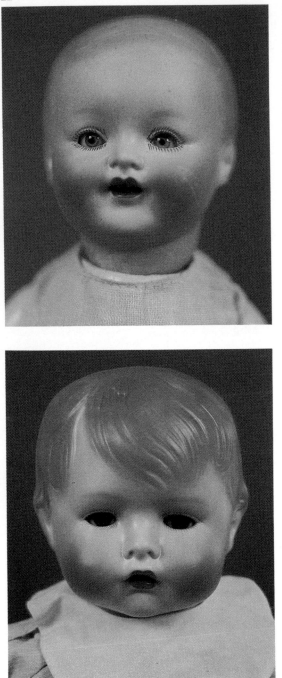

10in (25cm) Amberg *Vanta Baby* with bisque head, composition five-piece toddler body. For further information see page 71. *H & J Foulke, Inc.*

BELOW LEFT: 21in (53cm) *Baby Bo Kaye.* For further information see page 85. *Mary Barnes Kelley Collection.*

BELOW: 16in (41cm) Babyland Rag-type soldier, all original. For further information see page 86. *Jensen's Antique Dolls.*

7½in (19cm) Bähr & Pröschild 204 child, all original. For further information see page 87. *H & J Foulke, Inc.*

13in (33cm) Bähr & Pröschild 619 character baby. For further information see page 88. *Ruth West Antique Dolls.*

Bähr & Pröschild 604 character toddler. For further information see page 88. *H & J Foulke, Inc.*

23in (58cm) unmarked character toddler, probably by Bähr & Pröschild. For further information see page 88. *Ruth West Antique Dolls.*

14in (36cm) 137 Belton-type child. For further information see page 91. *H & J Foulke, Inc.*

LEFT: 22in (56cm) C.M. Bergmann child. For further information see page 92. *H & J Foulke, Inc.*

ABOVE: Kämmer & Reinhardt 100 *Baby.* For further information see page 95. *Richard Wright Antiques.*

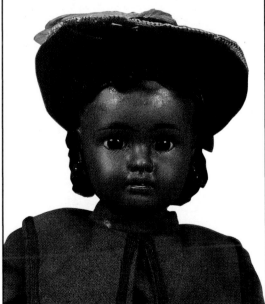

16in (41cm) Bähr & Pröschild 277 child. For further information see pages 94 and 95. *H & J Foulke, Inc.*

15in (38cm) brown Bébé Bru. For further information see page 94. *Private Collection.*

INSET: 18in (46cm) brown composition 134, probably German. For further information see page 113. *Kiefer Collection.*

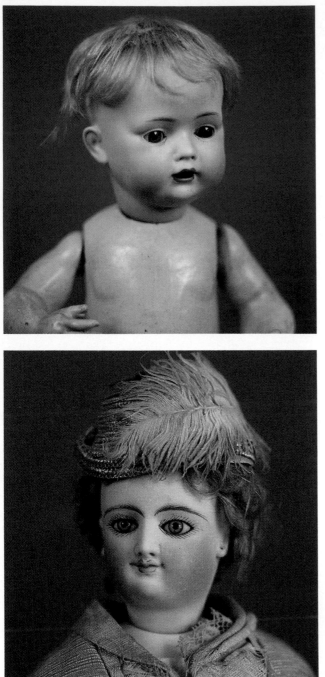

13in (33cm) George Borgfeldt character baby made by Bähr & Pröschild from their mold 620. For further information see page 115. *H & J Foulke, Inc.*

15in (38cm) smiling Bru fashion "D" with kid body and bisque hands. For further information see page 118. *Kay & Wayne Jensen Collection.*

BELOW RIGHT: 18in (46cm) Bru Brevete "2." For further information see page 119. *Jackie Kaner.*

22in (56cm) Circle Dot Bru. For further information see page 120. *Richard Wright Antiques.*

17in (43cm) Bru Bébé Teteur. For further information see page 120. *Private Collection.*

RIGHT: 11in (28cm) unmarked celluloid head character. For further information see page 131. *H & J Foulke, Inc.*

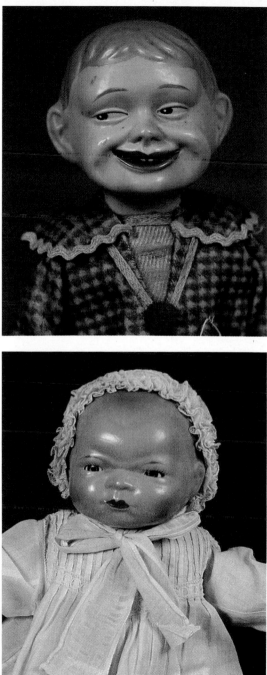

BELOW RIGHT: 13in (33cm) *Bye-Lo Baby* with composition head. For further information see page 125. *H & J Foulke, Inc.*

BELOW: 12in (31cm) Brückner cloth doll, all original. For further information see page 122. *Yvonne Baird Collection.*

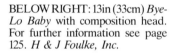

21in (53cm) all-celluloid baby with molded suit, butterfly mark with number 165. For further information see page 131. *Jensen's Antique Dolls*.

Alabama Indestructible Doll

Maker: Ella Smith Doll Co., Roanoke, Ala., U.S.A.
Date: 1900 - 1925
Material: All-cloth
Size: 11½ - 27in (29 - 69cm); 38in (96cm) black one known
Mark: On torso or leg, sometimes both:

PAT. NOV. 9, 1912

NO. 2
ELLA SMITH DOLL CO.

Alabama Baby: All-cloth painted with oils, tab-jointed shoulders and hips, flat derriere for sitting; painted hair (or rarely a wig), molded face with painted facial features, applied ears, (a few with molded ears); painted stockings and shoes (a few with bare feet); appropriate clothes; all in good condition, some wear acceptable.

or
"MRS. S. S. SMITH
Manufacturer and Dealer to
The Alabama Indestructible Doll
Roanoke, Ala.
PATENTED Sept. 26, 1905"
(also 1907 on some)

12in (31cm)	**$1800**
14 - 16in (36 - 41cm)	**1800 - 2000**
22 - 24in (56 - 61cm)	**2500 - 2900**
Black, 19in (48cm)	**6600****
Wigged 24in (61cm)	**3500****

**Not enough price samples to compute a reliable range.

19in (48cm) *Alabama Baby. Betty Harms Collection.*

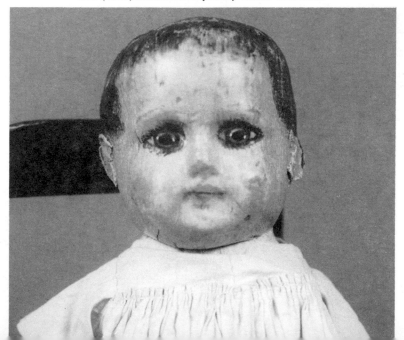

Madame Alexander

Maker: Alexander Doll Co. Inc., New York, N.Y., U.S.A.
Date: 1923 - on, but as early as 1912 the Alexander sisters were designing doll clothes and dressing dolls commercially.
Mark: Dolls themselves marked in various ways, usually "ALEXANDER". Clothing has a white cloth label with blue lettering sewn into a seam which says "MADAME ALEXANDER" and usually the name of the specific doll. Cloth and other early dolls are unmarked and identifiable only by the clothing label.

19in (48cm) *Little Shaver.* H & J Foulke, Inc.

CLOTH
Cloth Character Dolls: Ca. 1933 through the 1930s. All-cloth with one-piece arms and legs sewn on; mohair wig, molded mask face of felt or flocked fabric, painted eyes to the side, original clothes tagged with name of particular doll. Produced characters from *Little Women,* Charles Dickens, Longfellow and other literary works as well as storybook characters. (For photograph see *8th Blue Book,* page 21.)

16in (41cm) only
Fair	**$175 - 225**
Good	**325 - 375**
Mint	**650**

20in (51cm) *Alice*
Fair	**175 - 225**
Good	**325 - 375**
Mint	**650**

Cloth Baby: Ca. 1936: (For photograph see *7th Blue Book,* page 20.)
17in (43cm) Very good   **$375 - 425**
Cloth Dionne Quintuplet: Ca. 1935 (For photograph see *6th Blue Book,* page 18.)
17in (43cm) Very good   **$650 - 750**
Susie Q. & Bobby Q.: Ca. 1938. (For photograph see *6th Blue Book,* page 19.)
12 - 16in (31 - 41cm) Very good   **$500 - 550**
Little Shaver: 1942. Very good condition.
7in (18cm)	**$225 - 275**
10 - 12in (25 - 31cm)	**250 - 300**
16in (41cm)	**375 - 425**
20in (51cm)	**450 - 500**

COMPOSITION

Dionne Quintuplets: 1935. All-composition with swivel head, jointed hips and shoulders, toddler or bent-limb legs (some babies have cloth bodies with composition lower limbs); wigs or molded hair, sleep or painted eyes; original clothing, all in excellent condition.

Mark: "ALEXANDER" sometimes "DIONNE"

Clothing label:
"GENUINE
DIONNE QUINTUPLET DOLLS
ALL RIGHTS RESERVED
MADAME ALEXANDER, N.Y."
or
"DIONNE QUINTUPLET
(her name)
EXCLUSIVE LICENSEE
MADAM [sic] ALEXANDER
DOLL CO."

7 - 8in (18 - 20cm)	$ 250 - 275
matched set	1250 - 1500
10in (25cm) baby	325 - 350
11 - 12in (28 - 31cm) toddler	375 - 425
14in (36cm) toddler	475 - 525
16in (41cm) toddler	575 - 625
16in (41cm) baby with cloth body	400 - 450
Pins, each	85 - 95

16in (41cm) Dionne Quintuplet *Marie*, all original. *H & J Foulke, Inc.*

13in (33cm) *Betty*, all original. *H & J Foulke, Inc.*

Each Quint has her own color for clothing:
Yvonne — pink
Annette — yellow
Cecile — green
Emelie — lavender
Marie — blue

Foreign and Storyland: Ca. 1935 to mid 1940s. All-composition with one-piece head and body on smaller ones and separate head on larger ones, jointed shoulders and hips; mohair wig, painted eyes; original tagged clothes; all in excellent condition.
Mark: On back: "Mme. Alexander"

7 - 9in (18 - 23cm)	
Foreign Countries	$175 - 200
Storybook Characters	225 - 250
Birthday Dolls and other special outfits	250 up

Unnamed Girl: Ca. 1935.

13in (33cm)	$225 - 275

Betty: Ca. 1935. Painted or sleep eyes, wigged or molded hair.

13in (33cm)	$225 - 275
16in (41cm)	375 - 400

Topsy Turvy: Ca. 1936.

7½in (19cm)	$175 - 200

Madame Alexander Composition continued

Little Colonel: 1935. All-composition with swivel head, jointed hips and shoulders; mohair wig, sleep eyes, closed mouth, dimples; original clothes; all in excellent condition. *Betty* face.
Mark: On head:
    "ALEXANDER" or none
On dress tag:
    "Madame Alexander"
13 - 14in (33 - 36cm)   **$500 - 600**

Babies: 1936 - on. Composition head, hands and legs, cloth bodies; molded hair or wigged, sleep eyes, open or closed mouth; original clothes; all in excellent condition.
Mark: On dolls:
    "ALEXANDER"
On clothing: "Little Genius," "Baby McGuffey," "Pinky," "Precious," "Butch," "Bitsey."
11 - 12in (28 - 31cm)   **$200 - 225**
16 - 18in (41 - 46cm)   **275 - 325**
24in (61cm)   **375 - 425**

*Allow extra for *Pinky*.

18in (46cm) *Kate Greenaway*, all original. *H & J Foulke, Inc.*

13in (33cm) *Little Colonel*, all original. *H & J Foulke, Inc.*

Madame Alexander Composition continued

Princess Elizabeth Face: All-composition, jointed at neck, shoulders and hips; mohair or human hair wig, sleeping eyes, open mouth; original clothes; all in excellent condition.
Mark: On head:
"PRINCESS ELIZABETH
ALEXANDER DOLL CO."
Clothing tagged with individual name of doll
Princess Elizabeth, 1937 (For photograph see *9th Blue Book*, page 26.)

13in (33cm) *Betty* face	**$275 - 325**
14 - 16in (36 - 41cm)	**350 - 400**
20 - 22in (51 - 56cm)	**450 - 500**
24in (61cm)	**550 - 600**
27in (69cm)	**700**

McGuffey Ana, 1937, braids

9in (23cm) painted eyes, *Wendy* face	**$275 - 300**
11in (28cm) closed mouth	**325 - 375**
13 - 15in (33 - 38cm)	**400 - 450**
18 - 20in (46 - 51cm)	**500 - 550**
24in (61cm)	**650 - 700**

Snow White, 1937, closed mouth, black hair (For photograph see *6th Blue Book*, page 23.)

13in (33cm)	**350 - 400**
16 - 18in (41 - 46cm)	**450 - 500**

Flora McFlimsey, 1938, red hair, freckles (For photograph see *7th Blue Book*, page 27.)

15in (38cm)	**625 - 675**

Kate Greenaway, 1938

16 - 18in (41 - 46cm)	**525 - 575**

Wendy Ann Face: All-composition, jointed at neck, shoulders and hips; human hair or mohair wig, sleeping eyes, closed mouth; original clothes tagged with name of individual doll; all in excellent condition.
Mark:
"WENDY-ANN
MME ALEXANDER"
or
"ALEXANDER"

9in (23cm) *McGuffey Ana*, all original. *H & J Foulke, Inc.*

Wendy-Ann, 1936 (For photograph see *9th Blue Book*, page 28.)

9in (23cm) painted eyes	**$250 - 275**
11in (28cm)	**350**
14in (36cm) swivel waist	**350 - 375**
21in (53cm)	**550 - 600**

Scarlet O'Hara, 1937, black hair, blue or green eyes

11in (28cm)	**400 - 425**
14in (36cm)	**475 - 500**
18in (46cm)	**625 - 675**
21in (53cm)	**825 - 875**

Note: Sometimes the name is spelled "Scarlet;" other times "Scarlett."

Madame Alexander Composition continued

Bride & Bridesmaids, 1940 (For photograph see *9th Blue Book*, page 28.)

14in (36cm)	**250 - 275**
18in (46cm)	**375 - 400**
21in (53cm)	**450 - 475**

Portraits, 1940s

21in (53cm)	**850 up**

Carmen (Miranda), 1942 (For photograph see *7th Blue Book*, page 30.) (black hair):

9in (23cm) painted eyes	**225 - 250**
14 - 15in (36 - 38cm)	**325—375**

Fairy Princess or **Fairy Queen**, 1942 (For photograph see *8th Blue Book*, page 28.)

14in (36cm)	**275 - 325**
18in (46cm)	**450 - 475**

Armed Forces Dolls, 1942 (For photograph see *7th Blue Book*, page 29.) WAAC, WAVE, WAAF and Soldier

14in (36cm)	**450 - 475**

Miss America, 1939

14in (36cm)	**500 - 600**

18in (46cm) **Scarlett**, all original. *H & J Foulke, Inc.*

Madame Alexander Composition continued

14in (36cm) *Jeannie Walker*, all original. *H & J Foulke, Inc.*

Margaret Face: All-composition, jointed at neck, shoulders and hips; human hair, mohair, or floss wig, sleeping eyes, closed mouth; original clothes tagged with name of individual doll; all in excellent condition.
Mark: "ALEXANDER"
Margaret O'Brien, 1946 (For photograph sec *9th Blue Book*, page 30.)
(dark braided wig):

14in (36cm)	$500 - 525
18in (46cm)	675 - 725
21in (53cm)	800 - 825

Karen Ballerina, 1946 (For photograph see *8th Blue Book*, page 29.)
(blonde wig in coiled braids):

18in (46cm)	525 - 575

Alice-in-Wonderland, 1947 (For photograph see *5th Blue Book*, page 11.)

14in (36cm)	325 - 375
18in (46cm)	450 - 500

Special Face Dolls:
Dr. Dafoe, 1936 (The Quintuplets' doctor) (For photograph see *8th Blue Book*, page 24.)

14in (36cm)	$ 800

Jane Withers, 1937 (For photograph see *5th Blue Book*, page 11.)

13in (33cm)		
closed mouth	700 -	750
15 - 16in (38 - 41cm)	800 -	850
21in (53cm)	1000 -	1200

Sonja Henie, 1939; 14in (36cm) can be found on *Wendy-Ann* body with swivel waist.

14in (36cm)	375 -	400
18in (46cm)	500 -	550
21in (53cm)	575 -	625

Jeannie Walker, 1941

13 - 14in (33 - 36cm)	425 -	450
18in (46cm)	575 -	625

Baby Jane, 1935

16in (41cm)	800

21in (53cm) *Sonja Henie*, all original. *H & J Foulke, Inc.*

HARD PLASTIC

Margaret Face: 1948 - on. All-hard plastic, jointed at neck, shoulders and hips; lovely wig, sleep eyes, closed mouth; original clothes tagged with name of doll; all in excellent condition.
Mark: "ALEXANDER"

14in (36cm) *Nina Ballerina*, all original. *H & J Foulke, Inc.*

Nina Ballerina, 1949 - 1951	
14in (36cm)	**$350 - 375**
18in (46cm)	**425 - 450**
Fairy Queen, 1947 - 1948*	
14in (36cm)	**300 - 350**
Babs, 1948 - 1949*	
14in (36cm)	**375 - 400**
Mary Martin, 1950	
14in (36cm)	**600 - 650**
Margaret Rose, 1948 - 1953*	
14in (36cm)	**325 - 350**
Margaret O'Brien, 1948*	
14in (36cm)	**550 - 625**
Wendy-Ann, 1947 - 1948	
18in (46cm)	**400 - 425**
Wendy Bride, 1950*	
14in (36cm)	**325 - 375**
Cinderella, 1950*	
14in (36cm)	**575 - 625**
Prince Charming, 1950*	
14in (36cm)	**550 - 600**
Cynthia (black), 1952 - 1953	
14in (36cm)	**550 - 600**
Story Princess, 1954 - 1956	
14in (36cm)	**350 - 375**
Wendy (from Peter Pan set), 1953:	
14in (36cm)	**450 - 475**
Prince Philip, Ca. 1950*	
18in (46cm)	**550 - 600**
Snow White, 1952	
14in (36cm)	**500**
Bride, 1952:	
18in (46cm)	**375 - 425**
Margot Ballerina, 1953	
18in (46cm)	**425 - 450**
Glamour Girls, 1953*	
18in (46cm)	**700 - 800**
Queen Elizabeth, 1953	
18in (46cm)	**700**
Godey Ladies, 1950*	
14in (36cm)	**700 - 800**

*For photographs see *Treasury of Mme. Alexander Dolls.*

Madame Alexander Hard Plastic continued

Maggie Face: 1948 - 1956. All-hard plastic, jointed at neck, shoulders and hips; good quality wig, sleep eyes, closed mouth; original clothes tagged with the name of the doll; all in excellent condition.
Mark: "ALEXANDER"
Maggie, 1948 - 1953*
14in (36cm)   **$325 - 375**
17in (43cm)   **425 - 475**
Polly Pigtails, 1949
14in (36cm)   **350 - 375**
Kathy, 1951*
14in (36cm)   **400 - 425**

Alice in Wonderland, 1950-1951*
14in (36cm)   **350 - 375**
17in (43cm)   **425 - 475**
Annabelle, 1952*
17in (43cm)   **425 - 475**
Peter Pan, 1953*
Rosamund Bridesmaid, 1953*
15in (38cm)   **350 - 375**
Glamour Girls, 1953*
18in (46cm)   **700 - 800**
Me and My Shadow, 1954
18in (46cm)   **700 - 800**
Godey Man, 1950*
14in (36cm)   **700 - 800**

*For photographs see *Treasury of Mme. Alexander Dolls.*

Little Women: 1948 - 1956. All-hard plastic, jointed at neck, shoulders and hips; synthetic wig, sleep eyes, closed mouth; original clothes; all in excellent condition. Some models have jointed knees. "Maggie" and "Margaret" faces.
Mark: On head:
"ALEXANDER."
On clothes tag:
"Meg", "Jo", "Beth", "Amy" and "Marme"
14 - 15in (36 - 38cm)
Floss hair,
1948 - 1950   **$325 - 350**
Amy, loop curls   **375 - 400**
Dynel hair   **250 - 275**
Little Men, 1952   **750 up each**

14in (38cm) **Jo** with floss hair, all original. *H & J Foulke, Inc.*

Madame Alexander Hard Plastic continued

Winnie and Binnie: 1953 - 1955. All-hard plastic, walking body, later with jointed knees and vinyl arms; lovely wig, sleep eyes, closed mouth; original clothes; all in excellent condition.

15in (38cm)	**$275 - 300**
18in (46cm)	**300 - 325**
24in (61cm)	**375 - 400**
Mary Ellen,	
31in (79cm)	**450 - 500**

25in (64cm) **Winnie Walker**, all original. *H & J Foulke, Inc.*

Cissy: 1955 - 1959. Head, torso and jointed legs of hard plastic, jointed vinyl arms; synthetic wig, sleep eyes, closed mouth, pierced ears; original clothes; all in excellent condition with perfect hair and rosy cheeks. (For photograph see *9th Blue Book*, page 33.)
Mark: On head:
"ALEXANDER"
On dress tag:
"Cissy"
21in (53cm)

Street clothes	**$350 - 400**
Gowns	**450 up***
Elaborate fashion	
gowns	**700 up***

*Depending upon costume.

Alexander-Kins: 1953 - on. All-hard plastic, jointed at neck, shoulders and hips; synthetic wig, sleep eyes, closed mouth; original clothes; all in excellent condition.
7½ - 8in (19 - 20cm)
1953, straight leg non-walker
1954-1955, straight-leg walker
1956-1964, bent-knee walker
1965-1972, bent knee
1973-current, straight leg
Mark: On back of torso:
"ALEX"
After 1978:
"MADAME ALEXANDER"
On dress tag:
"Madame Alexander"
"Alexander-Kins" or
specific name of doll

Madame Alexander Hard Plastic continued

Wendy, in dresses
1953 - 1972   **$325 up**

Wendy Ballerina, 1956 - 1973
pink	**$250 - 300**
blue	**350**
yellow	**400**
Wendy, in riding habit	**450**
Wendy Nurse	**550 - 650**
Quizkin, 1953	**450 - 550**

Special Outfits:
Easter Girl	**$900 up**
Southern Belle	**750 up**
Cinderella	**550 up**
Baby Clown, 1955	**900 up**
Billy	**450**
Snow White (Disney)	**500**
Davy Crockett	**800 up**

8in (20cm) Alexander-Kin *Wendy*, all original. *H & J Foulke, Inc.*

Lissy: 1956 - 1958. All-hard plastic, jointed at neck, shoulders, hips, elbows and knees; synthetic wig, sleep eyes, closed mouth; original clothes; all in excellent condition. (For photograph see *8th Blue Book*, page 33.)
Mark: None on doll
On dress tag:
"Lissy" or name of character
12in (31cm)	**$ 300 - 400**
Kelly, 1959*	**400 - 450**
Little Women, 1957 - 1967	
	200 - 225
Southern Belle, 1963*	
	1000 up
McGuffey Ana, 1963*	
	1000 up
Laurie, 1967*	**400 - 450**
Pamela, 1962 - 1963*	**650**

*For photographs see *Treasury of Mme. Alexander Dolls*, pages 74 - 78.

12in (31cm) *Lissy Beth*, all original. *H & J Foulke, Inc.*

Madame Alexander Hard Plastic continued

Elise: 1957 - 1964. All-hard plastic with vinyl arms, completely jointed; synthetic wig, sleep eyes, closed mouth; original clothes; all in excellent condition.

16½ - 17in (42 - 43cm)

Street clothes	**$275 - 325**
Gowns	**350 up**
Bride, Ballerina	**325 - 350**
Elaborate Fashion	
Gowns	**500 up**

Cissette: 1957 - 1963. All-hard plastic, jointed at neck, shoulders, hips and knees; synthetic wig, sleep eyes, closed mouth, pierced ears; original clothes; all in excellent condition. (For photographs see *Treasury of Mme. Alexander Dolls*, pages 79 - 84.)

Mark: None on doll
On dress tag: "Cissette"

10in (25cm) *Cissette*	**$175 up**
Basic *Cissette*, mint and boxed	**190 - 210**
Portrettes, 1968 - 1973	**450 - 550**
Jacqueline, 1962	**450 - 550**

Shari Lewis: 1959. All-hard plastic with slim fashion body; auburn hair, brown eyes, closed mouth; original clothes; all in excellent condition. (For photograph see *5th Blue Book*, page 17.)

14in (36cm)	**$350 - 375**
21in (53cm)	**450 - 475**

16½in (42cm) *Elise* #1750, 1958, all original. *H & J Foulke, Inc.*

Madame Alexander Vinyl Dolls

Maggie Mixup: 1960 - 1961. All-hard plastic, fully-jointed; red straight hair, green eyes, closed mouth, freckles; original clothes; all in excellent condition. (For photographs see *6th Blue Book*, page 32.)

16½ - 17in (42 - 43cm)	**$ 350 - 375**
8in (20cm)	**450 - 550**
8in (20cm) angel	**1000 up**

VINYL

Kelly Face: 1958 - on. Vinyl character face with rooted hair, vinyl arms, hard plastic torso and legs, jointed waist; original clothes; all in excellent condition. (For photograph see *9th Blue Book*, page 37.)

Mark: On head:

Kelly, 1958 - 1959

15in (38cm)	**$225**
Pollyana, 1960 - 1961	
15in (38cm)	**225**

Marybel, 1959 - 1965

15in (38cm), in case	**250**
Edith, 1958 - 1959	
15in (38cm)	**225**
Elise, 1962	
15in (38cm)	**250 - 275**

Jacqueline: 1961 - 1962. Vinyl and hard plastic; rooted dark hair, sleep eyes, closed mouth; original clothes; all in excellent condition.

21in (53cm)	**$700 - 750**
Portrait Dolls,	
1965 to present	**250 up**

Caroline: 1961 - 1962. Hard plastic and vinyl; rooted blonde hair, smiling character face; original clothes; in excellent condition.

15in (38cm)	**$300**

21in (53cm) *Melanie* Portrait #2220, 1979-1981, all original. *Virginia Ann Heyerdahl Collection.*

Madame Alexander Vinyl Dolls continued

Janie: 1964 - 1966. Vinyl and hard plastic with rooted hair, impish face, pigeon-toed and knock-kneed; original tagged clothes; all in excellent condition.

12in (31cm)	**$225 - 250**
Lucinda, 1969 - 1970	**275 - 325**
Rozy, 1969	**325 - 375**
Suzy, 1970	**325 - 375**

12in (31cm) *Janie. H & J Foulke, Inc.*

Smarty: 1962 - 1963. Hard plastic and vinyl, smiling character face with rooted hair, knock-kneed and pigeon-toed; original clothes; in excellent condition.

12in (31cm)	**$200**
Katie (black), 1965	
	350 - 400

Polly Face: 1965. All-vinyl with rooted hair, jointed at neck, shoulders and hips; original tagged clothes; all in excellent condition.

17in (43cm):	
Polly	**$225 - 250**
Leslie (black)	**300 - 400**

17in (43cm) *Leslie* #1655, 1970, all original. *H & J Foulke, Inc.*

Mary Ann Face: Introduced in 1965 and used widely to present a variety of dolls. Only discontinued dolls are listed here. Vinyl head and arms, hard plastic torso and legs; appropriate synthetic wig, sleep eyes; original clothes; all in excellent condition.

Mark: On head:
"ALEXANDER
19©65"

14in (35cm) only:

Madame,
1967 - 1975 $ 200
Mary Ann,
1965   250
Orphant Annie,
1965 - 1966   250
Gidget, 1966   250
Little Granny,
1966   200
Riley's Little Annie, 1967   250
Renoir Girl,
1967 - 1971   200
Easter Girl,
1968   1200 - 1500
Scarlett #1495,
flowered gown,
1968   500
Jenny Lind & Cat,
1969 - 1971   300
Jenny Lind,
1970   400
Grandma Jane,
1970 - 1972   200
Disney Snow White,
to 1977   400
Goldilocks,
1978 - 1982   100

14in (36cm) *Jenny Lind & Her Listening Cat*, all original. *H & J Foulke, Inc.*

48

Madame Alexander Vinyl Dolls continued

Sound of Music: Large set 1965 - 1970; small set 1971 - 1973. All dolls of hard plastic and vinyl with appropriate synthetic wigs and sleep eyes; original clothes; all in excellent condition. **Mark:** Each doll tagged as to character.

Small set

8in (20cm) *Friedrich*	$200
8in (20cm) *Gretl*	200
8in (20cm) *Marta*	200
10in (25cm) *Brigitta*	200
12in (31cm) *Maria*	275
10in (25cm) *Louisa*	325
10in (25cm) *Liesl*	275

Large set*

11in (28cm) *Friedrich*	225
11in (28cm) *Gretl*	200
11in (28cm) *Marta*	200
14in (36cm) *Brigitta*	200
17in (43cm) *Maria*	275
14in (36cm) *Louisa*	250
14in (36cm) *Liesl*	250

*Allow considerably more for sailor outfits.

Coco: 1966. Vinyl and hard plastic, rooted blonde hair, jointed waist, right leg bent slightly at knee; original clothes; all in excellent condition. This face was also used for the 1966 portrait dolls.

21in (53cm)	**$1800 - 2000**

Elise: 1966 to present. Vinyl face, rooted hair; original tagged clothes; all in excellent condition.

17in (43cm)

Elise	$125*
Marlo, 1967	400 - 500
Maggie, 1972 - 1973	250
Portrait Elise, 1973	200

*Discontinued styles only.

Peter Pan Set: 1969. Vinyl and hard plastic with appropriate wigs and sleep eyes; original clothes; all in excellent condition.

14in (36cm) *Peter Pan*

("Mary Ann" face)	**$200 - 225**
14in (36cm) *Wendy* ("Mary Ann" face)	200 - 225
12in (31cm) *Michael* ("Janie" face)	250
11in (28cm) *Tinker Bell* ("Cissette")	250 - 275

Nancy Drew Face: Introduced in 1967 and used widely to present a variety of dolls. Vinyl head and arms, hard plastic torso and legs; appropriate synthetic wig, sleep eyes; original clothes; all in excellent condition.

12in (31cm) only:

Nancy Drew, 1967	$200
Renoir Child, 1967	200
Pamela with wigs, 1962 - 1963	350 - 400

First Ladies: Hard plastic and vinyl with rooted synthetic hair individually styled and sleep eyes; original tagged clothes; in mint condition. "Martha" and "Mary Ann" faces.

14in (36cm)

Series I: 1976 - 1978
Martha Washington, Abigail Adams, Martha Randolph, Dolley Madison, Elizabeth Monroe and *Louisa Adams.*

Set:	**$750**
Individual:	125
Martha Washington	210

Series II: 1979 - 1981
Sarah Jackson, Angelica Van Buren, Jane Findlay, Julia Tyler, Sarah Polk and *Betty Taylor Bliss.*

Set:	550
Individual:	90

Madame Alexander Vinyl Dolls continued

Series III: 1982 - 1984
Jane Pierce, Abigail Fillmore, Mary Todd Lincoln, Martha Johnson Patterson, Harriet Lane and *Julia Grant.*
Set: 500
Individual: 80
Mary Todd Lincoln: 110
Series IV: 1985 - 1987
Caroline Harrison, Mary McKee, Frances Cleveland, Mary McElroy, Lucretia Garfield, Lucy Hayes.
Set: 550
Individual: 90

Series V: 1988
Florence Harding, Edith Wilson, Helen Taft, Ellen Wilson, Ida McKinley, Edith Roosevelt.
Set: No secondary market yet.
Series VI: 1989
Lou Hoover, Eleanor Roosevelt, Grace Coolidge, Mamie Eisenhower, Bess Truman, Jacqueline Kennedy.
Set: No secondary market yet.

14in (36cm) First Lady *Sarah Polk*, all original. *H & J Foulke, Inc.*

Henri Alexandre

Maker: Henri Alexandre, Paris, France, 1888 - 1892; Tourrel 1892 - 1895; Jules Steiner and successors 1895 - 1901
Material: Bisque head, jointed composition body
Designer: Henri Alexandre
Trademark: Bébé Phénix

H.A. Bébé: 1889 - 1891. Perfect bisque socket head, closed mouth, paperweight eyes, pierced ears, good wig; jointed composition and wood body; lovely clothes; all in good condition. (For photograph see *9th Blue Book*, page 67.)
Mark:

H ⋈ A

17 - 19in (43 - 48cm)   **$6500****

**Not enough price samples to compute a reliable range.

Bébé Phénix: 1889 - 1900. Perfect bisque head, closed mouth, paperweight eyes, pierced ears, good wig; composition body sometimes with one-piece arms and legs; well dressed; all in good condition.
Mark: Red Stamp
Incised

PHÉNIX
★ 95

Approximate Size Chart:
  *81 = 10in (25cm)
  *85 = 14in (36cm)
  *88 = 17in (43cm)
  *90 = 18in (46cm)
  *92 = 19 - 21in (48 - 53cm)
  *93 = 22in (56cm)
  *94 = 23 - 24in (58 - 61cm)
  *95 = 23 - 25in (58 - 64cm)
17 - 18in (43 - 46cm)   **$4250 - 4500**
21 - 23in (53 - 58cm)   **4900 - 5400**
Open Mouth:
  19 - 21in (48 - 53cm)   **2400 - 2600**

See color photograph on page 17.

All-Bisque Dolls
(So-Called French)

Maker: Various French and/or German firms
Date: Ca. 1880 - on
Material: All-bisque
Size: Various small sizes, under 12in (31cm)
Mark: None, sometimes numbers

All-Bisque French Doll:
Jointed at shoulders and
hips, swivel neck, slender
arms and legs; good wig,
glass eyes, closed mouth;
molded shoes or boots and
stockings; appropriately
dressed; all in good condition, with proper parts.
5 - 6in (12 - 15cm)
$ 850 - 1000*
With bare feet,
5 - 6in (13 - 15cm)
900 - 1000*
With jointed elbows and knees,
5 - 6in (13 - 15cm)
2500 - 3000**
With jointed elbows,
5 - 6in (13 - 15cm)
2000 - 2500**
Painted eyes,
4½ - 5in (12 - 13cm)
all original   **450 - 550**
5½in (14cm) in original
presentation box with clothes
and accessories
5800
8½in (22cm) F.G. - type head,
barefoot, at auction
3000

*Allow extra for original clothes.
**Not enough price samples to
compute a reliable range.

5in (13cm) French all-bisque, all original. *H & J Foulke,
Inc.*

All-Bisque Dolls
(German)

Maker: Various German firms
Date: Ca. 1880 - on
Material: Bisque
Size: Various small sizes, most under 12in (31cm)
Mark: Some with "Germany" and/or numbers; some with paper labels on stomachs

---

All-Bisque French-type or Slender Dolls: Ca. 1880 - on. Jointed usually by wire or pegging at shoulders and hips, stationary neck, slender arms and legs; good wig, glass eyes, closed mouth; molded shoes or boots and stockings; dressed or undressed; many in regional costumes; all in good condition, with proper parts.

3in (8cm) **$225 - 250**
3¾ - 4in (10cm)
              185 - 210
5 - 6in (13 - 15cm)
              300 - 350
Swivel neck:
4in (10cm) **325 - 375**
6 - 6½in (15 - 17cm)
              475 - 525
Black or Mulatto:
4 - 4½in (10 - 12cm)
              300 - 350

3¾in (10cm) French-type or Slender German all-bisque, all original. *H & J Foulke, Inc.*

All-Bisque Dolls (German) continued

All-Bisque with molded clothes: Ca. 1890 - on. Many by Hertwig & Co. Jointed at shoulders (sometimes hips), molded and painted clothes or underwear; molded and painted hair, sometimes with molded hat, painted eyes, closed mouth; molded shoes and socks (if in underwear often barefoot); good quality work; all in good condition, with proper parts.

Children:

3¼in (8cm)	**$ 95 - 110**
4 - 5in (10 - 13cm)	**135 - 160**
6 - 7in (15 - 18cm)	**200 - 250**

Glass Eyes, molded underwear,
5½in (14cm) **350**

Punch, Judy and other white bisque characters, 3 - 4in (8 - 10cm) **95 - 110**

Molded Hats:
See page 205.

All-Bisque with painted eyes: Ca. 1880 - 1910. Jointed at shoulders, stiff or jointed hips, stationary neck; molded and painted hair or mohair wig, painted eyes, closed mouth; molded and painted shoes and stockings; fine quality work; dressed or undressed; all in good condition, with proper parts.

1¼in (3cm) crocheted clothes	**$ 65 - 75**
1½ - 2in (4 - 5cm)	**75 - 85**
4 - 5in (10 - 13cm)	**140 - 175**
6 - 7in (15 - 18cm)	**200 - 225**

Swivel neck:

2½in (9cm) all original	**150**
4 - 5in (10 - 13cm)	**200 - 250**

Knees bent for sitting:
5½in (14cm) **175 - 200**

Early round face, stiff hips, bootines: (For photograph see *8th Blue Book*, page 42.)

4½in (12cm)	**250 - 275**
6 - 7in (15 - 18cm)	**400 - 450**

Early face, stiff hips, pink or blue shirred hose: (For photograph see *9th Blue Book*, page 45.)

4½in (12cm)	**175 - 200**
6in (15cm)	**350 - 375**
8in (20cm)	**550 - 575**

Early face with molded hair:

2¾in (7cm)	**100 - 110**
5in (13cm)	**150 - 175**
7in (18cm)	**250 - 300**

7in (18cm) Hertwig boy with molded clothes. *H & J Foulke, Inc.*

All-Bisque Dolls (German) continued

All-Bisque with glass eyes: Ca. 1890 - 1910. Very good quality bisque, jointed at shoulders, stiff or jointed hips; good wig, glass eyes, closed mouth (sometimes open); molded and painted shoes and stockings; dressed or undressed; all in good condition, with proper parts.

5in (13cm) all-bisque Kestner 184 girl with yellow boots. *H & J Foulke, Inc.*

3in (8cm)	**$ 275 - 325***
4 - 5in (10 - 13cm)	**225 - 275***
6in (15cm)	**325 - 375***
7in (18cm)	**400 - 450***
8in (20cm)	**500 - 550***
9in (23cm)	**700 - 750**
10in (25cm)	**900 - 950**
12in (31cm)	**1200**

Early style model, stiff hips, shirred hose or bootines:

3in (8cm)	**275 - 325**
4½in (12cm)	**250 - 275**
6in (15cm)	**400 - 425**

*Allow $25 - 50 extra for yellow boots or unusual footwear and/or especially fine quality.

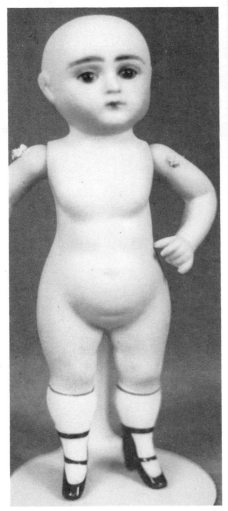

7in (18cm) fine early all-bisque with round face and bootines. *H & J Foulke, Inc.*

See also Kestner, Kling, Limbach, and Alt, Beck & Gottschalck.

All-Bisque Dolls (German) continued

All-Bisque with swivel neck and glass eyes: Ca. 1880 - 1910. Swivel neck, pegged shoulders and hips; good wig, glass eyes, closed or open mouth; molded and painted shoes or boots and stockings; dressed or undressed; all in good condition, with proper parts.

3¼in (8cm)	**$ 350**
4 - 4½in (10 - 12cm)	**375 - 400***
5 - 6in (13 - 15cm)	**450 - 500***
7in (18cm)	**600 - 700***
8in (20cm)	**800 - 900***
10in (25cm)	**1200 - 1300**

Early Kestner or S&H type:
(For photograph see *8th Blue Book*, page 44.)

5in (13cm)	**750 - 850**
6in (15cm)	**1000 - 1100**
8in (20cm)	**1500 - 1600**
11in (28cm)	**2200 - 2500**

With jointed knee:

5½in (14cm)	**2100**
8in (20cm)	**3200**

Swivel waist:

5½in (14cm)	**2800**

So-called "Wrestler" (***#102***):

6½in (16cm)	**1100 - 1250**
8½in (22cm)	**1500 - 1650**
9½in (24cm)	**1850 - 2000**

Bare feet:

5 - 6in (13 - 15cm)	**1300 - 1600**
8 - 9in (20 - 23cm)	**2200 - 2500**
11 - 12in (28 - 31cm)	**3000 - 3500**

Round face, Bootines:

6in (15cm)	**750 - 850**
8in (20cm)	**1100 - 1200**

Long black or blue stockings:
See page 383.

*Allow $50 extra for yellow boots or unusual footwear.

8½in (22cm) all-bisque 102 Kestner with swivel neck and yellow boots. *H & J Foulke, Inc.*

6in (15cm) Kestner all-bisque with swivel neck and bare feet. *H & J Foulke, Inc.*

All-Bisque Dolls (German) continued

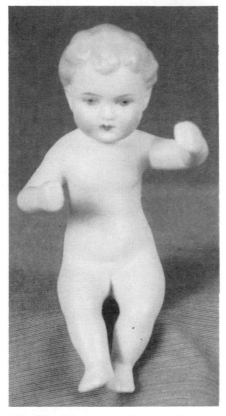

5¼in (13cm) fine early quality immobile baby.
H & J Foulke, Inc.

All-Bisque Baby: 1900 - on. Jointed at shoulders and hips with curved arms and legs; molded and painted hair, painted eyes; not dressed; all in good condition, with proper parts.

2½ - 3½in (6 - 9cm)	**$ 75 - 95**
4 - 5in (10 - 13cm)	**150 - 175**

Fine early quality, blonde molded hair:

4½in (12cm)	**150 - 175**
5 - 6in (13 - 15cm) immobile	**150 - 175**
6 - 7in (15 - 18cm)	**225 - 275**
9in (23cm)	**550 - 650**
13in (33cm)	**900 - 1100**

All-Bisque Character Baby: Ca. 1910. Jointed at shoulders and hips, curved arms and legs; molded hair, painted eyes, character face; undressed; all in good condition, with proper parts.

3½in (9cm)	**$ 95**
4½in - 5½in (12 - 14cm)	**175 - 225**
7in (18cm)	**275**
8in (20cm)	**375**

With glass eyes, *#830* and others

4 - 5in (10 - 13cm)	**275 - 300**
6in (15cm)	**400**
8in (20cm)	**600**

#497 Baby Darling

6in (15cm)	**500**
8in (20cm)	**800 - 850**

Swivel neck, glass eyes:

6in (15cm)	**425 - 475**
8in (20cm)	**625 - 675**
10in (25cm)	**850 - 950**

Toddler, swivel neck, glass eyes, *#178* Kestner. (For photograph see *9th Blue Book*, page 48.)

6in (15cm)	**600 - 700**
8in (20cm)	**1000**

Swivel neck, painted eyes:

5 - 6in (13 - 15cm)	**300 - 350**
8in (20cm)	**450**
11in (28cm)	**750**

#880 Mildred, the **Prize Baby:**

6½in (17cm)	**1800**
9in (23cm)	**2200**

6in (15cm) all-bisque character baby with swivel neck. *H & J Foulke, Inc.*

All-Bisque Dolls (German) continued

Later All-Bisque with glass eyes: Ca. 1915. Many of pretinted pink bisque. Jointed at shoulders and hips; good wig, glass eyes, closed or open mouth; molded and painted black one-strap shoes and stockings; undressed or dressed; all in good condition, with proper parts.

2½in (6cm) all-bisque character girl, all original. *H & J Foulke, Inc.*

6½in (17cm) later all-bisque Kestner 257 girl. *H & J Foulke, Inc.*

Good smooth bisque:

4 - 5in (10 - 13cm)	**$140 - 175**
6in (15cm)	**210 - 235**
7in (18cm)	**275 - 300**

Grainy bisque:

4½in (12cm)	**95**
6in (15cm)	**150**

All-Bisque Character Dolls: 1913 - on. Character faces with well- painted features and molded hair; usually jointed only at arms. Also see individual listings. See color photograph on page 18.

All-Bisque Dolls (German) continued

Pink bisque, 2 - 3in (5 - 8cm)	$ 45	
Thumbsucker, 3in (8cm)	165	
Girl with molded hair bow loop, 2½in (6cm)	50 -	65
Whistling boy, 3in (8cm)	95	
HEbee, SHEbee, 4½in (12cm)	425	
Little Annie Rooney, 4in (10cm)	250 - 300	
Baby Bud, glass eyes, wig, boxed, 7in (18cm)	750	
Orsini: *MiMi* or *DiDi,* 5in (13cm) glass eyes	1100 - 1250	
DiDi, 5in (13cm) painted eyes.	900	
ViVi or *FiFi,* 5in (13cm) glass eyes	1250 - 1450	
Max and *Moritz* (Kestner), 5½in (14cm)	2200 - 2500	

All-Bisque with character face: Ca. 1915. Jointed at shoulders and hips; smiling character face, closed or open mouth; molded and painted black one-strap shoes and stockings; dressed or undressed; all in good condition, with proper parts. Very good quality.

#150 open/closed mouth with two painted teeth. (For photograph see *9th Blue Book,* page 49.)

Glass eyes:
4½in (12cm) $275 - 300
6in (15cm) 350 - 400
Painted eyes:
4½in (12cm) 150 - 175
6in (15cm) 250 - 275

#602 Kestner, swivel neck glass eyes,
5 - 6in (13 15cm)
500 - 650

#155, smiling face, (For photograph see *8th Blue Book,* page 48.)
5½in (14cm) 350 - 400
7in (18cm) 450 - 500

5in (13cm) Kestner 602 character girl with swivel neck. *H & J Foulke, Inc.*

All-Bisque Dolls (German) continued

Later All-Bisque with painted eyes: Ca. 1920. Many by Hertwig. Some of pretinted bisque. Jointed at shoulders and hips, stationary neck; mohair wig or molded hair, painted eyes, closed mouth; molded and painted one-strap shoes and white stockings; dressed or undressed; all in good condition, with proper parts.

3½in (9cm)	$ 65 - 75
4½ - 5in (12 - 13cm)	90 - 100
6 - 7in (15 - 18cm)	140 - 175
8in (20cm)	225

2⅞in (7cm) all-bisque *Candy Baby* with unusual open mouth, all original. *H & J Foulke, Inc.*

All-Bisque "Flapper" (tinted bisque): Ca. 1920. Jointed at shoulders and hips; molded bobbed hair with loop for bow, painted features; long yellow stockings, one-strap shoes with heels; undressed or dressed; all in good condition, with proper parts, very good quality. (For photograph see *6th Blue Book*, page 49.)

5in (13cm)	$225 - 275
6 - 7in (15 - 18cm)	325 - 375
Standard quality,	
5in (13cm)	150 - 175

All-Bisque Baby: Ca. 1920. Pink bisque, so-called "Candy Baby," jointed at shoulders and hips, curved arms and legs; painted hair, painted eyes; original factory clothes; all in good condition, with proper parts.

2½ - 3in (6 - 8cm)	$65 - 70

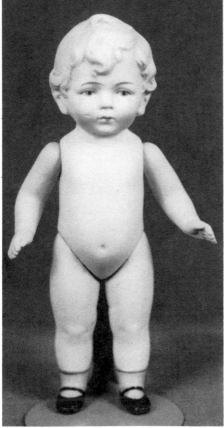

7in (18cm) later all-bisque boy with painted eyes. *H & J Foulke, Inc.*

All-Bisque Dolls (German) continued

All-Bisque "Flapper:" Ca. 1920. Pink bisque with wire joints at shoulders and hips; molded bobbed hair and painted features; painted shoes and socks; original factory clothes; all in good condition, with proper parts. See color photograph on page 18.

3in (8cm)	$ 50 - 60
Molded hats	165 - 185
Groom with molded top hat and *Bride,* boxed and all original.	350

Bathing Beauty: 1920s. All-bisque lady, either nude or partially dressed in painted-on clothing; modeled in various sitting, lying or standing positions; painted features; molded hair; possibly with bathing cap or bald head with mohair wig; may be dressed in bits of lace. (For photograph see *9th Blue Book*, page 51.)

Common type, 3 - 4in (8 - 10cm)	$ 75 - 90
Fine quality, 4 - 5in (10 - 13cm)	500 up
6 - 7in (15 - 18cm)	600 up
4 - 5in (10 - 13cm) 2 figures joined together	1300
5 - 6in (13 - 15cm) lady with dog or cat	1500 - 1800

All-Bisque Nodder Characters: Ca. 1920. Many made by Hertwig & Co. Nodding heads, elastic strung, molded clothes; all in good condition. Decoration is usually not fired so it wears and washes off very easily. Marked "Germany." See color photograph on pages 18 and 360.

3 - 4in (8 - 10cm)	$ 50 - 60
Comic characters	75 up*
Dressed Animals	100 - 135
Dressed Teddy Bears	165 - 195
Santa	150 - 200

*Depending upon rarity.

All-Bisque Immobiles: Ca. 1920. All-bisque figures with molded clothes, molded hair and painted features. Decoration is not fired, so it wears and washes off very easily. Marked "Germany." See color photographs on page 19.

Adults and *children*, 1½ - 2¼in (4 - 6cm)	$ 35 - 45
Children, 3¼in (8cm)	45 - 50
Santa, 3in (8cm)	110 - 125
Children with animals on string, 3in (8cm)	90 - 100
Bride and Groom cake top, 5in (13cm)	150 - 200
6½in (17cm)	295

All-Bisque Dolls
(Made in Japan)

Maker: Various Japanese firms
Date: Ca. 1915 - on
Material: Bisque
Size: Various small sizes
Mark: "Made in Japan" or "NIPPON"

Baby		
White, 4in (10cm)	**$ 25 -**	**30**
Black, 4 - 5in (10 - 13cm)	**50 -**	**60**
Betty Boop-type,		
4 - 5in (10 - 13cm)	**18 -**	**22**
6 - 7in (15 - 18cm)	**30 -**	**35**
Child,		
4 - 5in (10 - 13cm)	**25**	
6 - 7in (15 - 18cm)	**35 -**	**40**
Comic Characters,		
3 - 4in (8 - 10cm)	**25 up***	
Stiff Characters,		
3 - 4in (8 - 10cm)	**5 -**	**10**
6 - 7in (15 - 18cm)	**25 -**	**30**
Cho-Cho San, 4½in (12cm)	**65 -**	**75**
Nodders, 4in (10cm)	**25 -**	**35**
Orientals, 3 - 4in (8 - 10cm)	**20 -**	**25**
Queue San, 4in (10cm)	**65 -**	**75**
Marked "Nippon" Characters,		
4 - 5in (10 - 13cm)	**45 -**	**50**
Three Bears boxed set	**150 - 165**	
Snow White boxed set	**350 - 450**	
Black Character Girl, molded hair bow		
loop 4½in (12cm)	**35 -**	**40**

*Depending upon rarity.

3½in (9cm) all-bisque Made in Japan Orientals, all original. *H & J Foulke, Inc.*

Alt, Beck & Gottschalck

Maker: Alt, Beck & Gottschalck, porcelain factory, Nauendorf near Ohrdruf, Thüringia, Germany. Made heads for many producers including Wagner & Zetzsche.

Date: 1854 - on

Material: China and bisque heads for use on composition, kid or cloth bodies; all-bisque or all-china dolls.

China Shoulder Head: Ca. 1880. Black or blonde-haired china head; old cloth body with china limbs; dressed; all in good condition. Mold numbers, such as *784, 1000, 1008, 1028, 1046, 1142, 1210.* (For photograph see *9th Blue Book*, page 54.)

Mark: *1008 ✗9*

Also ✗ or *№* in place of ✗

15 - 18in (38 - 46cm)	**$300 - 350**
20 - 22in (51 - 56cm)	**400 - 450**
25 - 26in (64 - 66cm)	**550 - 650**

Bisque Shoulder Head: Ca. 1880. Molded hair, painted or glass eyes, closed mouth; cloth body with bisque lower limbs; dressed; all in good condition. Mold numbers, such as *890, 990, 1000, 1008, 1028, 1064, 1142, 1254, 1288, 1304.* See color photograph on page 21.

Mark: See above

Painted eyes,
13 - 14in (33 - 36cm)	**$275 - 350***
16 - 18in (41 - 46cm)	**400 - 475***
22 - 24in (56—61cm)	**550 - 600***

Glass eyes,
12 - 14in (31 - 36cm)	**450 - 500***
18 - 20in (46 - 51cm)	**750 - 850***

Blue Scarf Lady, glass eyes,
20in (51cm)	**1300 - 1500**

Molded orange bonnet, glass eyes **#1024**
26in (66cm)	**3200**

*Allow extra for unusual or elaborate hairdo or molded hat.

Bisque shoulder head #1064 by ABG. *H & J Foulke, Inc.*

Alt, Beck & Gottschalck continued

Bisque Shoulder Head: Ca. 1885 - on. Turned shoulder head, mohair or human hair wig, plaster dome or bald head, glass sleeping or set eyes, closed mouth; kid body with gusseted joints and bisque lower arms, or cloth body with kid lower arms; dressed; all in good condition. Mold numbers, such as *639, 698, 912, 1032, 1123, 1235.*

Mark: 639 ⊁ 6

with DEP after 1888

13½in (34cm) 1235 ABG shoulder head. *H & J Foulke, Inc.*

18in (46cm) 911 ABG socket head on early composition and wood body. See color photograph on page 20. *Maxine Salaman Collection.*

15 - 17in (38 - 43cm)
    $ 700 - 800
20 - 22in (51 - 56cm)
    950 - 1150
26 - 27in (69cm)
    1400 - 1500
#911, 916, swivel neck:
17 - 19in (43 - 48cm)
    1700 - 2000

20½in (52cm) ABG 1362 character girl, all original. *H & J Foulke, Inc.*

With open mouth:
Mark:

698 ½ Germany Dep N° 10

14 - 16in (36 - 41cm)	$ 475 - 550
20 - 22in (51 - 56cm)	650 - 725
25in (64cm)	750 - 800

All-Bisque Baby: Ca. 1890. Bisque head with swivel neck, closed mouth, glass eyes, appropriate wig; jointed shoulders and hips. Mold *#915* (on crown rim).
9in (23cm) at auction   **$2300**

Alt, Beck & Gottschalck continued

14in (36cm) ABG 1352 character baby. *H & J Foulke, Inc.*

Child Doll: Perfect bisque head, good wig, sleep eyes, open mouth; ball-jointed body in good condition; appropriate clothes.
Mark:

#1362 *Sweet Nell:*

12 - 14in (31 - 37cm)	$ 400 - 425
19 - 22in (48 - 56cm)	500 - 550
26 - 28in (66 - 71cm)	800 - 900
31 - 32in (79 - 81cm)	1000 - 1200
36in (91cm)	1500 - 1600
39 - 42in (99 - 107cm)	2300 - 2500

#911, closed mouth:

18in (46cm)	2500**

#630, closed mouth:

23in (68cm)	2200 - 2500**

**Not enough price samples to compute a reliable range.

All-Bisque Girl: 1911. Chubby body, loop strung shoulders and hips, inset glass eyes, open/closed mouth, painted eyelashes, full mohair or silky wig; molded white stockings, blue garters, black Mary Janes. (For photograph see *9th Blue Book*, page 56.)
Mark:

Also *#100, 125* or *150* in place of *225.* Bottom number is centimeter size.

5 - 6in (13 - 15cm)	$200 - 250
7in (18cm)	275 - 325
8in (20cm)	400 - 450
10in (25cm)	600 - 650

Character: 1910 - on. Perfect bisque head, good wig, sleep eyes, open mouth; some with open nostrils; composition body; all in good condition; suitable clothes.
Mark:

#1322, 1352, 1361: See color photograph on page 21.

10 - 12in (25 - 31cm)	$350 - 400*
15 - 17in (38 - 43cm)	500 - 550*
23 - 24in (58 - 61cm)	850 - 900*

#1357:
(For photograph, see *7th Blue Book*, page 55.)

18 - 20in (46 - 51cm)	850 - 950**
toddler	

#1358:
(For photograph, see *7th Blue Book*, page 180.)

18 - 20in (46 - 51cm)	3000 - 3500**

*Allow $50 extra for flirty eyes or toddler body.
**Not enough price samples to compute a reliable average.

Louis Amberg & Son

Maker: Louis Amberg & Son, New York, N.Y., U.S.A.
Date: 1907 - on (although Amberg had been in the doll business under other names since 1878)

Jointed Girl: 1912. Composition dolly face head, sleeping eyes, open mouth, human hair wig; jointed composition body; all in good condition with appropriate clothes. (For photograph see *7th Blue Book*, page 56.)
Mark: Body:

"AMBERG
VICTORY
DOLL"

Head: "L.A. &S"
22 - 24in (56 - 61cm)   **$250 - 300**

Newborn Babe: 1914, reissued 1924. Designed by Jeno Juszko. Bisque head of an infant with painted hair, sleep eyes, closed or open mouth; soft cloth body with celluloid, rubber or composition hands; appropriate clothes; all in good condition. Mold **886** by Recknagel. Mold **371** with open mouth by Marseille. (For photograph of closed mouth doll see *9th Blue Book*, page 57.)
Mark:

L · A · & · S ·
371 · 3⁄0 D · R · G · M ·
Germany

THE ORIGINAL
NEWBORN BABE
(C) Jan. 9th 1914 — No. G. 45520

AMBERG DOLLS
The World Standard

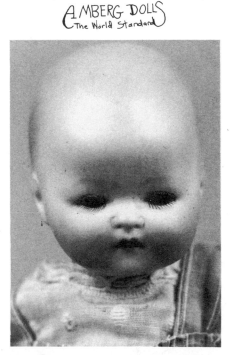

Length:
8in (20cm)	**$325 - 350**
10 - 11in (25 - 28cm)	**425 - 450**
14 - 15in (36 - 41cm)	**550 - 650**

Charlie Chaplin: 1915. Composition portrait head with molded and painted hair, painted eyes to the side, closed full mouth, molded mustache; straw-filled cloth body with composition hands; original clothes; all in good condition with wear. (For photograph see *8th Blue Book*, page 57.)
Mark: cloth label on sleeve:

"CHARLIE CHAPLIN DOLL
World's Greatest Comedian
Made exclusively by Louis Amberg
& Son, N.Y.
by Special Arrangement with
Essamay Film Co."

14in (36cm)   **$450 - 500**

8½in (22cm) head circumference *Newborn Babe* with label, head incised "LA&S 371." *H & J Foulke, Inc.*

Louis Amberg & Son continued

Composition Character Child: Ca. 1916. Composition character head, flange neck, molded and painted hair, painted eyes, open mouth with painted teeth; cloth body with composition hands: original clothes; all in good condition. (For photograph see *9th Blue Book*, page 58.)

Mark: "L. A. & S."

16½ (42cm)   **$150 - 165**

Composition Mibs: 1921. Composition shoulder head designed by Hazel Drucker with wistful expression, molded and painted blonde or reddish hair, blue painted eyes, closed mouth; cloth body with composition arms and legs with painted shoes and socks; appropriate old clothes; all in good condition.

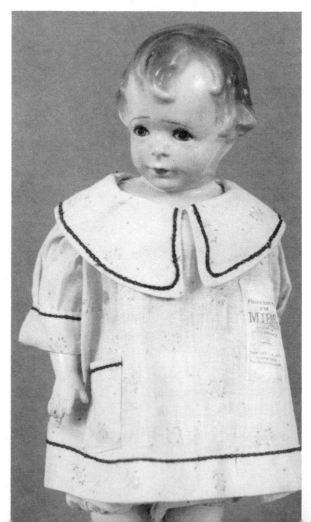

Mark: None on doll; paper label only:
"Amberg Dolls
Please Love Me
I'm Mibs"
16in (41cm) **$850 up****

Baby Peggy: 1923. Composition head, arms and legs, cloth body; molded brown bobbed hair, painted eyes, smiling closed mouth; appropriately dressed; all in good condition. (For photograph see *6th Blue Book*, page 57.)

20in (51cm) **$550 - 600****

**Not enough price samples to compute a reliable range.

Mibs, all original with label. See color photograph on page 359. *Nancy A. Smith Collection.*

Louis Amberg & Son continued

Baby Peggy: 1924. Perfect bisque head with character face; brown bobbed mohair wig, brown sleep eyes, closed mouth; composition or kid body, fully-jointed; dressed or undressed; all in very good condition.
Mark:

"19 © 24
LA & S NY
Germany
—50—
982/2"

also:
973 (smiling socket head)
972 (pensive socket head)
983 (smiling shoulder head)
982 (pensive shoulder head)
18 - 22in (46 - 56cm)
$2500 - 2850

20in (51cm) ***Baby Peggy***
with bisque shoulder head.
Jensen's Antique Dolls.

Louis Amberg & Son continued

All-Bisque Character Children: 1920s. Made by a German porcelain factory. Pink pretinted bisque with molded and painted features, molded hair; jointed at shoulders and hips; molded stockings with blue garters, brown strap shoes, white stockings. See color photograph on page 18.

4in (10cm)   **$125**
5 - 6in (13 - 15cm)   **160 - 185**
girl with molded bow (For photograph see *9th Blue Book*, page 59.)
  6in (15cm)   **250 - 275**
girl with downward gaze, glass eyes, wig
  5 - 6in (13 - 15cm)   **325 - 375**

Mibs
  3in (8cm)   **$225**
  4¾in (12cm)   **325 - 350**
Baby Peggy
  3in (8cm)   **225**
  5½in (14cm)   **350**
Coquette
  5½in (14cm)   **160 - 175**

Vanta Baby: 1927. A tie-in with Vanta baby garments. Composition or bisque head with molded and painted hair, sleep eyes, open mouth with two teeth (closed mouth and painted eyes in all-composition small dolls); muslin body jointed at hips and shoulders, curved composition arms and legs; suitably dressed; all in good condition. **Mark:** Bisque Head

Vanta Baby
L ABS · 3/0 D·R·G·M
Germany.

5½in (14cm) pink bisque coquette character. *H & J Foulke, Inc.*

Louis Amberg & Son continued

Composition head
  20in (51cm)
    $ 250 - 275
Bisque head
  10in (25cm) Toddler
    500
  25in (64cm) Baby
    1000 - 1100

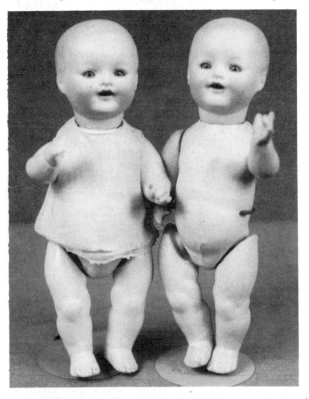

10in (25cm) *Vanta Baby* twins. See color photograph on page 22. *H & J Foulke, Inc.*

Sue, Edwina or It: 1928. All-composition with molded and painted hair, painted eyes; jointed neck, shoulders and hips, a large round ball joint at waist; dressed; all in very good condition. (For photograph see *7th Blue Book*, page 59).
Mark:

> "AMBERG
> PAT. PEND.
> L.A. & S. © 1928"

14in (36cm)   **$425 - 475**

Tiny Tots Body Twists: 1928. All-composition with jointed shoulders and a large round ball joint at the waist; molded and painted hair in both boy and girl styles, painted eyes; painted shoes and socks; dressed; all in good condition. (For photograph see *8th Blue Book*, page 60.)
Mark: tag on clothes:

> "An Amberg Doll with
> BODY TWIST
> all its own
> PAT. PEND. SER. NO.
> 32018"

8in (20cm)   **$165 - 185**

American Character

Maker: American Character Doll Co., New York, N.Y., U.S.A.
Date: 1919 - on
Trademark: Petite

Marked Petite or American Character Mama Dolls: 1923 - on. Composition head, arms and legs, cloth torso; mohair or human hair wig, sleep eyes, closed or open mouth; original clothes; all in good condition. (For photograph see *9th Blue Book*, page 61.)

16 - 18in (41 - 46cm)	**$200 - 225**
24in (61cm)	**275 - 325**

Puggy: 1928. All-composition chubby body jointed at neck, shoulders and hips; molded and painted hair, painted eyes to the side, closed mouth, pug nose, frowning face; original clothes; all in good condition.
Mark:
"A PETITE DOLL"

12in (31cm)	**$500**

Marked Petite Girl Dolls: 1930s. All-composition jointed at neck, shoulders and hips; human hair or mohair wig, lashed sleeping eyes, open mouth with teeth; original or appropriate old clothes; all in good condition.

16 - 18in (41 - 46cm)	**$225 - 250**
24in (61cm)	**275 - 325**

19in (48cm) Petite girl. *H & J Foulke, Inc.*

Sally: 1930. All-composition jointed at neck, shoulders and hips; molded and painted hair, painted side-glancing eyes, closed mouth; original or appropriate old clothes; all in good condition. (For photograph see *9th Blue Book*, page 61.)

Mark:
"PETITE
SALLY"

12in (31cm) **$175 - 200**
16in (41cm)
  sleeping eyes **225 - 250**

12in (31cm) *Puggy*, all original. *Jensen's Antique Dolls.*
24in (61cm) *Sweet Sue Walker*, all original. *H & J Foulke, Inc.*

Sweet Sue: 1953. All-hard plastic or hard plastic and vinyl, some with walking mechanism, some fully-jointed including elbows, knees and ankles; original clothes; all in excellent condition.

Marks: "A.C."
        "Amer. Char."

14in (36cm) **$150 - 185**
18 - 20in (46 - 51cm)
        200 - 250
24in (61cm)   **250 - 275**
30in (76cm)   **325 - 375**
20 - 21in (51 - 53cm)
  Mint-in-box **300 - 375**

74

American Character continued

Eloise: Ca. 1955. All-cloth with molded face, painted side-glancing eyes, smiling mouth, yellow yarn hair; flexible arms and legs; original clothing; in excellent condition. Designed by Bette Gould from the fictional little girl "Eloise" who lived at the Plaza Hotel in New York City.

Mark: Cardboard tag

21in (53cm)   **$250**

21in (53cm) *Eloise,* all original. *H & J foulke, Inc.*

8½in (22cm) hard plastic *Betsy McCall,* all original. *H & J Foulke, Inc.*

Betsy McCall: 1957. All-hard plastic with legs jointed at knees; rooted Saran hair on a wig cap, round face with sleep eyes, plastic eyelashes; original clothes; all in excellent condition.

Mark:

8in (20cm)   **$135 - 150**

Betsy McCall: 1960. All-vinyl with rooted hair, lashed sleep eyes, round face, turned-up mouth; slender arms and legs; original clothes; all in excellent condition.

Mark:
McCALL
19©56
CORP.

13 - 14in (33 - 36cm)	**$200**
18 - 20in (46 - 51cm)	**225 - 250**
30 - 36in (76 - 91cm)	**350 - 400**

Artist Dolls

Modern Artist Dolls: 1930s - on. Original dolls which were created as works of art and decorative objects, not intended as playthings.

Martha Armstrong-Hand, porcelain babies and children.	**$1200 up**
Bob & June Beckett, carved wood children.	**300 - 400**
Halle Blakeley, High-fired clay lady dolls.	**450 - 550**
Helen Bullard, carved wood	
Holly	**100 - 125**
Hitty	**150 - 175**
American Family Series (16 dolls)	**225 - 250 each**
Charlotte Byrd, Bear Bryant	**400**
Astry Campbell, porcelain, *Ricky & Becky*	**850 pair**
Emma Clear, porcelain	
George & Martha Washington	**400 - 700 pair**
depending upon clothes and sharpness of detail	
28in (71cm) glass-eyed Parian models	**1000 - 1100**
Danny	**350 - 400**
Gibson Girl	**350 - 400**
Gertrude Florian, ceramic composition dressed ladies	**300**
Madeline Fox. Gibson Girl	**1000**
Dorothy Heiser, cloth sculpture	
Early dolls	**350 - 450**
Queens 10 - 12in (25 - 31cm)	**900 - 1000**
Maggie Head Kane, porcelain	
Gypsy Mother	**400**
Lil Miss Ohio	**150 - 175**
Irma Park, wax-over-porcelain miniatures	**35 - 100**
depending upon elaborateness of detail	
Kathy Redmond, porcelain ladies with elaborately molded shoulder plates and hair	**400**
Lewis Sorensen, wax	
Gibson Girl	**300 - 350**
Abraham & Mary Todd Lincoln	**400 pair**
Sherman Smith, carved wood	
Angelita, dressed	**150**
Miss Unity, 6in (15cm)	**175**
Linda Steele, porcelain	
Wilmington Regional Souvenir	**300 - 350**
John Clendenien, UDFC Souvenir, 1989	**150**
Martha Thompson, porcelain	
Princess Caroline, Prince Charles, Princess Ann	**900 - 1000 each**
Little Women	**1000 each**
Queen Elizabeth with molded crown	**1500**
Princess Margaret Rose	**1200**
Eunice Tuttle, porcelain miniature children	**250 - 300**
Beverly Walters, porcelain	
Miniature Fashions	**500 up**
Santa Claus	**400 - 500**

Artist Dolls continued

Lita Wilson, porcelain
  Jackie & Jack Kennedy   **400 each**
  Marilyn Monroe   **300 - 400**
  Scarlett O'Hara   **300 - 400**
Phyllis Wright, porcelain children   **300 - 450**
John Wright, cloth adult characters   **1500 - 2000**
Fawn Zeller, porcelain
  Miami Miss   **$300 - 350**
  Piedmont Polly   **900**
  Jeannie, Angela   **500 - 600 each**
  Jackie & Jack Kennedy   **500 each**

Catherine de Medici by Kathy Redmond. *H & J Foulke, Inc.*

Artist Dolls continued

16½in (42cm) lady by Gertrude Florian. *H & J Foulke, Inc.*

Danny by Emma Clear. *H & J Foulke, Inc.*

Arranbee

Maker: Arranbee Doll Co., New York, N.Y., U.S.A.
Date: 1922 - 1960
Mark: "ARRANBEE" or "R & B"

18in (46cm) *My Dream Baby*, AM 341 with 14in (36cm) head circumference. *H & J Foulke, Inc.*

Baby: 1924. Perfect solid dome bisque head with molded and painted hair, sleep eyes, open mouth with teeth, dimples; cloth body with celluloid or composition hands, may have a molded celluloid bottle in hand, "Nursing Bottle Baby;" dressed; all in good condition. (For photograph see *6th Blue Book*, page 61.)
Head circumference:
12 - 13in (31 - 33cm) **$400 - 450**

My Dream Baby: 1924. Perfect bisque head with solid dome and painted hair, sleep eyes, closed or open mouth; all-composition or cloth body with composition hands; dressed; all in good condition. Some heads incised "A.M.," *"341"* or *"351";* some incised "ARRANBEE."
Head circumference:
10in (25cm) **$275**
12 - 13in (31 - 33cm) **350 - 425**
15in (38cm) **600 - 650**

Storybook doll *Bo-Peep*, all original and boxed. *H & J Foulke, Inc.*

Arranbee continued

Storybook Dolls: 1930s. All-composition with swivel neck, jointed arms and legs; molded and painted hair, painted eyes; all original storybook costumes; all in good condition.

Mark: R. & B.
DOLL CO.

9 - 10in (23 - 25cm) **$150 - 175**
Boxed *Bo-Peep* with lamb **225 - 250**

Nancy: 1930. All-composition, jointed at neck, shoulders and hips, molded hair, painted eyes and closed mouth; original or appropriate old clothes; all in good condition. (For photograph see *8th Blue Book*, page 81.)
Mark: "ARRANBEE" or "NANCY"
12in (31cm) **$175 - 200**
16in (41cm) sleep eyes, wig, open mouth (For photograph see *9th Blue Book*, page 82.) **225 - 250**

18in (46cm) hard plastic *Nanette,* all original. *H & J Foulke, Inc.*

14in (36cm) *Debu' Teen* all original. *H & J Foulke, Inc.*

Debu' Teen and Nancy Lee: 1938 - on. All-composition or composition swivel shoulder head and limbs on cloth torso; mohair or human hair wig, sleep eyes, closed mouth, original clothes; all in good condition.
Mark: "R & B"
14in (36cm) **$200 - 225**
18in (46cm) **250**
21in (53cm) **300**
Skating doll, 14in (36cm) **225 - 250**

Little Angel: 1940s. Composition head and lower limbs, cloth torso, molded hair, sleep eyes, closed mouth; original clothes; all in good condition.
16in (41cm) **$175 - 200**
Boxed and excellent condition **250**

Nanette and Nancy Lee: 1950s. All-hard plastic, jointed at neck, shoulders and hips; synthetic wig, sleep eyes, closed mouth; original clothes; all in excellent condition. This face mold was also used for dolls which were given other names.
Mark: "R & B"
14in (36cm) **$150 - 200**
18in (46cm) **250 - 275**

Georgene Averill
(Madame Hendren)

Maker: Averill Mfg. Co. and Georgene Novelties, Inc., New York, N.Y., U.S.A.
Date: 1915 - on
Designer: Georgene Averill (See also Maud Tousey Fangel and Grace Drayton)
Trademarks: Madame Hendren, Georgene Novelties

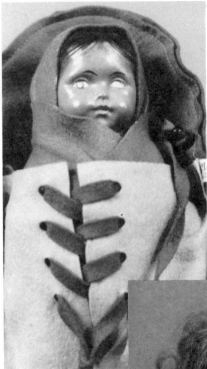

Tagged Mme. Hendren Character: Ca. 1915 - on. Composition character face, usually with painted features, molded hair or wig (sometimes yarn); hard-stuffed cloth body with composition hands; original clothes often of felt, included Dutch children, Indians, sailors, cowboys, blacks; all in good condition.

Cloth Label:

MADAME HENDREN
CHARACTER   DOLL
COSTUME PAT. MAY 9TH 1916

10 - 14in (25 - 36cm)   **$110 - 135**

Mama & Baby Dolls: Ca. 1918 - on. Composition shoulder head, lower arms and legs, cloth torso with cry box; mohair wig or molded hair, sleep eyes, open mouth with teeth or closed

12in (31cm) papoose, all original with Madame Hendren label. *H & J Foulke, Inc.*

22in (56cm) Madame Hendren mama doll 222. *Miriam Blankman Collection.*

Georgene Averill (Madame Hendren) continued

mouth; appropriately dressed; all in good condition. Names such as *Baby Hendren, Baby Georgene* and others.

15 - 18in (38 - 46cm)	**$165 - 185**
22in (56cm)	**250 - 275**
24in (61cm)	**350 - 400**

Dolly Reckord: 1922. Record playing mechanism in torso. Good condition with records.

26in (66cm)	**$500**

26in (66cm) *Dolly Reckord*, all original. *H & J Foulke, Inc.*

Infant Baby Dolls: Ca. 1924. Composition infant head with flange neck. Good condition with light crazing. Sometimes stamped on body. (For photograph see *8th Blue Book*, page 83.)

Mark:

Genuine
Madame Hendren
Doll
522
Made in U.S.A.

16in (41cm)	**$150 - 165**
22in (56cm)	**250 - 275**

Whistling Doll: 1925 - 1929. Composition head with molded hair, side-glancing eyes, mouth pursed to whistle through round opening; composition arms, cloth torso; legs are coiled spring bellows covered with cloth; when head is pushed down or feet are pushed up, the doll whistles. Original or appropriate clothes; all in good condition. (For photographs see *7th Blue Book*, page 198 and *9th Blue Book*, page 84.)

Mark: None

Original Cardboard Tag:

"I whistle when you dance me on one foot and then the other.
Patented Feb. 2, 1926
Genuine Madame Hendren Doll."

14 - 15in (36 - 38cm) sailor, cowboy, (*Dan*)	**$165 - 185**
Black *Rufus* or *Dolly Dingle*	**350****

**Not enough price samples to compute a reliable range.

Georgene Averill (Madame Hendren) continued

Bonnie Babe: 1926. Bisque heads by Alt, Beck & Gottschalck; cloth bodies by K & K Toy Co.; distributed by George Borgfeldt, New York. Perfect bisque head with smiling face, molded hair, glass sleep eyes, open mouth with two lower teeth; cloth body with composition arms (sometimes celluloid) and legs often of poor quality; all in good condition. Mold *#1386* or *1402*. (For photograph see *9th Blue Book*, page 85.)

Mark:
Copr. by Georgene Averill Germany 1005/3652 1386

Head circumference:	
9 - 10in (23 - 25cm)	$ 900
12 - 13in (31 - 33cm)	1100 - 1200
14½ - 15in (37 - 38cm)	1500 - 1600
Composition body, 8in (20cm) tall	1250**
Celluloid head, 16in (41cm) tall	550 - 650**

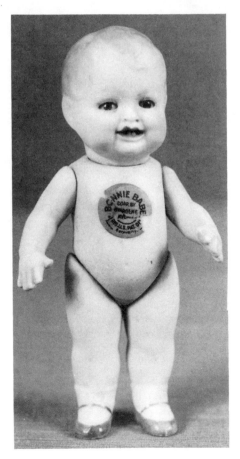

All-Bisque Bonnie Babe: 1926. Jointed at neck, shoulders and hips; pink or blue molded slippers. Unmarked except for round paper label on stomach.

5in (13cm)	$ 675 - 725
with original clothes, mint-in-box, at auction	1150
7in (18cm)	950 - 1000
With molded clothes,	
5in (13cm)	1250**

All-Bisque Sonny: Jointed at neck, shoulders and hips; glass eyes; bare-feet.

5½in (14cm)	$2000**

**Not enough price samples to compute a reliable range.

4½in (12cm) all-bisque **Bonnie Babe.** *H & J Foulke, Inc.*

Georgene Averill (Madame Hendren) continued

Body Twists: 1927. All-composition, jointed at neck, shoulders and hips, with a large round ball joint at waist; molded and painted hair, painted eyes, closed mouth; dressed; all in good condition. Advertised as **Dimmie** and **Jimmie**.
14½in (37cm)   **$425**

14½in (37cm) Body Twist **Dimmie**, all original. *H & J Foulke, Inc.*

Sunny Boy and Girl: Ca. 1927. Celluloid "turtle" mark head with molded hair and glass eyes; stuffed body with composition arms and legs; appropriate or original clothes; all in good condition. (For photograph see *9th Blue Book*, page 86.)
15in (38cm)   **$300 - 350**

Snookums: 1927. Composition shoulder head, molded and painted hair with hole for one tuft of hair, painted eyes, smiling face with open/closed mouth; composition yoke and arms; cloth body and legs; dressed; all in good condition. From the comic strip "The Newlyweds" by George McManus. (For photograph see *5th Blue Book*, page 169.)
14in (36cm)   **$275 - 325**

Patsy-Type Girl: 1928. All-composition, jointed at neck, shoulders, and hips; molded hair, sleeping eyes, tiny closed mouth; bent right arm; original or appropriate old clothing; good condition with light crazing. (For photograph see *9th Blue Book*, page 86.)
Mark: A.D. Co.
14in (36cm)   **$200 - 225**

Georgene Averill (Madame Hendren) continued

Harriet Flanders: 1937. All-composition with jointed neck, shoulders and hips; chubby toddler body; solid dome head with tufts of molded blonde hair, lashed sleeping eyes, closed mouth; original clothes. Very good condition. Designed by Harriet Flanders. (For photograph see *7th Blue Book*, page 167.)

Mark: HARRIET ©
   FLANDERS

16in (41cm)   **$250**
Painted eyes, 12in (31cm) **150**

Cloth Dolls: Ca. 1930s - on. Mask face with painted features, yarn hair, painted and/or real eyelashes; cloth body with movable arms and legs; attractive original clothes; all in excellent condition.

Children or Babies:
12in (31cm)   **$ 85 - 125**
24 - 26in (61 - 66cm) **175 - 225**

Topsy & Eva
 10in (25cm)   **$125 - 135**
International and Costume Dolls:
 12in (31cm)   **65 - 75**
 Mint in box with wrist tag **85 - 95**
Uncle Wiggily,
 13in (33cm)   **350****
Characters, 14in (36cm):
 Little Lulu, 1944   **375 - 425****
  40in (100cm)   **750****
 Nancy, 1944   **375 - 425****
 Sluggo, 1944   **375 - 425****
 Tubby Tom, 1951   **375 - 425****

Baby Yawn: 1946. Composition head and hands. Closed eyes, yawning expression, all original. (For photograph see *5th Blue Book*, page 143.)
14in (36cm)   **$450 - 500****

**Not enough price samples to compute a reliable range.

13in (34cm) cloth girl of the type made by Averill, all original. *H & J Foulke, Inc.*

Baby Bo Kaye

Maker: Composition heads by Cameo Doll Company; bisque heads made in Germany, by Alt, Beck & Gottschalck; bodies by K & K Toy Co., New York, N.Y., U.S.A.
Date: 1925
Material: Bisque, composition or celluloid head with flange neck; composition or celluloid limbs, cloth body
Designer: J. L. Kallus
Mark:

"Copr. by
J. L. Kallus
Germany
1394/30"

Baby Bo Kaye: Perfect bisque head marked as above, molded hair, glass eyes, open mouth with two lower teeth; body as above; dressed; all in good condition. See color photograph on page 22.
17 - 19in (43 - 48cm)
$2600 - 3000
Celluloid head,
16in (41cm)
650 - 750

All-Bisque Baby Bo Kaye: Molded hair, glass sleep eyes, open mouth with two teeth; swivel neck, jointed shoulders and hips; molded shoes and socks; unmarked.
Mark:

5in (13cm) **$1250 - 1350**
6in (15cm) **1600 - 1700**

5in (14cm) *Baby Bo Kaye*, all original. *H & J Foulke, Inc.*

Babyland Rag

Maker: E. I. Horsman, New York, N.Y., U.S.A
Date: 1904 - 1920
Material: All-cloth
Size: 12 - 30in (31 - 76cm)
Mark: None

15in (38cm) hand-painted Babyland Rag. *H & J Foulke, Inc.*

Babyland Rag: Cloth face with hand-painted features, later with printed features, sometimes mohair wig; cloth body jointed at shoulders and hips; original clothes. See color photograph on page 22.

Early hand-painted face:
13 - 15in (33 - 38cm)	
very good	$ 750 - 850*
fair	400 - 500
22in (56cm) fair	550 - 600
30in (76cm) very good	2000**

Topsy Turvy,
13 - 15in (33 - 38cm) good	700 - 800*
Black, 15in (38cm)	650 - 700**
20in (51cm)	1000 - 1200*

Life-like face:
13 - 15in (33 - 38cm)	
very good	600 - 650*

*Allow more for mint condition doll.
**Not enough price samples to compute a reliable range.

Babyland Rag-type (lesser quality):
White, 14in (36cm) good	**$375 - 475**
Topsy Turvy,	
14in (36cm) good	450 - 550

Bähr & Pröschild

Maker: Bähr & Pröschild, porcelain factory, Ohrdruf, Thüringia, Germany. Made heads for Bruno Schmidt, Heinrich Stier, Kley & Hahn and others.
Date: 1871 - on
Material: Bisque heads for use on composition or kid bodies, all-bisque dolls

---

Marked Belton-type Child Doll: Ca. 1880. Perfect bisque head, solid dome with flat top having two or three small holes, paperweight eyes, closed mouth with pierced ears; wood and composition jointed body with straight wrists; dressed; all in good condition. Mold numbers in *200* series, usually *204* or *224*.
   Mark: 204
11 - 13in (28 - 33cm)
      $1600 - 1800
15 - 16in (38 - 41cm)
      1900 - 2200
20 - 22in (51 - 56cm)
      2500 - 2800
24in (61cm) **3200 - 3500**

7½in (19cm) 204 girl with open mouth, all original. See color photograph on page 23. *H & J Foulke, Inc.*

Bähr & Pröschild continued

Marked Child Doll: 1888 - on. Perfect bisque shoulder or socket head, sleeping eyes, open mouth with four or six upper teeth, good human hair or mohair wig; gusseted kid or jointed composition body (many of French-type); dressed; all in good condition. Mold numbers in *200* and *300* series.

Mark: 224
dep

#204, 224, 239, 273, 275, 277, 289, 297, 325, 340, 379, 394 and other socket heads:

7 - 8in (18 - 20cm)	
five-piece body	**$ 350 - 400**
10in (25cm)	**500 - 600**
15 - 17in (38 - 43cm)	**675 - 725**
20 - 22in (51 - 56cm)	**825 - 900**
25in (64cm)	**1100 - 1200**

#246, 309 and other shoulder heads:

16 - 18in (41 - 46cm)	**425 - 475**
22 - 24in (56 - 61cm)	**575 - 650**

All-bisque Girl, yellow stockings

5in (13cm)	**275 - 325**

20in (51cm) 340 girl. *H & J Foulke, Inc.*

Marked B. P. Character Child: Ca. 1910. Perfect bisque socket head, good wig, sleep or painted eyes, closed mouth; toddler or jointed composition body; dressed; all in good condition. Mold *#2072, 536* and other child *500* series models made for Kley & Hahn and Bruno Schmidt. (For photograph see *9th Blue Book*, page 91.)

Mark:

15 - 16in (36 - 38cm)	**$3000 - 3200***
19 - 21in (48 - 53cm)	**4000 - 4500***

*Allow $500 extra for glass-eyed models.

Marked B. P. Character Baby: Ca. 1910 - on. Perfect bisque socket head, solid dome or good wig, sleep eyes, open mouth; composition bent-limb baby body; dressed; all in good condition. Mold *#585, 604, 624, 678, 619, 641* and *587.* See color photographs on pages 23 and 24.

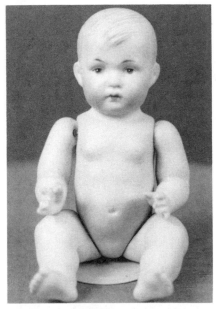

6½in (17cm) 425 all-bisque baby with incised heart. *H & J Foulke, Inc.*

Bähr & Pröschild continued

Mark:

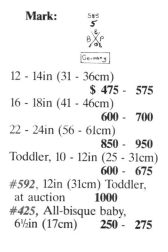

12 - 14in (31 - 36cm)
$ 475 - 575
16 - 18in (41 - 46cm)
600 - 700
22 - 24in (56 - 61cm)
850 - 950
Toddler, 10 - 12in (25 - 31cm)
600 - 675
#592, 12in (31cm) Toddler,
at auction **1000**
#425, All-bisque baby,
6½in (17cm) **250 - 275**

12in (31cm) 585 character toddler. *H & J Foulke, Inc.*

E. Barrois

Maker: E. Barrois, doll factory, Paris, France. Heads purchased from an unidentified French or German porcelain factory.
Date: 1844 - 1877
Material: Bisque or china head, cloth or kid body (some with wooden arms)
Mark:

$$E. \ I \ \text{DÉPOSÉ} \ B.$$

E.B. Fashion Lady: Perfect bisque shoulder head (may have a swivel neck), glass eyes (may be painted with long painted eyelashes), closed mouth; appropriate wig; kid body, some with jointed wood arms or wood and bisque arms; appropriate clothing. All in good condition.
16 - 19in (41 - 48cm)
$3100 - 3600*

*Allow $500 extra for wood or bisque arms.

16½in (42cm) fashion lady shoulder head of the type made by Barrois. *Private Collection.*

Bawo & Dotter

Maker: Bawo & Dotter, Bavaria, France and New York, N.Y., U.S.A.
Date: 1880s
Material: China head, cloth body, china lower limbs
Mark: On back shoulders:

7
Pat. Dec. 7/80

Marked Bawo & Dotter China Head: Perfect china shoulder head with black or blonde molded hair (several styles with a high forehead exposed and one with soft curly bangs), painted eyes, closed mouth, rosy cheeks; cloth body with patented printed corset, china lower arms and lower legs with molded boots (limbs often marked with same size number as head).

16 - 18in (41 - 46cm)
$250 - 275
20 - 22in (51 - 56cm)
300 - 350
24in (61cm) **400 - 450**
28in (71cm) **550 - 600**

25in (64cm) china head incised "B & D//H" with pink tint, unusually large eyes. *H & J Foulke, Inc.*

Belton-type
(So-called)

Maker: Various French and German firms such as Bähr & Pröschild
Date: 1875 - on
Material: Bisque socket head, ball-jointed wood and composition body with straight wrists
Mark: None, except sometimes numbers

Belton-type Child Doll: Perfect bisque socket head, solid but flat on top with two or three small holes for stringing; paperweight eyes, closed mouth, pierced ears; wood and composition ball-jointed body with straight wrists; dressed; all in good condition.

Fine early quality, French-type face (some mold *#137*):

10 - 12in (25 - 31cm)	$1750 - 2150
14 - 16in (36 - 41cm)	2400 - 2700
18 - 21in (46 - 53cm)	2900 - 3200
23 - 24in (58 - 61cm)	3500 - 4000

Standard quality, German-type face:

10 - 12in (25 - 31cm)	1250 - 1350
14 - 16in (36 - 41cm)	1500 - 1700

Tiny with five-piece body:

8 - 9in (20 - 23cm)	750 - 850

#200 Series see Bähr & Pröschild, page 87.

14in (36cm) Belton-type 137, fine quality bisque. See color photograph on page 25. *H & J Foulke, Inc.*

C. M. Bergmann

Maker: C. M. Bergmann doll factory of Waltershausen, Thüringia, Germany; heads manufactured for this company by Armand Marseille, Simon & Halbig, Alt, Beck & Gottschalck and perhaps others.

Date: 1888 - on

Material: Bisque head, composition ball-jointed body

Trademarks: Cinderella Baby (1897), Columbia (1904), My Gold Star (1926)

Mark:

C.M. BERGMANN

A - H ½ - M:

Made in Germany

C. M. Bergmann
Waltershausen
Germany
1916
6½ a

Distributor: Louis Wolfe & Co., New York, N.Y., U.S.A.

22in (56cm) Bergmann/S&H child. See color photograph on page 26. *H & J Foulke, Inc.*

Bergmann Character Baby: 1909 - on. Marked bisque socket head, mohair wig, sleep eyes, composition bent-limb baby body; dressed; all in good condition.

Mark:

C. M. Bergmann
Spezial

16 - 18in (41 - 46cm)	**$ 500 - 550**
#612 (open/closed mouth)	
14 - 16in (36 - 41cm)	**1200 - 1500****

**Not enough price samples to compute a reliable range.

Bergmann Child Doll: Ca. 1889 - on. Marked bisque head, composition ball-jointed body, good wig, sleep or set eyes, open mouth; dressed; all in nice condition.

Heads by A.M. and unknown makers:

10in (25cm)	**$ 450**
18 - 21in (46 - 53cm)	**425 - 475**
24 - 26in (61 - 66cm)	**525 - 575**
30in (76cm)	**900 - 1000**
35in (89cm)	**1250 - 1350**
39in - 42in (99 - 111cm)	**2000 - 2200**

C. M. Bergmann continued

Heads by Simon & Halbig:

10in (25cm)	500 - 525	30in (76cm)	1000 - 1100
14 - 16in (36 - 41cm)	400 - 450	33 - 35in (84 - 89cm)	1350 - 1550
18 - 21in (46 - 53cm)	500 - 550	39in (99cm)	2200
24 - 26in (61 - 66cm)	600 - 700	*Eleonore,* 25in (64cm)	800

Bing Art Dolls

Maker: Bing Werke (Bing Kunstlerpuppen) Nürnberg, Germany
Date: 1921 - 1932
Material: All-cloth, all-felt or composition head and cloth body
Size: 6 - 17½in (15 - 45cm)
Designer: Prof. Vogt of Nürnberg & Emil Wagner of Sonneberg
Mark: "Bing" on sole of shoe or unmarked

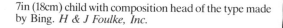

Bing Art Doll: Cloth or composition head, molded
face, handpainted features, painted hair or
wigged; cloth body with pin jointed shoulders
and hips; original clothing; very good condition.
Cloth head,
   painted hair, 10 - 12in (25 - 31cm) **$625 - 675****
   14in (36cm) **775 - 825****
   wigged, 10½in (27cm) **300 - 400****
Composition head, 7in (18cm) **95 - 110****

**Not enough price samples to compute a reliable range.

7in (18cm) child with composition head of the type made
by Bing. *H & J Foulke, Inc.*

Black Dolls*

Black Bisque Doll: Ca. 1880 - on. Various French and German manufacturers from their regular molds or specially designed ones with Negroid features. Perfect bisque socket head either painted dark or with dark coloring mixed in the slip, this runs from light brown to very dark; composition or sometimes kid body in a matching color, cloth bodies on some baby dolls; appropriate clothes; all in good condition. See color photographs on pages 26 and 27.

17½in (45cm) French Fashion-type black lady. *Private Collection.*

FRENCH Makers:
Bru, Circle Dot,
  13 - 15in (33 - 38cm)
                                    $20,000
Fashion Lady, shoulder head,
  open mouth, 17in (43cm)
                          4000 -   5000
  swivel neck, original African clothes
                  15,000 -   20,000

F.G. Child
  18in (46cm)   **3500 -   4000**

GERMAN Makers:
  A.M. 341, 11 - 12in (28 - 31cm), cloth body
                          375 -   400
  351, 15 - 16in (38 - 41cm), compo body
                          600 -   700
  362, 15in (38cm)   **675 -   700**
  1894, 12in (31cm)   **475 -   500**
  B.P. 277, 16in (41cm) **1600 -   1800**
  Gebr. Heubach 7658, 7657, 7671,
  12in (31cm)   **1500 -   1800**

18½in (47cm) F. G. in Scroll black Bébé. *Private Collection.*

Black Dolls continued

E. Heubach 399, 414
7 - 8in (18 - 20cm) baby
| | | **300 -** | **350** |
11 - 12in (28 - 31cm) toddler
| | | **450 -** | **550** |
444, 12 - 14in (31 - 36cm)
| | | **650 -** | **750** |
418, 10 - 12in (25 - 31cm)
| | | **600 -** | **650** |
K&R 100, 19in (48cm) **1600**
101, 15in (38cm), at auction
| | | **5000**** | |
Child 16in (41cm) **1500**
Kestner 134, 10in (25cm)
| | | **650 -** | **700** |
Hilda 13in (33cm) **3200 - 3500**
20in (51cm) **7000**
Kuhnlenz 34, 7 - 8in (20 - 23cm)
fully jointed **450**
21in (53cm) **7500****

*Also see entries for specific doll makers or
material of doll.
**Not enough price samples to compute a
reliable range.

16in (41cm) B.P. 277 brown child. For color
photograph see page 26. *H & J Foulke, Inc.*

S PB H Hanna, 8in (20cm)	**$ 300**
1909, 15in (38cm)	**550**
Simon & Halbig 739, 20 - 21in (51 - 53cm)	**1800 - 2200**
1079, 31in (79cm)	**3400**
1039, 16 - 18in (41 - 46cm)	**1300 - 1500**
939 O.M., 28in (71cm) at auction	**6000**
1368, For photograph see page 12. 14in (36cm)	**3100**
All-Bisque, 4in (10cm), glass eyes	**300 - 350**
61, swivel neck, 5 - 6in (13 - 15cm)	**600 - 700**
Kestner-type, 6½in (17cm)	**950**
Unmarked, good quality:	
10 - 13in (25 - 33cm), jointed body	**375 - 425**
8 - 9in (20 - 23cm), five-piece body	**275 - 300**
5in (13cm), closed mouth	**275 - 325**

Black Dolls continued

Cloth Black Doll: *1880s-on. American-made cloth doll with black face, painted, printed or embroidered features; jointed arms and legs; original clothes; all in good condition.

Mammy-type,
18 - 22in (46 - 56cm)
$ 350 up +

Stockinette (so-called Beecher-type), (For photograph see *8th Blue Book*, page 98.)
2000 - 2500

1930s Mammy,
14 - 16in (36 - 41cm)
150 up +

WPA, molded cloth face, (For photograph see *7th Blue Book*, page 83.)
22in (56cm)
1300 - 1500

Paint over molded stockinette (Chase-type), (For photograph see *9th Blue Book* page 100.)
18in (46cm)
2000 - 2500

Black cloth, embroidered face, 18 - 21in (46 - 53cm)
1000 up +

+ Greatly depending upon appeal.
*Also check under manufacturer if known.

Black primitive rag doll. *Nancy A. Smith Collection.*

18in (46cm) Century Doll Co. mama doll with composition head. For further information see page 132. *H & J Foulke, Inc.*

Very rare Chase character man. For further information see page 134. *Nancy A. Smith Collection.*

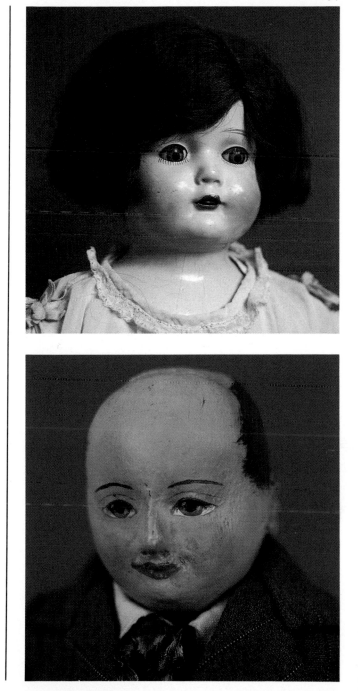

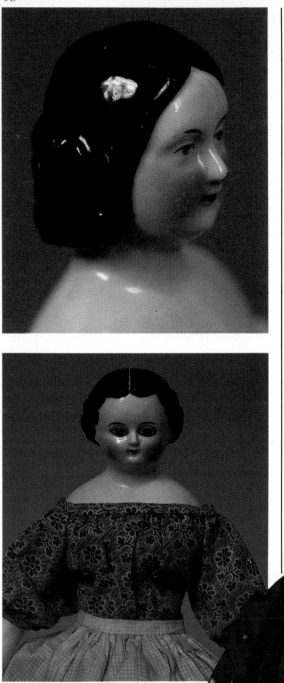

LEFT: China head girl with molded long curls. For further information see page 136. *H & J Foulke, Inc.*

BELOW LEFT: 14in (36cm) china head lady with brown glass eyes. For further information see page 137. *Private Collection.*

BELOW: 14in (36cm) china head lady with rare early hair style. For further information see page 136. *Richard Wright Antiques.*

9in (23cm) china child with swivel neck, china hips and lower limbs, cloth midsection and upper limbs, papier-mâché shoulder plate. "Alice" hairdo. For further information see page 137. *H & J Foulke, Inc.*

14in (36cm) child lady with glass eyes, very rare for this model. For further information see page 138. *Private Collection.*

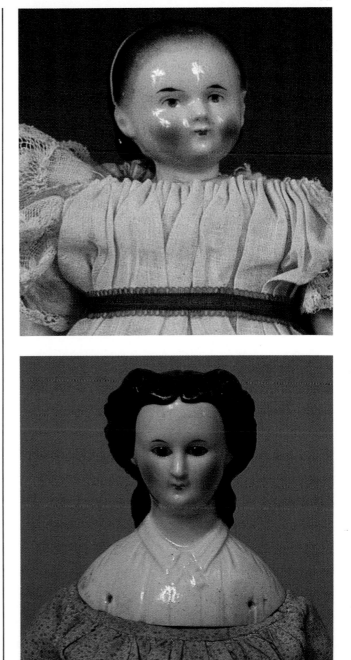

16in (41cm) china head with boy hairdo. For further information see page 141. *Richard Wright Antiques.*

9½in (24cm) china head lady with 1860s hairdo, all original. For further information see page 138. *H & J Foulke, Inc.*

RIGHT: 15in (38cm) Russian cloth pair *Village Boy* and *Smolensk District Woman*, all original. For further information see page 144. *H & J Foulke, Inc.*

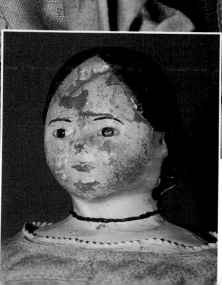

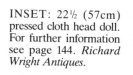

Peter Ponsett at three different ages by Dewees Cochran. For further information see page 161. *Esther Schwartz Collection.*

Susan Stormalong at three different ages by Dewees Cochran. For further information see page 161. *Esther Schwartz Collection.*

17in (43cm) unmarked composition *Patsy*-type doll, all original. For further information see page 165. *Jensen's Antique Dolls.*

13in (33cm) early unmarked American composition character doll. For further information see page 165. *H & J Foulke, Inc.*

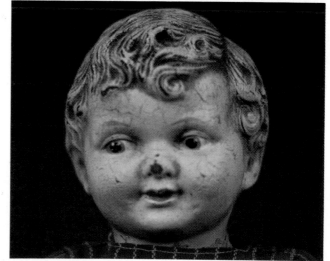

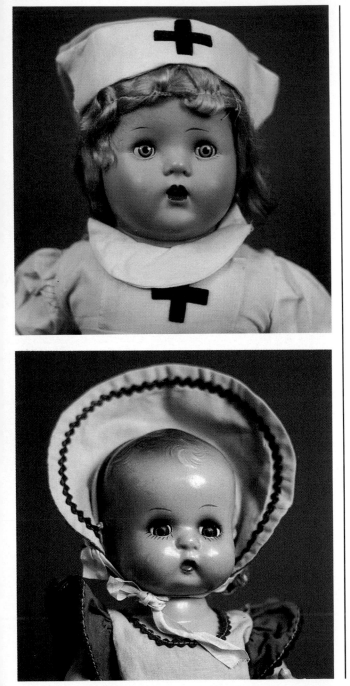

18½in (47cm) unmarked composition mama doll, all original. For further information see page 166. *H & J Foulke, Inc.*

12in (31cm) Eugenia composition toddler, all original. For further information see page 169. *H & J Foulke, Inc.*

17in (43cm) Sayco composition child, all original. For further information see page 169. *H & J Foulke, Inc.*

17in (43cm) *Paris Bébé* by Danel & Cie. For further information see page 173. *Ruth West Antique Dolls.*

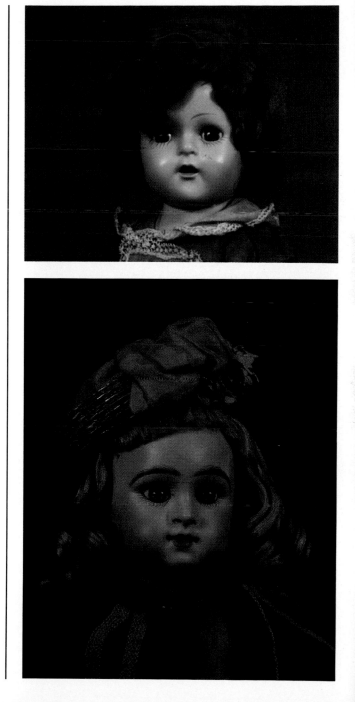

22in (56cm) Cuno & Otto Dressel 93 child, excellent quality, probably one of the first heads made by Armand Marseille. For further information see page 178. *H & J Foulke, Inc.*

23in (58cm) Cuno & Otto Dressel 1912 child. For further information see page 178. *H & J Foulke, Inc.*

19in (48cm) Effanbee *Patsy Ann*, all original. For further information see page 187. *H & J Foulke, Inc.*

BELOW: 14in (36cm) Effanbee *Patsy*, all original. For further information see page 187. *H & J Foulke, Inc.*

21in (53cm) Effanbee Historical Doll *1841 Pre-Civil War*, all original. For further information see page 191. *Rosemary Dent Collection.*

RIGHT: 24in (61cm) Effanbee *Mickey*, all original. For further information see page 185. *H & J Foulke, Inc.*

BELOW RIGHT: 16½in (42cm) "H" Bébé, size "0." For further information see page 195. *Private Collection.*

BELOW: 14in (36cm) Effanbee Historical Doll *1608 Virginia Colony*, all original. For further information see page 192. *Rosemary Dent Collection.*

13in (33cm) shoulder head French fashion, original clothes. For further information see page 197. *H & J Foulke, Inc.*

17in (43cm) French fashion lady. For further information see page 197. *H & J Foulke, Inc.*

RIGHT: 17in (43cm) French fashion lady with cup and saucer neck, kid body, bisque hands. For further information see page 197. *Kay & Wayne Jensen Collection.*

BELOW RIGHT: 13½in (34cm) French fashion lady incised "1," probably by François Gaultier. For further information see page 202. *H & J Foulke, Inc.*

BELOW: Freundlich *Baby Sandy* with original pin. For further information see page 198. *H & J Foulke, Inc.*

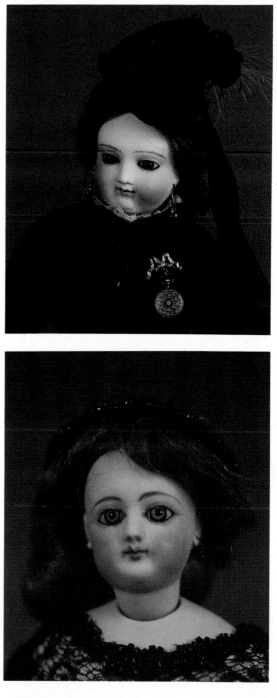

11½in (29cm) French fashion lady incised "2/0," probably by François Gaultier. For further information see page 202. *H & J Foulke, Inc.*

Black Dolls continued

Papier-Mâché Black Doll: Ca. 1890. By various German manufacturers. Papier-mâché character face, arms and legs, cloth body; glass eyes; original or appropriate clothes; all in good condition.

10 - 12in (25 - 31cm)   **$275 - 300**
18 - 20in (46 - 51cm) character with broad smile **700 - 800**

Black Composition Doll: Ca. 1920 on. German made character doll,all-composition, jointed at neck, shoulders and hips; molded hair or wig, glass eyes (sometimes flirty); appropriate clothes; all in good condition. See color photograph on page 27.

15 - 17in (38 - 43cm)   **$500 - 600**

Black Composition Doll: Ca. 1930. American-made bent-limb baby or mama-type body, jointed at hips, shoulders and perhaps neck; molded hair, painted or sleep eyes; original or appropriate clothes; some have three yarn tufts of hair on either side and on top of the head; all in good condition.

"Topsy" Baby,
10 - 12in (25 - 31cm)   **$ 95 - 110**
16 - 17in (41 - 43cm)   **175 - 200**
Mama Doll,
20 - 22in (51 - 56cm)   **200 - 250**
Patsy-type, (For photograph see page 11.)
12 - 14in (31 - 36cm)   **175 - 225**
Toddler,
18in (46cm)   **250 - 275**
Amos, Andy and Madame Queen,
18in (46cm) all original,
mint, at auction   **1900**
Tony Sarg's Mammy with baby (For photograph see *6th Blue Book*, page 74.)
18in (46cm)   **450 - 500**

17in (43cm) Hugo Wiegand German all-composition toddler. *Kiefer Collection.*

Black Dolls continued

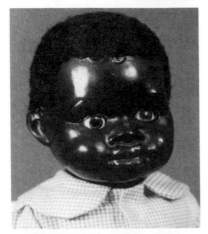

Black Hard Plastic Characters: Ca. 1950. English made by Pedigree and others. All hard plastic, swivel neck, jointed shoulders and hips, sleeping eyes, curly black wig sometimes over molded hair.

16in (41cm)	**$125 - 150**
21in (53cm)	**175 - 200**

16in (41cm) English hard plastic black character. *Kiefer Collection.*

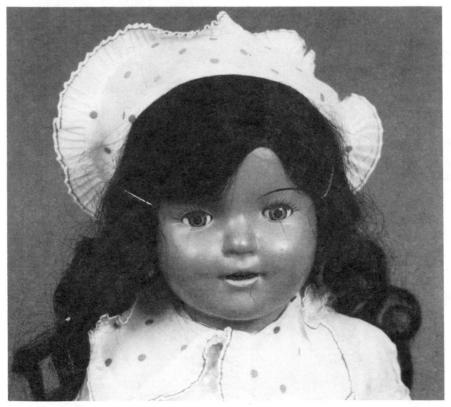

25in (64cm) brown composition mama doll with label: Suntan Dolls by Lujon. *H & J Foulke, Inc.*

George Borgfeldt & Co.

Maker: George Borgfeldt, New York, N.Y., U.S.A., importer, assembler and distributor contracted with various doll factories, particularly in Germany and Japan, to make dolls and doll parts of all types and materials.

G.B. Character Baby: Ca. 1910. Perfect bisque head with smiling face, dimples, sleeping eyes, open mouth with teeth, human hair or mohair wig; composition baby body; appropriate clothing. All in good condition.

Mark:

Germany

G. B.

12 - 14in (31 - 36cm)	$475 - 525
20 - 22in (51 - 56cm)	800 - 900
B.P. 620, 13 - 15in (33 - 38cm)	475 - 525

G.B./A.M. Character Baby: 1913. Perfect bisque socket head, molded hair or mohair wig, sleeping eyes, open smiling mouth; composition bent-limb baby body; appropriate clothes. All in good condition. Mold *#327, #328* and *#329*.

Mark:

G.327.B.

Germany

A.2M

10 - 11in (25 - 28cm)	$325 - 350
14 - 16in (36 - 41cm)	400 - 450
19 - 21in (48 - 53cm)	525 - 625
23 - 24in (58 - 61cm)	700 - 800

13in (33cm) 620 G.B. & Co. made by Bähr & Pröschild for Borgfeldt. See color photograph on page 28. *H & J Foulke, Inc.*

George Borgfeldt & Co. continued

Child Dolls: 1910 - 1922. Perfect bisque socket head, sleep eyes, open mouth with teeth, good wig; ball-jointed composition body; nicely dressed; all in good condition.

Mark:

My Girlie
III
Germany

My Girlie, My Dearie, Pansy:
  23 - 25in (58 - 64cm)   **$550 - 600**
  S&H/G.B., 23 - 26in (58 - 66cm)   **550 - 650**

25in (64cm) *My Dearie. H & J Foulke, Inc.*

Boudoir Dolls

Maker: Various French, U.S. and Italian firms
Date: Early 1920s into the 1940s
Material: Heads of composition and other materials; bodies mostly cloth but also of composition and other substances
Size: Many 24 - 36in (61 - 91cm); some smaller
Mark: Mostly unmarked

Boudoir Doll: Head of composition, cloth or other material, painted features, mohair wig, composition or cloth stuffed body, unusually long extremities, usually high-heeled shoes; original clothes elaborately designed and trimmed; all in excellent condition.

1920s Art Doll, exceptional quality, silk hair,
  28 - 30in (71 - 76cm)
  $ 350 - 450
Standard quality, dressed,
  28 - 30in (71 - 76cm)
  125 - 150
  undressed **65 - 75**
1940s composition head
  75 - 85
Lenci, 24 - 28in (61 - 71cm)
  1600 up
Smoking Doll, 25in (64cm)
  300 up
Mme de Lafayette, 36in (91cm)
  boxed, elaborate clothes,
  at auction **1100**

See color photograph on page 232.

27in (69cm) felt boudoir doll by Lenci of dancer Raquel Meller. *H & J Foulke, Inc.*

Bru

Maker: Bru Jne. & Cie, Paris, and Montreuil-sous-Bois, France
Date: 1866 - 1899
Bru Marked Shoes: $500 - 600

Fashion Lady: 1866 - on. Perfect bisque swivel head on shoulder plate, cork pate, appropriate old wig, closed smiling mouth, paperweight eyes, pierced ears; gusseted kid lady body; original or appropriate old clothes; all in good condition. Incised with letters A through O in sizes 11in (28cm) to 36in (91cm) tall. See color photograph on page 28.

12 - 13in (31 - 33cm)	$ 2400 - 2700*
15in (38cm)	3000 - 3500*
17 - 18in (43 - 46cm)	3800 - 4300*
20in (51cm)	5000 - 5500*
28in (71cm)	12,500*
Wood body, 14in (36cm), naked	5000

*Allow $500 extra for wood arms.

14½in (37cm) Bru fashion with plate incised "B. Jne & Cie." *Private Collection.*

36in (91cm) smiling lady fashion by Bru. *Crandall Collection.*

Fashion Lady: 1866 - on. Perfect bisque swivel head on shoulder plate, cork pate, old mohair wig, closed mouth, paperweight eyes, pierced ears; gusseted or straight kid body; original or appropriate old clothes; all in good condition. Oval face, incised with numbers only. Shoulder plate sometimes marked "B. Jne & Cie."

12 - 13in (31 - 33cm)	$2200 - 2600
15 - 16in (38 - 41cm)	2900 - 3200
20in (51cm)	4000 - 4500
Wood body, 14in (36cm)	4300 - 4500

Bru continued

Marked Brevete Bébé: Ca. 1870s. Perfect bisque swivel head on shoulder plate, cork pate, skin wig, paperweight eyes with shading on upper lid, closed mouth with white space between lips, full cheeks, pierced ears; gusseted kid body pulled high on shoulder plate and straight cut with bisque lower arms (no rivet joints); dressed; all in good condition. See color photograph on page 29.

Mark: Size number only on head.

Oval sticker on body:

or

rectangular sticker like Bébé Bru one, but with words Bébé Breveté

Size 2/0 = 14in (36cm)
Size 1 = 16in (41cm)
Size 2 = 18in (46cm)
Size 3 = 19in (48cm)

10in (25cm) all original **$19,000 - 24,000**
13 - 15in (33 - 38cm) **15,000 - 18,000**
18 - 21in (46 - 53cm) **20,000 - 25,000**
Size 8 head with shoulder plate (no body)
18,000

Bru Brevete model incised "4." *Photograph courtesy of Lesley Hurford.*

Bru continued

Marked Crescent or Circle Dot Bébé: Ca. late 1870s. Perfect bisque swivel head on a
deep shoulder plate with molded breasts, cork pate, attractive wig, paperweight
eyes, closed mouth with slightly parted lips, molded and painted teeth, plump
cheeks, pierced ears; gusseted kid body with bisque lower arms (no rivet joints);
dressed; all in good condition. See color photograph on page 29.

Mark: ⌒ ◐

Sometimes with "BRU Jne"

Approximate size chart:

0 = 11in (28cm)
1 = 12in (31cm)
2 = 13in (33cm)
5 = 17in (43cm)
8 = 22in (56cm)
10 = 26in (66cm)
12 = 30in (76cm)
14 = 35in (89cm)

12in (31cm) with 5 additional original dresses	**$25,000**
13in (33cm) all original	**25,000**
16 - 17in (41 - 43cm)	**21,000 - 23,000**
20 - 22in (51 - 56cm)	**25,000 - 28,000**
30in (76cm)	**38,000 - 40,000**

Marked Nursing Bru (Bébé Teteur): 1878 - 1898. Perfect bisque head, shoulder plate and
lower arms, kid body; upper arms and upper legs of metal covered with kid, lower
legs of carved wood, or jointed composition body; attractive wig, lovely glass eyes,
open mouth with hole for nipple, mechanism in head sucks up liquid, operates by
turning key; nicely clothed; all in good condition. See color photograph on page 30.

13 - 15in (33 - 38cm)	**$7000 - 8000**

Bru continued

Marked Bru Jne Bébé: Ca. 1880s. Perfect bisque swivel head on deep shoulder plate with molded breasts, cork pate, attractive wig, paperweight eyes, closed mouth, pierced ears; gusseted kid body with scalloped edge at shoulder plate, bisque lower arms with lovely hands, kid over wood upper arms, hinged elbow, all kid or wood lower legs (sometimes on a jointed composition body); dressed; all in good condition. (For body photograph see *6th Blue Book*, page 79.)

Mark: "BRU J^ne"

Body Label:

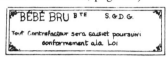

12in (31cm)	**$22,000 - 24,000**
15 - 16in (38 - 41cm)	**19,000 - 22,000**
19 - 21in (48 - 53cm)	**25,000 - 29,000**
23in (58cm)	**32,000**
26 - 28in (66 - 71cm)	**38,000 - 40,000**
24in (61cm) *Bébé Marchant*, all original and boxed, at auction	**19,000**

Marked Bru Jne R Bébé: Ca. Early 1890s. Perfect bisque head on a jointed composition body; attractive wig, paperweight eyes, closed mouth, pierced ears; dressed all in good condition.

Mark: BRU J^ne R
11

Body Stamp: "Bebe Bru" with size number

11in (28cm) **$4000**

23 - 26in (58 - 66cm)
8000 - 8500

Open mouth
22 - 24in (56 - 61cm)
4500 - 5000

18½in (47cm) Bru Jne. *Private Collection.*

Brückner Rag Doll

Maker: Albert Brückner, Jersey City, N.J., U.S.A.
Date: 1901 - on
Material: All-cloth with stiffened mask face
Size: 12 - 14in (31 - 36cm)
Mark: On right front shoulder: PAT'D. JULY 8ᵀᴴ 1901

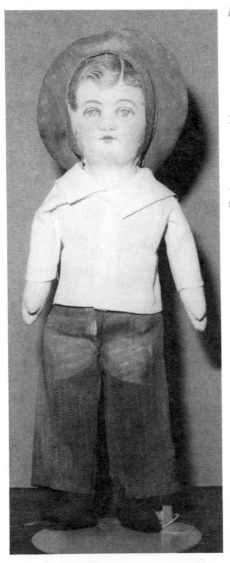

Marked Brückner: Cloth head with printed features on stiffened mask face, cloth body flexible at shoulders and hips; appropriate clothes; all in good condition. These dolls were sold by Horsman as part of their "Babyland Rag" line. See color photograph on page 31.

12 - 14in (31 - 36cm)

White	**$200 - 225**
Black	**250 - 275**
Topsy Turvy	**400 - 500**
Dollypop	**250****

**Not enough price samples to compute a reliable range.

12in (31cm) Brückner doll, all original. *Pat Brown.*

Bucherer

Maker: A. Bucherer, Amriswil, Switzerland
Date: 1921
Material: Composition head, hands and feet, metal ball-jointed body
Size: 8in (20cm) average
Mark:

"MADE IN
SWITZERLAND
PATENTS
APPLIED FOR"

Bucherer Doll: Composition character head often with molded hat; metal ball-jointed body; original clothes, often felt; all in good condition.
Comic characters: *Mutt, Jeff, Maggie, Jiggs, Katzenjammer Kids,* etc.
$250
Regular People: lady, man, fireman, clown, black man, Becassine, baseball player and others.
$135 - 160

Bucherer baseball player, all original including mitt. *H & J Foulke, Inc.*

Bye-Lo Baby

Maker: Bisque heads — J. D. Kestner; Alt, Beck & Gottschalck; Kling & Co.; Hertel, Schwab & Co.; all of Thüringia, Germany.
Composition heads — Cameo Doll Company, New York, N.Y.
Celluloid heads — Karl Standfuss, Saxony, Germany
Wooden heads (unauthorized) — Schoenhut of Philadelphia, Pa.
All-Bisque Baby — J. D. Kestner
Cloth Bodies and Assembly — K & K Toy Co., New York, N.Y.
Composition Bodies — König & Wernicke
Date: 1922 - on
Designer: Grace Storey Putnam
Distributor: George Borgfeldt, New York, N.Y., U.S.A.

Bisque Head Bye-Lo Baby: Ca. 1923. Perfect bisque head, cloth body with curved legs (sometimes with straight legs), composition or celluloid hands; sleep eyes; dressed. Made in seven sizes 9 - 20in (23 - 51cm). (May have purple "Bye-Lo Baby" stamp on front of body.) Sometimes Mold *#1373* (ABG)

Mark: © 1923 by
Grace S. Putnam
MADE IN GERMANY

Head circumference:

8in (20cm)	$ 475 - 500
9 - 10in (23 - 25cm)	475 - 500*
12 - 13in (31 - 33cm)	550 - 600*
15in (38cm)	900*
17in (43cm)	1100 - 1200*
18in (46cm)	1250 - 1500*
Black, 13in (33cm)	2600*

*Allow extra for original tagged gown and button. (For photograph see *9th Blue Book*, page 73.)

Baby Aero or *Fly-Lo Baby* bisque head Mold *#1418.*
10in (25cm) long $3000 - 3500

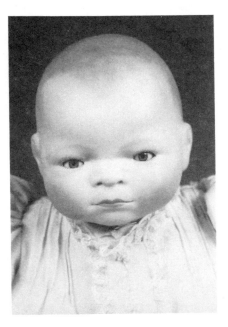

12½in (32cm) head circumference **Bye-Lo Baby** with bisque head. *H & J Foulke, Inc.*

Mold *#1369* (ABG) socket head on composition body, some marked "K&W." (For photograph see page 7.)
12 - 13in (30 - 33cm) long
$1350 - 1550
Mold *#1415*, smiling with painted eyes
13½in (34cm) h.c.　　**3000 - 3300**
Composition head, 1924. See color photograph on page 31.
　12 - 13in (31 - 33cm) h.c.
　　　　　　　350 - 375
Celluloid head,
　10in (25cm) h.c.　　**300****
Painted bisque head, late 1920s.
　12 - 13in (31 - 33cm) h.c.　**325****
Wooden head, (Schoenhut), 1925.
　　　　　　　1500 - 1600
Vinyl head, 1948.
　16in (41cm)　　**150 - 200**

**Not enough price samples to compute a reliable range.

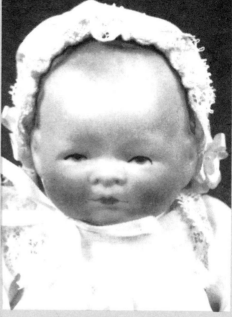

6in (15cm) all-bisque **Bye-Lo Baby.** *H & J Foulke, Inc.*

Marked All-Bisque Bye-Lo Baby: 1925 - on. Sizes 10cm (4in) to 20cm (8in).
　Mark:　Dark green paper label on front torso often missing; incised on back "20-12" (or other stock and size number).

"Copr. by G.S. Putnam"

Solid head with molded hair and painted eyes, jointed shoulders and hips.
　4 - 5in (10 - 13cm)　　$ 275 - 375
　6in (15cm)　　450 - 500
　8in (20cm)　　650 - 700
Solid head with swivel neck, glass eyes, jointed shoulders and hips.
　4 - 5in (10 - 13cm)　　500 - 575
　6in (15cm)　　700 - 750
Head with wig, glass eyes, jointed shoulders and hips.
　4 - 5in (10 - 13cm)　　600 - 700
　6in (15cm)　　800 - 900
　8in (20cm)　　1250 - 1350
Action **Bye-Lo Baby**, immobile in various positions, painted features.
　3in (8cm)　　350 - 400
　Celluloid, 4in (10cm)　　125 - 150

Cameo Doll Company

Maker: Cameo Doll Company, New York, N.Y. U.S.A. later Port Allegany, Pa.,
U.S.A. Original owner: Joseph L. Kallus.
Date: 1922 - on
Material: Wood-pulp composition and wood

Baby Bo Kaye: 1925. (See page 85.)
Kewpie: 1913. (See page 283.)
Scootles: 1925. Designed by Rose O'Neill.
All-composition, unmarked, jointed
at neck, shoulders and hips; molded
hair, blue or brown painted eyes looking to the side, closed smiling mouth;
not dressed; all in very good condition.
Mark: Wrist tag only

7 - 8in (18 - 20cm)	**$300 - 350****
12in (31cm)	**425 - 475**
15 - 16in (38 - 41cm)	**500 - 600**
20in (51cm)	**800****
Black, 14in (36cm)	**750****
All-bisque, marked on feet	
5 - 6in (13 - 15cm) Germany	**500 - 600**

Wood Segmented Characters: Designed
by Joseph L. Kallus. Composition
head, molded hair, painted features;
segmented wood body; undressed; all
in very good condition. (For photographs see *8th Blue Book*, pages 110
and 111.)
Mark: Label with name on chest.

Margie, 1929. 10in (25cm)	**$225 - 250**
Pinkie, 1930. 10in (25cm)	**275 - 325**
Joy, 1932. 10in (5cm)	**275 - 325**
15in (38cm)	**375 - 425**
Betty Boop, 1932.	
12in (31cm)	**500 - 600**

With molded bathing suit and composition legs; wearing a cotton print dress,
650

Pete the Pup, 1932.
9in (23cm)	**200**
Bimbo, 1932.	
9in (23cm)	**250****

Giggles: 1946. Designed by Rose O'Neill.
All-composition, un- marked, jointed
at neck, shoulders and hips, molded
hair with bun in back, large painted
sideglancing eyes, closed mouth; original romper; all in very good condition.
(For photograph see *9th Blue Book*,
page 113.)
Mark: Paper wrist tag only
14in (36cm)   **$500 - 550****

**Not enough price samples to compute a
reliable range.

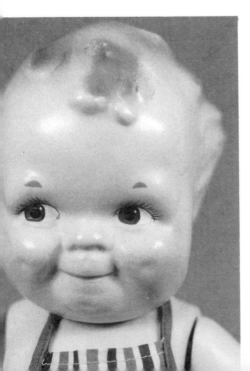

13in (33cm) *Scootles. H & J Foulke, Inc.*

Campbell Kid

Maker: E. I. Horsman Co., Inc., New York, N.Y., U.S.A.; American Character Doll
   Co., New York, N.Y., U.S.A.
Date: 1910 - on
Material: Composition head and arms, cloth body and legs; or all-composition
Size: Usually 9 - 16in (23 - 41cm)
Designer: Grace G. Drayton

Campbell Kid: 1910 - 1914. By Horsman. Marked composition head with flange neck,
   molded and painted bobbed hair, painted round eyes to the side, watermelon mouth;
   original cloth body, composition arms, cloth legs and feet; all in fair condition.
   Mark: On head:
      Cloth label on sleeve: **E.I.H. © 1910**

The Campbell Kids
Trademark by
Joseph Campbell
Mfg. by E. I. HORSMAN Co.

Indian complexion, all original
$400 - 450
Brown complexion, all original
300 - 350
10 - 13in (25 - 33cm) 200 - 225

Campbell Kid: 1948. By Horsman. Unmarked all-composition, molded
painted hair, painted eyes to the side,
watermelon mouth; painted white
socks and black slippers; original
clothes; all in good condition.
12in (31cm) $300

10in (25cm) 1910 *Campbell Kid*, all original
with label. *H & J Foulke, Inc.*

12in (31cm) *Campbell Kid*, all original. *H & J
Foulke, Inc.*

Catterfelder Puppenfabrik

Maker: Catterfelder Puppenfabrik, Catterfeld, Thüringia, Germany. Heads by J. D. Kestner and other porcelain makers
Date: 1902 - on
Material: Bisque head; composition body
Trademark: My Sunshine
Mark:

C. P.
208
45
N

C.P. Child Doll: Ca. 1902 - on. Perfect bisque head, good wig, sleep eyes, open mouth with teeth; composition jointed body; dressed; all in good condition.

#264 (made by Kestner):
17 - 18in (43 - 46cm)
$650 - 700
22 - 24in (56 - 61cm)
800 - 900

17in (43cm) 264 child. *Sheila Needle Collection. Photograph by Morton Needle.*

Catterfelder Puppenfabrik continued

Rare C.P. character child. *Richard Wright Collection.*

C.P. Character Child: Ca. 1910 - on. Perfect bisque character face with wig, painted eyes; composition jointed body; dressed; all in good condition. Sometimes mold **#207** or **#219**.

15 - 16in (38 - 41cm)   **$3000 - 3500****

**Not enough price samples to compute a reliable range.

C.P. Character Baby: Ca. 1910 - on. Perfect bisque character face with wig or molded hair, painted or glass eyes; jointed baby body; dressed; all in good condition. (For photograph see *8th Blue Book*, page 121.)

#200, 201, 208, 209, 262, 263:
15 - 17in (38 - 43cm)   **$500 - 600**
22 - 24in (56 - 61cm)   **850 - 950**

Celluloid Dolls

Makers: Germany:
Rheinische Gummi und Celluloid Fabrik Co. (Turtle symbol)
Buschow & Beck. *Minerva* trademark. (Helmet symbol)
E. Maar & Sohn. *Emasco* trademark. (3 M symbol)
Cellba. (Mermaid symbol)
Poland:
P.R. Zask. (ASK in triangle)
France:
Petitcolin. (Eagle symbol)
Société Nobel Française. (SNF in diamond)
Neumann & Marx. (Dragon symbol)
Société Industrielle de Celluloid (Sicoine)
United States:
Parsons-Jackson Co., Cleveland, Ohio and other companies
England:
Cascelloid Ltd. (Palitoy)

Date: 1895—1940s

Material: All-celluloid or celluloid head with jointed kid, cloth or composition body.

Marks: Various as indicated above: sometimes also in combination with the marks of J. D. Kestner, Kämmer & Reinhardt, Bruno Schmidt, Käthe Kruse and König & Wernicke

Celluloid head Child doll: Ca. 1900 - on. Molded hair or wig, painted or glass eyes, open or closed mouth; cloth or kid body, celluloid or composition arms; dressed; all in good condition. Some with character faces.

22in (56cm) Palitoy all-celluloid toddler. *H & J Foulke, Inc.*

Painted eyes:
13 - 15in (33 - 38cm)	**$125 - 150**

Glass eyes:
13 - 15in (33 - 38cm)	**150 - 175**
18 - 20in (46 - 51cm)	**200 - 225**
22 - 24in (56 - 61cm)	**250 - 275**

12in (31cm) character child with celluloid turtle mark head, so-called *Tommy Tucker* mold, cloth body, all original. *H & J Foulke, Inc.*

All-Celluloid Child Doll: Ca. 1900 - on. Jointed at neck, shoulders, and hips; molded hair or wig, painted eyes; dressed; all in good condition.

Celluloid Dolls continued

17in (43cm) all-celluloid Minerva child with glass eyes. *H & J Foulke, Inc.*

6 - 7in (13 - 15cm)	**$ 50 -**	**60**
9 - 10in (23 - 25cm)	**80 -**	**90**
13 - 14in (33 - 36cm)	**135 -**	**165**

Tommy Tucker-type character,
12 - 13in (31 - 33cm) **150 - 165**

Glass eyes:
12 - 13in (31 - 33cm) **165 - 185**
15 - 16in (38 - 41cm) **250 - 275**
18in (46cm) **325 - 375**
Parsons-Jackson toddler with stork
trademark, 13in (33cm) **275 - 300**
K★R 717 or *728:*
14 - 16in (36 - 41cm) **350 - 450**

All-Celluloid Baby: Ca. 1910 - on. Bent-limb baby, molded hair, painted eyes, closed mouth; jointed arms and/or legs; no clothes; all in good condition.
6 - 8in (15 - 20cm) **$ 60 - 80**
10 - 12in (25 - 31cm) **110 - 125***
15in (38cm) **165 - 175***
21in (53cm) **250 - 275**
23in (58cm) toddler **350**
Japanese, 18 - 21in (46 - 53cm)
  225 - 275
Black, French SNF, 19in (48cm)
  275 - 325
Parsons-Jackson Baby, 11½in (29cm)
  165 - 185

Celluloid Head Infant: Ca. 1920s - on. Celluloid baby head with glass eyes, painted hair, open or closed mouth; cloth body sometimes with celluloid hands; appropriate clothes; all in good condition.
12 - 15in (31 - 38cm) **$135 - 165**

Celluloid socket head Doll: Ca. 1910 - on. Wig, glass eyes, sometimes flirty, open mouth with teeth; ball-jointed or bent-limb composition body; dressed; all in good condition.
15 - 18in (38 - 46cm) **$300 - 350**
22 - 24in (56 - 61cm) **450 - 500**
Characters:
K★R 701,
12 - 13in (31 - 33cm) **700****
K★R 717 child,
16 - 18in (41 - 46cm) **425 - 475**
28in (71cm) **750**
K★R 700,
14 - 15in (36 - 38cm) **300 - 325**
K★R 728,
12 - 13in (31 - 33cm) baby **300 - 350**
18in (46cm) toddler **475 - 525**
K&W toddler,
16in (41cm) **400 - 450**

*Allow $25 - 35 extra for glass eyes.
**Not enough price samples to compute a reliable range.

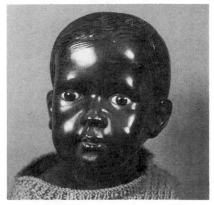

21in (53cm) black all-celluloid Turtle mark baby with glass eyes. *Kiefer collection.*

Century Doll Co.

Maker: Century Doll Co., New York, N.Y., U.S.A.; bisque heads by J.D. Kestner, Germany
Date: 1909 - on
Material: Bisque or composition head, cloth body, composition arms (and legs)
Mark:

Germany
CENTURY DOLL C°.
────── *200/0½* ──────

Marked Century Infant: Ca. 1925. Perfect bisque solid-dome head, molded and painted hair, sleep eyes, open/closed mouth; cloth body, composition hands or limbs; dressed; all in good condition. (For photographs see *Kestner, King of Dollmakers*, pages 193 and 194.) Some with smiling face are mold **#277.**

Head circumference:

10 - 11in (25 - 28cm)	**$475 - 525**
13 - 14in (33 - 36cm)	**650 - 700**

Mama doll, bisque shoulder head #281, (for photograph see *Kestner, King of Dollmakers*, page 194.)
21in (53cm)   **650 - 750****
Child with molded hair #200
12in (31cm)   **350****

**Not enough price samples to compute a reliable average.

Marked "Mama" Doll: Ca. 1920s. Composition shoulder head with character face, molded hair, smiling open mouth with two teeth, dimples, tin sleep eyes. Cloth torso with cryer, composition arms and legs; appropriate clothing. All in good condition. See color photograph on page 97.
16in (41cm)   **$185 - 210**
"Chuckles" Baby, 1927.
16½in (42cm)   **200 - 225**

12in (31cm) character child 200. *H & J Foulke, Inc.*

Chad Valley

Maker: Chad Valley Co. (formerly Johnson Bros., Ltd.), Birmingham, England
Date: 1917 - on
Material: All-cloth
Mark: Cloth label usually on foot:
"HYGENIC TOYS
Made in England by
CHAD VALLEY CO. LTD."

Chad Valley Doll: All-cloth, usually felt face and velvet body, jointed neck, shoulders and hips; mohair wig, glass or painted eyes; original clothes; all in excellent condition.

Characters, painted eyes,
10 - 12in (25cm)	$ 80 -	110

Children, painted eyes,
9in (23cm)	135 -	150
13 - 14in (33 - 36cm)	350 -	400
16 - 18in (41 - 46cm)	500 -	600

Children, glass eyes,
16 - 18in (41 - 46cm)	650 -	750

Royal Children, glass eyes,
16 - 18in (41 - 46cm)	1300 -	1600

Mabel Lucie Attwell, glass inset side-glancing eyes, smiling watermelon mouth, for photograph (see *6th Blue Book,* page 63.)
14in (36cm)	600 -	650

Bobby with glass eyes, 17in (43cm) mint with tag, at auction **935**

15in (38cm) Chad Valley smiling character, all original. *H & J Foulke, Inc.*

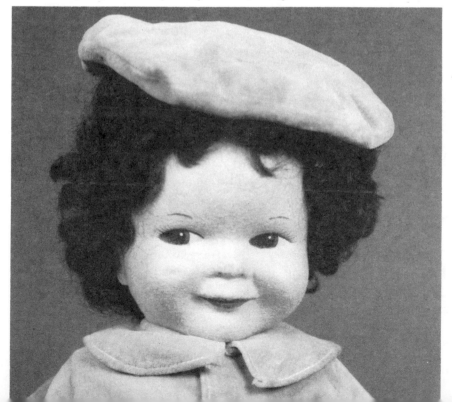

Martha Chase

Maker: Martha Jenks Chase, Pawtucket, R.I., U.S.A.
Date: 1889 on
Material: Stockinette and cloth, painted in oils; some fully painted washable models; some designed for hospital training use.
Size: 9in (23cm) to life-size
Designer: Martha Jenks Chase
Mark: "Chase Stockinet Doll" stamp on left leg or under left arm, paper label on back (usually gone)

PAWTUCKET, R.I
MADE IN U.S.A.

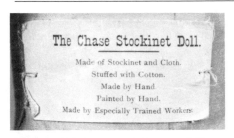

Cardboard label sewn on cloth torsos of Chase dolls. *H & J Foulke, Inc.*

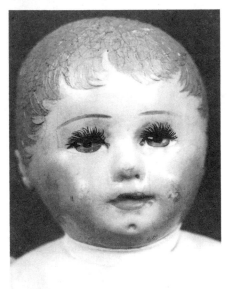

20in (51cm) Chase baby. *H & J Foulke, Inc.*

Chase Doll: Head and limbs of stockinette, treated and painted with oils, large painted eyes with thick upper lashes, rough-stroked hair to provide texture, cloth bodies jointed at shoulders, hips, elbows and knees, later ones only at shoulders and hips; some bodies completely treated; showing wear.

Baby,

13 - 15in (33 - 38cm)	**$ 575 - 675**
17 - 20in (43 - 51cm)	**750 - 850**
24 - 26in (61 - 66cm)	**950 - 1000**
37 - 40in (94 - 102cm)	**1800 - 2000**

Child, molded bobbed hair. (For photograph see *6th Blue Book*, page 95.)

12in (31cm)	**1000 - 1200**
15in (38cm)	**1300 - 1600**
22in (56cm)	**2200 - 2400**
Lady, 13 - 15in (33 - 38cm)	**2500 - 3000**
Man, 15 - 16in (38 - 41cm)	**2500 - 3000**

See color photograph on page 97.

Black, 24in (61cm)	**8500 - 9500**

(For photograph see *9th Blue Book* page 74.)

Hospital Lady,

64in (163cm)	**1600 - 2000**
George Washington	**4500 - 5000**

China Heads*
(French)

Maker: Various French doll firms; some heads may have been made in Germany
Date: 1850s
Material: China head, shapely kid fashion body, some with large china arms
Mark: None

French China Head Doll: China shoulder head, glass or beautifully painted eyes, painted eyelashes, feathered eyebrows, closed mouth, open crown, cork pate, good wig; shapely kid fashion body (may have china arms curved to above elbow); appropriately dressed; all in good condition.

15 - 17in (38 - 43cm)
$ 3000 - 4000
19 - 21in (48 - 53cm)
4500 - 5000
28in (71cm) wire controlled eyes
13,000
Painted short black hair, pink kid body
5in (13cm) pair   **1250**
15in (38cm)   **1400 - 1500**

*For dolls marked "Huret" or "Rohmer," see appropriate entry under those names.

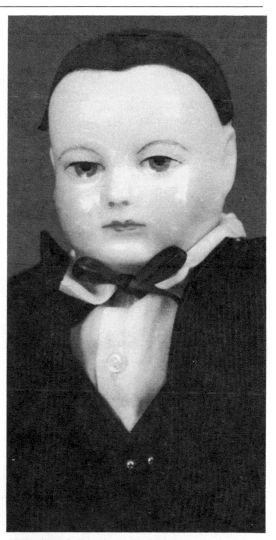

15½in (39cm) French china with painted eyes. *Private Collection.*

China Heads
(German)

Maker: Some early dolls by K.P.M., Meissen and Royal Copenhagen (Denmark), but most by unidentified makers. Later dolls by firms such as Kling & Co., Alt, Beck & Gottschalck, Kestner & Co., Hertwig & Co., and others

Material: China head, cloth or kid body, leather arms or china limbs

Mark: K.P.M., Meissen and Royal Copenhagen usually marked inside the shoulders; later dolls by Kling & Co. and A.B.G. are identifiable by their mold numbers.

1840s Hairstyles: China shoulder head with black molded hair; may have pink tint complexion; old cloth body; (may have china arms); appropriate old clothes; all in good condition.

Hair swept back into bun. See color photograph on page 98.

18 - 21in (46 - 53cm)	**$2500 - 5000***

With Wood Body, china lower limbs

6in (15cm)	**1200 - 1400**
9in (23cm)	**2500 - 2800**

Brown hair with bun (For photograph see *5th Blue Book*, page 93.)

18in (46cm)	**4000 up***

Young Man, brown hair

16 - 18in (41 - 46cm)	**2500 - 2800**

Kinderkopf (china head)

15 - 16in (38 - 41cm)	**850 - 950****
Long Curls, 14in (36cm)	**900 - 1000**

See color photograph on page 98.

16in (41cm) curls falling onto shoulders	**2250****

Molded pink, yellow and blue hat,

13in (33cm)	**3400****

*Depending upon quality, hairdo and rarity.
**Not enough price samples to compute a reliable range.

16in (41cm) black-haired china head lady with molded bun. *Richard Wright Antiques.*

China Heads (German) continued

28in (71cm) black-haired china head lady with high molded bun. *Richard Wright Antiques.*

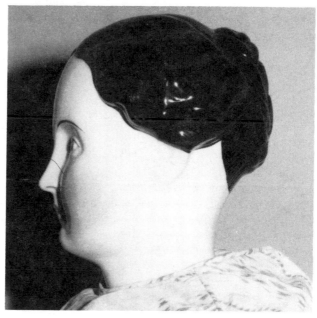

1850s Hairstyles: China shoulder head (some with pink tint), molded black hair (except bald), painted eyes; old cloth body with leather or china arms; appropriate old clothes; all in good condition.

Bald head, some with black areas on top, proper wig. Allow extra for original human hair wig in fancy style.

Fine quality:

15 - 17in (38 - 43cm)	**$ 900 - 1000**
22 - 24in (56 - 61cm)	**1400 - 1600**

With Glass eyes, fine quality,

20in (51cm)	**2200 - 2400****

Standard quality:

8 - 10in (20 - 25cm)	**250 - 300**
9in (23cm) all original	**385 - 410**
12 - 15in (31 - 38cm)	**400 - 500**
18 - 20in (46 - 51cm)	**650 - 750**

Covered Wagon

16 - 17in (41 - 43cm)	**550 - 600**
22in (56cm)	**850 - 950**

With brown eyes,

18 - 21in (46 - 53cm)	**1100 - 1300**

Greiner-style, with brown eyes

17 - 19in (43 - 48cm)	**1100 - 1400**

With glass eyes. See color photograph on page 98.

15 - 16in (38 - 41cm)	**3500****
22in (56cm)	**4800****

Waves framing face, brown eyes. (For photograph see *7th Blue Book*, page 114.)

17 - 19in (43 - 48cm)	**900 - 1000**

With glass eyes,

16in (41cm)	**2600****

Child or Baby, flange swivel neck; china or papier-mâché shoulder plate and hips, china lower limbs; cloth midsection (may have voice box) and upper limbs. (For photograph see *9th Blue Book*, page 76.)

10in (25cm)	**3200****

Alice Hairstyle, See color photograph on page 99.

10in (25cm)	**3500****

**Not enough price samples to compute a reliable range.

China Heads (German) continued

1860s and 1870s Hairstyles: China shoulder head with black molded hair (a few blondes), painted eyes, closed mouth; old cloth body may have leather arms or china lower arms and legs with molded boots; appropriate old clothes; all in good condition.

Plain style with center part (so-called flat top and high brow) See color photograph on page 100.

6 - 7in (15 - 18cm)	**$ 90 - 100**
10in (25cm) original factory clothes	**200**
14 - 16in (36 - 41cm)	**225 - 250**
19 - 22in (48cm) - 56cm)	**300 - 350**
24 - 26in (61 - 66cm)	**400 - 500**
34 - 35in (86 - 89cm)	**700 - 800**
Molded necklace, 21 - 24in (53 - 61cm)	**700**
Brown Eyes, 20 - 21in (51 - 53cm)	**550**

Mary Todd Lincoln with snood. (For photograph see *8th Blue Book*, page 130.)

17 - 19in (43 - 48cm)	**750**

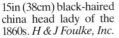

15in (38cm) black-haired china head lady of the 1860s. *H & J Foulke, Inc.*

18in (46cm) black-haired china head lady of the 1860s. *H & J Foulke, Inc.*

China Heads (German) continued

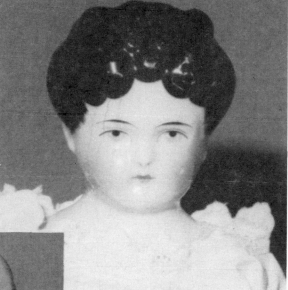

19in (48cm) fancy black-haired china head lady of the 1870s with hair cascading down back. *Sheila Needle Antique Dolls.*

15in (38cm) blonde-haired *Alice*-style china head with curls and black ribbon. *Jackson/Pearson Collection.*

Fancy style (only a sampling can be covered because of the wide variety). See color photograph on page 99.

Jenny Lind (For photograph see *Doll Classics*, page 130.)
   18 - 20in (46 - 51cm)   **1000**

Curly Top (For photograph see *7th Blue Book*, page 115.)
   20 - 21in (51 - 53cm)   **675 - 775**

Grape Lady (For photograph see *8th Blue Book*, page 130.)
   19 - 21in (48 - 53cm)   **1600 - 1800**

Countess Dagmar with pierced ears (For photograph see *6th Blue Book*, page 102 top.)
   19in (48cm)   **900 - 950**

Spill Curl (For photograph see *5th Blue Book*, page 98.)
   18in (46cm)   **700 - 800**

Flat face, molded hairband
   20in (51cm)   **500 - 600**

Morning Glory, 21in (53cm)
      5000 - 6000**

**Not enough price samples to compute a reliable range.

Dolley Madison with molded bow or flowers
   19 - 22in (48 - 56cm)   **500 - 550**
   27in (69cm)   **650 - 750**

Adelina Patti (For photograph see *Doll Classics*, page 130.)
   15 - 17in (38 - 43cm)   **300 - 350**
   22 - 24in (56 - 61cm)   **500 - 550**
   32in (81cm)   **850**

China Heads (German) continued

22in (56cm) fancy black-haired china head lady with hair pulled back and side rolls. *Jackson/ Pearson Collection.*

20in (51cm) fancy black-haired china head lady with side wings and molded beads. *Jackson/ Pearson Collection.*

China Heads (German) continued

Young Victoria. (For photograph see *9th Blue Book*, page 77.)

22 - 24in (56 - 61cm)   **$3200**

Man or boy. See color photograph on page 100.

Fine quality 20in (51cm)   **1600 - 1800**
Standard quality
16in (41cm)   **475 - 525**
Curls clustered on neck
20in (51cm)   **2500**
Coiled braided bun high in back,
24in (61cm)   **1000 - 1100**
Loose bun, gold beads, side "wings,"
16in (41cm)   **850 - 950**
Blonde "Alice" hairdo with snood,
21in (53cm)   **850 - 950**
Blonde hair with pink scarf and snood.
18in (46cm)   **750 - 850**

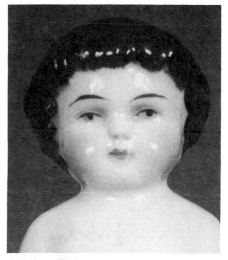

Black-haired china head child of the 1880s with bangs. *H & J Foulke, Inc.*

20in (51cm) blonde-haired china head of the 1880s with bangs by Alt, Beck & Gottschalck, *#1046*, size 7. *H & J Foulke, Inc.*

China Heads (German) continued

1880s Hairstyles: China shoulder head with black or blonde molded hair, blue painted eyes, closed mouth; cloth body with china arms and legs or kid body; appropriate old clothes; all in good condition. Many made by Alt, Beck & Gottschalck (see page 63 for mold numbers) or Kling & Co. (see page 286 for mold numbers).

Bangs on forehead,

13 - 15in (33 - 38cm)	$250 - 300
18 - 20in (46 - 51cm)	350 - 400
24 - 25in (61 - 64cm)	500 - 550

Short wavy hair, exposed ears (ABG #*784*) (For photograph see *8th Blue Book*, page 133.)

14 - 16in (36 - 41cm)	250 - 275
22 - 23in (56 - 58cm)	400 - 425

For photographs, see page 141.

1890s Hairstyle: China shoulder head with black or blonde molded wavy hair, blue painted eyes, closed mouth; old cloth or kid body with stub, leather, bisque or china limbs; appropriate clothes; all in good condition.

7 - 8in (18 - 20cm)	$ 65 - 75
12 - 13in (31 - 33cm)	110 - 135
16 - 18in (41 - 46cm)	185 - 210
22 - 24in (56 - 61cm)	250 - 300
Open mouth, 16in (41cm)	400
Molded poke bonnet,	
13in (33cm)	185
8in (20cm)	125
Molded "Jewel" necklace,	
22in (56cm)	300

Pet Name: Ca. 1905. Made by Hertwig & Co. for Butler Bros., N.Y. China shoulder head, molded yoke with name in gold; black or blonde painted hair (one-third were blonde), blue painted eyes; old cloth body (some with alphabet or other figures printed on cotton material), china limbs; properly dressed; all in good condition. Used names such as ***Agnes, Bertha, Daisy, Dorothy, Edith, Esther, Ethel, Florence, Helen, Mabel, Marion*** and ***Pauline.***

9 - 10in (23 - 25cm)	$125 - 140
14 - 16in (36 - 41cm)	200 - 225
19 - 21in (48 - 53cm)	275 - 300

4in (10cm) blonde-haired china head lady of the 1890s. *H & J Foulke, Inc.*

Cloth, Printed

Maker: Various American companies, such as Cocheco Mfg Co., Lawrence & Co., Arnold Print Works, Art Fabric Mills and Selchow & Righter and Dean's Rag Book Company in England.
Date: 1896 - on
Material: All-cloth
Size: 6 - 30in (15 - 76cm)
Mark: Mark could be found on fabric part which was discarded after cutting

---

Cloth, Printed Doll: Face, hair, underclothes, shoes and socks printed on cloth; all in good condition, some soil acceptable. Dolls in printed underwear are sometimes found dressed in old petticoats and frocks. Names such as: *Dolly Dear, Merry Marie, Improved Foot Doll, Standish No Break Doll,* and so on.

6 - 7in (15 - 18cm)	$ 85 - 95
16 - 18in (41 - 46cm)	175 - 200
22 - 24in (56 - 61cm)	225 - 250

Uncut sheet, bright colors
20in (51cm) doll   **225 - 250**

Brownies: 1892.
Designed by Palmer Cox; marked on foot.
8in (20cm)   **90 - 95**
15in (38cm)   **200**

Boys and Girls with printed outer clothes, Ca. 1903,
12 - 13in (31 - 33cm)   **175 - 200**
17in (43cm)   **240 - 265**

Darkey Doll, made up
16in (41cm)   **275 - 325**

Aunt Jemima Family,
(four dolls)   **85 - 95 each**

Punch & Judy,   **425 - 450 pair**

Soldier, 12in (31cm)   **125 - 135**

Hen and Chicks,
uncut sheet   **75 - 85**

Gutsell, 16in (41cm) made up with shirt and jacket   **650 - 750**

Mother's Congress Doll, Baby Steuart,
fading and wear,
at auction   **1100**

Ball, Uncut   **250 - 275**

Peck 1886 Santa   **225**

E.T. Gibson, red sailor dress with separate skirt,
at auction   **495**

Black Child, Art Fabric,
18in (46cm)   **400 - 450**

George & Martha Washington   **450 pair**

Dean's Rag Book Children and Characters
10in (25cm)   **85**
16 - 18in (41 - 46cm)   **150 - 165**

9in (23cm) printed cloth girl. *H & J Foulke, Inc.*

Cloth, Russian

Maker: Unknown craftsmen
Date: Ca. 1930
Material: All-cloth
Size: 10 - 15in (25 - 38cm)
Mark: "Made in Soviet Union" sometimes with identification of doll, such as "Ukranian Woman," "Village Boy," "Smolensk District Woman"

Russian Cloth Doll: All-cloth with stockinette head and hands, molded face with hand-painted features; authentic regional clothes; all in very good condition. See color photograph on page 101.

11in (28cm) child	**$ 85 - 95**
15in (38cm)	**135 - 165**

15in (38cm) Russian cloth Village Boy. *H & J Foulke, Inc.*

Cloth Shoulder Head

Maker: Unknown
Date: Ca. 1850
Material: All-cloth
Size: 22in (56cm)

Cloth Shoulder Head: Cloth shoulder head with molded features, painted black hair, glass or painted eyes, closed mouth; cloth body; appropriate old clothes. Very rare. 22in (56cm)

Very good condition	**$2000 up****
Fair condition	**950****

See color photograph on page 101.

**Not enough price samples to compute a reliable range.

20in (51cm) François Gaultier Bébé F 9 G with block letters. For further information see page 203. *Kay & Wayne Jensen Collection.*

13in (33cm) German bisque boy with blonde molded hair. For further information see page 204. *Private Collection.*

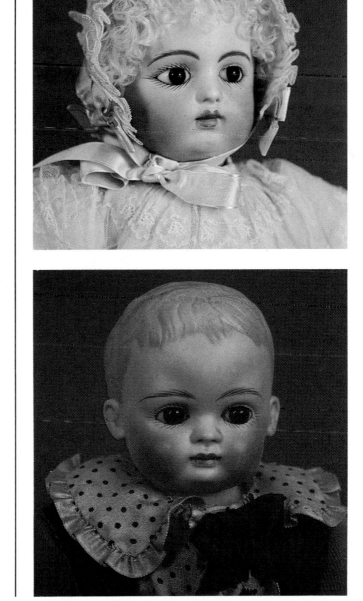

22in (56cm) German bisque shoulder head lady with painted eyes. For further information see page 206. *Becky & Jay Lowe.*

RIGHT: 19in (48cm) unmarked Bébé with French look, but probably of German origin. For further information see page 206. *H & J Foulke, Inc.*

BELOW RIGHT: Rare German character girl "111." For further information see page 208. *Jackie Kaner.*

BELOW: 14in (36cm) German bisque character boy incised "163." For further information see page 208. *H & J Foulke, Inc.*

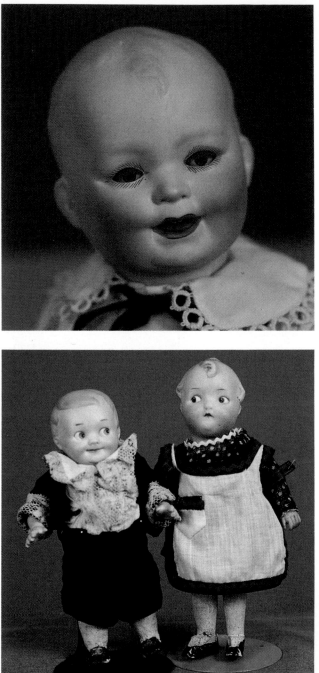

Rare German toddler incised "926." For further information see page 208. *Private Collection.*

Googlies by Armand Marseille and Gebrüder Heubach with painted eyes. For further information see page 214. *H & J Foulke, Inc.*

149

RIGHT: 16½in (42cm) *Gladdie*. For further information see page 210. *H & J Foulke, Inc.*

BELOW RIGHT: 15in (38cm) character incised "4B" probably by Goebel. For further information see page 213. *H & J Foulke, Inc.*

BELOW LEFT: Pair of all-bisque Kestner googlies with jointed elbows and knees. For further information see page 214. *H & J Foulke, Inc.*

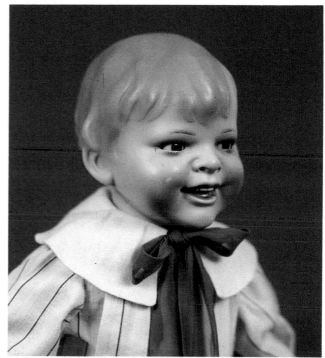

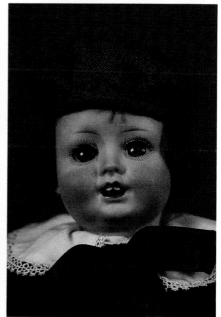

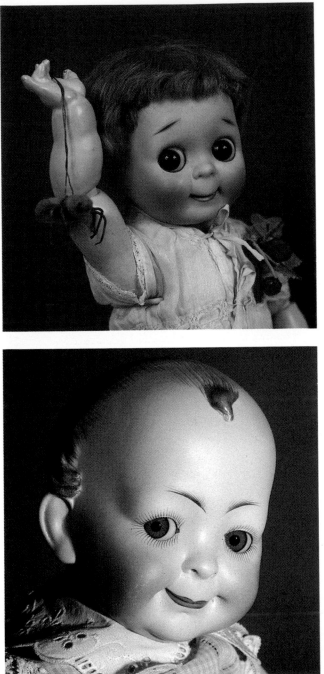

15½in (39cm) J. D. Kestner 221 googly. For further information see page 215. *Private Collection.*

18in (46cm) Hertel, Schwab & Co. 172 googly. For further information see page 216. *Richard Wright Antiques.*

ABOVE: Pair of composition face German googlies, all original. For further information see page 216. *H & J Foulke, Inc.*

32in (81cm) doll with Greiner head, 1858 label. For further information see page 233. *H & J Foulke, Inc.*

LEFT: 16in (41cm) Heinrich Handwerck child. For further information see page 234. *Esther Schwartz Collection.*

BELOW LEFT: 23in (58cm) K. Hartmann doll. For further information see page 236. *H & J Foulke, Inc.*

BELOW: 16in (41cm) Gunther Heine cloth doll. For further information see page 236. *Becky & Jay Lowe.*

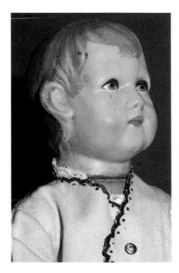

20in (51cm) Hertel, Schwab & Co. 151 character baby. For further information see page 237. *H & J Foulke, Inc.*

18in (46cm) Hertel, Schwab & Co. 136 child. For further information see page 238. *H & J Foulke, Inc.*

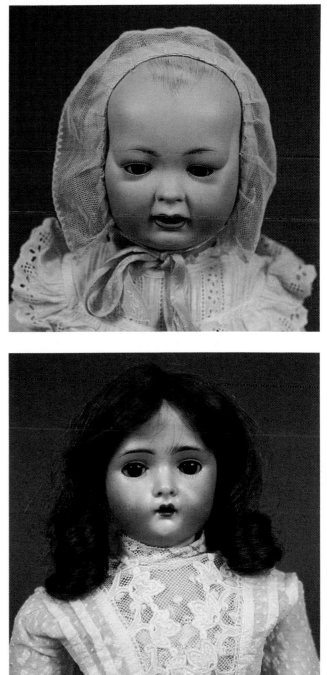

15in (38cm) E. Heubach (Köppelsdorf) 320 character baby. For further information see page 241. *H & J Foulke, Inc.*

11½in (29cm) Gebrüder Heubach 8724 character boy. For further information see page 244. *H & J Foulke, Inc.*

LEFT: 16½in (42cm) Hertel, Schwab & Co. 149 character girl. For further information see page 238. *Mary Barnes Kelley Collection.*

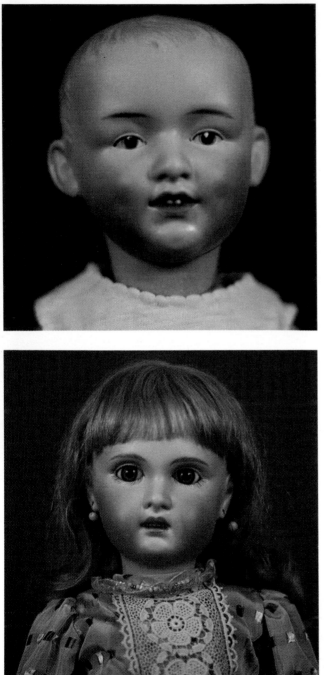

15½in (39cm) Gebrüder Heubach character boy (no mold number). For further information see page 244. *H & J Foulke, Inc.*

BELOW LEFT: 1907 Jumeau mold made by Gebrüder Heubach from pink pretinted bisque. For further information see page 245. *Lesley Hurford Collection.*

INSET: 15in (38cm) Gebrüder Heubach 8556 character. For further information see page 243. *Richard Wright Antiques.*

RIGHT: 18in (46cm) Gebrüder Heubach character girl with molded hair bow. For further information see page 244. *Richard Wright Antiques.*

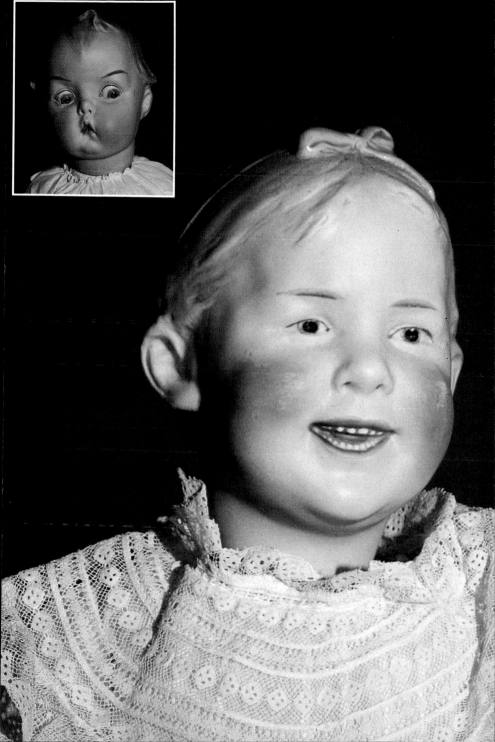

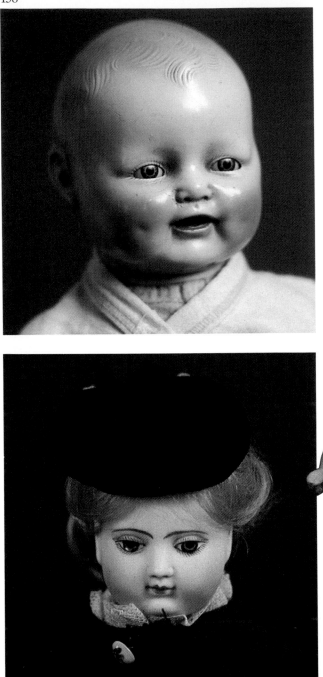

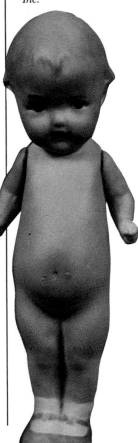

Horsman composition head *Baby Dimples*. For further information see page 249. *H & J Foulke, Inc.*

BELOW LEFT: 17in (43cm) signed Huret French fashion lady with jointed wood body. For further information see page 252. *H & J Foulke, Inc.*

BELOW: 6in (15cm) Gebrüder Heubach all-bisque character with clenched fists. For further information see page 245. *H & J Foulke, Inc.*

16in (41cm) Ideal *Judy Garland*, replaced dress but original tag. For further information see page 255. *H & J Foulke, Inc.*

21in (53cm) Ideal *Flossie Flirt*. For further information see page 253. *H & J Foulke, Inc.*

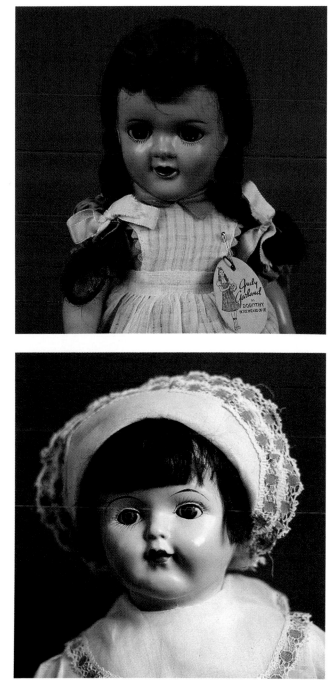

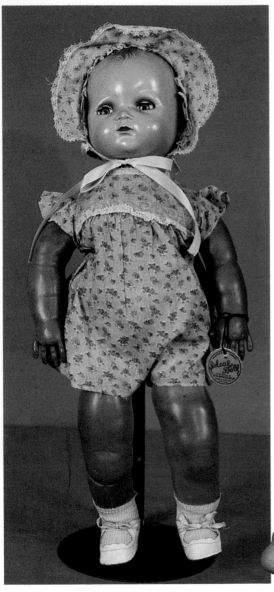

Ideal *Magic Skin Baby*, all original. For further information see page 255. *H & J Foulke, Inc.*

BELOW: 10in (25cm) Ideal wood-segmented *Pinocchio*. For further information see page 255. *Jensen's Antique Dolls.*

Dewees Cochran

Maker: Dewees Cochran, Fenton, Calif., U.S.A.
Date: 1940 - on
Material: Latex
Size: 9 - 18in (23 - 46cm)
Designer: Dewees Cochran
Mark: Signed under arm or behind right ear

Dewees Cochran Doll: Latex with jointed neck, shoulders and hips; human hair wig, painted eyes, character face; dressed; all in good condition.

15 - 16in (38 - 41cm) *Cindy*, 1947-1948.	**$ 750 - 850**
Grow-up Dolls: Stormy, Angel, Bunnie, J.J. and *Peter Ponsett* each at ages 5, 7, 11, 16 and 20, 1952-1956. See color photographs on page 102.	**1400 - 1800**
Look-Alike Dolls (6 different faces)	**1200 - 1400**
Baby, 9in (23cm)	**1300 - 1500**
Individual Portrait Children	**1500 - 1800**
Composition American Children (see Effanbee, page 189).	

15in (38cm) *Cindy*, all original. *Dolly Valk Collection.*

Columbian Doll

Maker: Emma and Marietta Adams
Date: 1891 - 1910 or later
Material: All-cloth
Size: 15 - 29in (38 - 74cm)
Mark: Stamped on back of body
Before 1900:

"COLUMBIAN DOLL
EMMA E. ADAMS
OSWEGO CENTRE
N.Y."

After 1906:

"THE COLUMBIAN DOLL
MANUFACTURED BY
MARIETTA ADAMS RUTTAN
OSWEGO, N.Y."

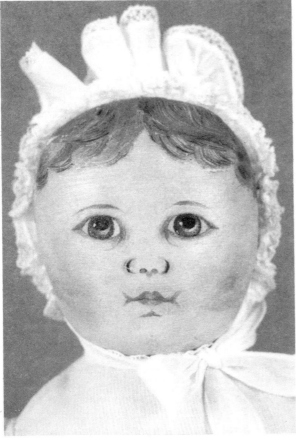

Columbian Doll: All-cloth with hair and features hand-painted on a flat face; treated limbs; appropriate clothes; all in good condition, showing wear.
15in (38cm) some repaint
$3000 - 4000
20 - 22in (51 - 56cm)
6200 - 6800
20 - 22in (51 - 56cm) fair condition
3000 - 4000
20in (51cm) excellent, at auction **9500**

21in (53cm) Columbian rag doll, all original except shoes. *Nancy A. Smith Collection.*

Composition
(American)

Maker: Various United States firms, many unidentified
Date: 1912 - on
Material: All-composition or composition head and cloth body, some with composition
limbs

All-Composition Child Doll: 1912 - 1920. Various firms, such as Bester Doll Co., New
Era Novelty Co., New Toy Mfg. Co., Superior Doll Mfg. Co., Artcraft Toy Product
Co., Colonial Toy Mfg. Co. Composition with mohair wig, sleep eyes, open mouth;
ball-jointed composition body; appropriate clothes; all in good condition. These are
patterned after German bisque head dolls.
22 - 24in (56 - 61cm)   **$250 - 300**

21in (53cm) Bester Doll Co. all-composition doll with ball-jointed body. *H & J Foulke,
Inc.*

Composition (American) continued

18in (46cm) early unmarked composition character. *H & J Foulke, Inc.*

26in (66cm) unmarked composition mama-type doll, all original. *H & J Foulke, Inc.*

Composition (American) continued

Early Composition Character Head: Ca. 1912. Composition head with molded hair and painted features; hard cloth body with composition hands; appropriate clothes; all in good condition. See color photograph on page 103.

10 - 12in (25 - 31cm)	**$100 - 125**
16 - 18in (41 - 46cm)	**225 - 250**
24 - 26in (61 - 66cm)	**350 up**

Girl-type Mama Dolls: Ca. 1920 - on. Made by various American companies. Composition head with hair wig, sleep eyes, open mouth with teeth; composition shoulder plate, arms and legs, cloth body; original clothes; all in good condition, of good quality.

16 - 18in (41 - 46cm)	**$175 - 200**
20 - 22in (51 - 56cm)	**250 - 300**
24 - 26in (61 - 66cm)	**350 - 400**

Molded Loop Dolls: Ca. 1930s. All-composition with molded bobbed hair and loop for tying on a ribbon, painted eyes, closed mouth; composition or cloth torso, composition arms and legs; original or appropriate clothing; all in good condition. Quality is generally mediocre.

12 - 15in (31 - 38cm)
    $100 - 125

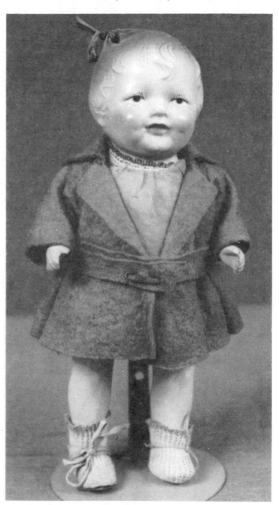

Patsy-type Girl: Ca. 1930s. All-composition with molded bobbed hair, sleep or painted eyes, closed mouth; jointed at neck, shoulders and hips; original clothes; all in very good condition, of good quality. See color photograph on page 103.

9 - 10in (23 - 25cm)	**$110 - 135**
14 - 16in (36 - 41cm)	**185 - 210**
20in (51cm)	**250 - 275**

12in (31cm) Toy Products Mfg. Co. all-composition child with molded loop, all original. *H & J Foulke, Inc.*

Composition (American) continued

Composition Baby: Ca. 1930. All-composition or composition head, arms and legs, cloth torso; with molded and painted hair, sleep eyes; appropriate or original clothes; all in very good condition, of good quality. See color photograph on page 104.

10 - 12in (25 - 31cm)	**$100 - 125**
16 - 18in (41 - 46cm)	**175 - 200**
24in (61cm)	**350 - 400**

Dionne-type Doll: Ca. 1935. All-composition with molded hair or wig, sleep or painted eyes, closed or open mouth; jointed at neck, shoulders and hips; original clothes; all in very good condition, of good quality.

7 - 8in (18 - 20cm)	**$ 65 - 75**
18 - 20in (46 - 51cm) toddler	**250 - 275**

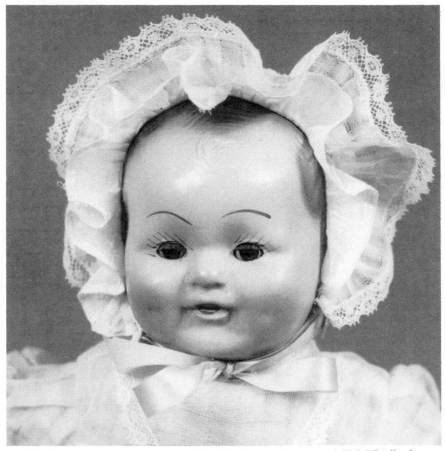

13in (33cm) unmarked composition baby with cloth body, all original. *H & J Foulke, Inc.*

Composition (American) continued

Alexander-type Girl: Ca. 1935. All-composition, jointed at neck, shoulders and hips; sleeping eyes, mohair wig, closed mouth, dimples. Original or appropriate clothing. All in good condition, of good quality.

13in (33cm) **$165 - 175**
17 - 18in (43 - 46cm) **250 - 300**

20in (51cm) unmarked all-composition Alexander-type girl, all original. *H & J Foulke, Inc.*

Shirley Temple-type Girl: Ca. 1935 - on. All-composition, jointed at neck, shoulders and hips; blonde curly mohair wig, sleep eyes, open smiling mouth with teeth; original clothes; all in very good condition, of good quality.

16 - 18in (41 - 46cm)
　　　　　　$250 - 300

17in (43cm) unmarked all-composition *Shirley Temple*-type girl, all original. *H & J Foulke, Inc.*

Composition (American) continued

Costume Doll: Ca. 1940. All-composition, jointed at neck, shoulders and hips, sleep or
painted eyes, mohair wig, closed mouth; original costume; all in good condition.
11in (28cm)

Excellent quality	**$75 - 85**
Standard quality	**45 - 50**

11in (28cm) unmarked all-composition costume doll, all original. *H & J Foulke, Inc.*

Composition (American) continued

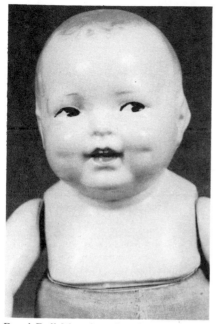

Regal Doll Manufacturing Co. *Kiddie Pal* baby. *H & J Foulke, Inc.*

Miscellaneous Specific Dolls: Orphan Annie, 1920s. See color photograph on page 359.

12 - 15in (31 - 38cm)	**$150 - 175**
Jackie Robinson	
13½in (34cm)	**500 - 550**
Trudy 3 faces, 1946.	
14in (36cm)	**225 - 235**
Lone Ranger	
16in (41cm)	**350 - 375**
Kewpie-type characters,	
12in (31cm)	**70 - 80**
Mountie (Reliable)	
16in (41cm)	**150 - 165**
HEbee, SHEbee,	
10½in (27cm)	**500 - 550**
Buddy Lee,	
12in (31cm) all original	**150 - 200***
Eugenia *Janie* toddler	

See color photograph on page 104.

12in (31cm)	**125 - 135**

Sayco composition girl
See color photograph on page 105.

17in (43cm)	**250**
Regal *Kiddie Pal*,	
18in (46cm) undressed	**125 - 150**
20in (51cm) all original	**275**
Monica, 1941 - 1951.	
18in (46cm)	**400 - 500**
Famlee, 1921. Boxed with 3 heads and 4 costumes at auction	**750**

Our Gang 1926. Dancing Dolls, boxed, all original (composition cracked and peeling), five dolls at auction

550

Puzzy, 1948. H. of P.	
15in (38cm)	**350 - 375**
Sizzy, 1948. H. of P.	
14in (36cm)	**250 - 275**

*Depending upon costume.

12in (31cm) Eugenia Doll Co. *Janie*, original clothes. *H & J Foulke, Inc.*

Composition

(German)

Maker: Various German firms such as König & Wernicke, Kämmer & Reinhardt and others
Date: Ca. 1925
Material: All-composition or composition head and cloth body
Size: Various

All-Composition Child Doll: Socket head with good wig, sleep (sometimes flirty) eyes, open mouth with teeth; jointed composition body; appropriate clothes; all in good condition, of excellent quality. (For photograph see *6th Blue Book*, page 111.)

12 - 14in (31 - 36cm)	**$200 - 225**
18 - 20in (46 - 51cm)	**300 - 350**

Character face, (For photograph see *7th Blue Book*, page 128.)
18 - 20in (46 - 51cm)
350 - 450

Patsy-type girl
13in (33cm)   **225**

Character Baby: Composition head with good wig, sleep eyes, open mouth with teeth; bent-limb composition baby body or hard-stuffed cloth body; appropriate clothes; all in good condition, of excellent quality. (For photograph see *9th Blue Book*, page 135.)

All-composition baby,
  16 - 18in (41 - 46cm)
$250 - 275
Cloth body,
  14 - 16in (36 - 41cm)
175 - 200
All composition toddler,
  16 - 18in (41 - 46cm)
325 - 375

13in (33cm) German composition *Patsy*-type girl A/2, all original. *H & J Foulke, Inc.*

Composition Shoulder Head

(Patent Washable Dolls)

Maker: Various German firms, such as Heinrich Steir, J.D. Kestner, F.M. Schilling and
C. & O. Dressel
Date: 1880 - 1915
Material: Composition shoulder head, cloth body, composition lower limbs
Size: 10 - 42in (25 - 107cm)
Mark: None

14in (36cm) composition shoulder head, Patent Washable-type, superior quality, probably intended to be a baby with short mohair wig, smiling face with painted teeth and bare feet, original shift. *H & J Foulke, Inc.*

Composition Shoulder Head continued

Composition Shoulder Head: Composition shoulder head with mohair or skin wig, glass eyes, closed or open mouth; cloth body with composition arms and lower legs, sometimes with molded boots; appropriately dressed; all in good condition.

Superior Quality:		Standard Quality:	
13 - 15in (33 - 38cm)	$ 325 - 375	11 - 12in (28 - 31cm)	**125 - 150**
19 - 21in (48 - 53cm)	**450 - 550**	14 - 16in (36 - 41cm)	**175 - 200**
24in (61cm)	**650 - 750**	18 - 20in (45 - 51cm)	**225 - 250**
30in (76cm)	**950**	22 - 24in (56 - 61cm)	**275 - 325**
Painted hair, Täufling		30 - 33in (76 - 84cm)	**475 - 525**
13in (33cm), at auction	**500**	38in (97cm)	**600 - 700**
		Lady, 13 - 16in (33 - 41cm)	**650 - 750**
		23in (58cm), at auction	**3800**
		Oriental, 12in (31cm)	**225 - 250**

29in (74cm) composition shoulder head, standard quality, Patent Washable-type. *H & J Foulke, Inc.*

Danel

Maker: Danel & Cie., Paris & Montreuil-sous-Bois, France
Date: 1889 - 1895
Material: Bisque socket head, composition body
Trademarks: Paris Bébé, Bébé Français (Also used by Jumeau)

Marked Paris Bébé: 1889. Perfect bisque socket head, good wig, paperweight eyes, closed mouth, pierced ears; composition jointed body; appropriately dressed; all in good condition. See color photograph on page 105.

Mark: On head

TÊTE DÉPOSÉ
PARIS BEBE

On body

PARIS BEBE
Bréveté

17 - 19in (43 - 48cm)	$4500 - 4900
23 - 24in (58 - 61cm)	5300 - 5500

Marked B.F.: Ca. 1891. Perfect bisque head, appropriate wig, paperweight eyes, closed mouth, pierced ears; jointed composition body; appropriate clothes; all in good condition.

Mark: B 9 F

16 - 19in (41 - 48cm)	$4000 - 4500
25 - 26in (64 - 66cm)	5500 - 6000

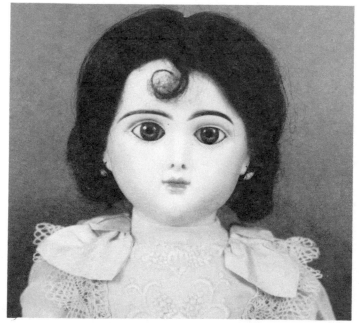

24½in (62cm) B 11 F child. *Private Collection.*

D E P*

(Open Mouth)

Maker: Maison Jumeau, Paris, France; (heads possibly by Simon & Halbig, Gräfenhain, Thüringia, Germany)
Date: Late 1890s
Material: Bisque socket head, French jointed composition body (sometimes marked Jumeau)
Size: About 12 - 33in (31 - 84cm)
Mark: "DEP" and size number (up to 16 or so); sometimes stamped in red "Tete Jumeau;" body sometimes with Jumeau stamp or sticker

DEP 8

DEP: Perfect bisque socket head, human hair wig, sleep eyes, painted lower eyelashes only, upper hair eyelashes (sometimes gone), deeply molded eye sockets, open mouth, pierced ears; jointed French composition body; lovely clothes; all in good condition.

11 - 12in (28 - 31cm)	$ 600 - 650
13 - 15in (33 - 38cm)	700 - 800
18 - 20in (46 - 51cm)	1000 - 1150
23 - 25in (58 - 64cm)	1450 - 1650
29 - 30in (74 - 76cm)	2200 - 2400
19in (48cm) all original and boxed	1500
16in (41cm) elaborate original costume	2100

*The letters DEP appear in the mark of many dolls, but the particular dolls priced here have only "DEP" and a size number (unless they happen to have the red stamp "Tete Jumeau"). The face is characterized by deeply molded eye sockets and no painted upper eyelashes.

*For closed mouth **DEP**, see page 194.

21in (53cm) **DEP** Jumeau. *H & J Foulke, Inc.*

Doll House Dolls

Maker: Various German firms
Date: Ca. 1890 - 1920
Material: Bisque shoulder head, cloth
body, bisque arms and legs
Size: Under 7in (18cm)
Mark: Sometimes "Germany"

Doll house lady with glass eyes. *H & J Foulke, Inc.*

Doll House Doll: Man or lady as above
with molded hair, painted eyes; original clothes or suitably dressed; all in
nice condition.
4½ - 7in (12 - 18cm)
Victorian man with mustache

	$ 175 - 225
Victorian lady	150 - 175
Lady with glass eyes and wig	325 - 375
Man with mustache, original Military uniform	700
Molded hair, glass eyes, Ca. 1870	400
Swivel neck, French-type head,	750
Molded hair, painted eyes. Ca. 1870	250 - 275
Man with molded hair, glass eyes, mustache, all original and boxed, at auction	1675
1920s man or lady	100 - 125
Girl with bangs, Ca. 1880	125 - 150

Doll house child, ca. 1880. *H & J Foulke, Inc.*

Door of Hope

Maker: Door of Hope Mission, China; heads by carvers from Ning-Po
Date: 1901 - on
Material: Wooden heads; cloth bodies, some with carved wooden hands
Size: Usually under 13in (33cm)
Mark: Sometimes "Made in China" label

Door of Hope: Carved wooden head with painted and/or carved hair, carved features; cloth body, some with stubby arms, some with carved hands; original handmade clothes, exact costuming for different classes of Chinese people; all in good condition. 25 dolls in the series.

Adult, 11 - 13in (28 - 33cm)	**$ 375 - 475**
Child, 7 - 8in (18 - 20cm)	**500 - 550**
Mother and Baby, 11in (28cm)	**650 - 700**
Manchu Lady, at auction	**1025**
Kindergarten Girl, 6in (15cm)	**550 - 650**
Woman with carved flowers in hair	**550**
Brides, old or new style	**800 - 850**

Door of Hope man, all original. *H & J Foulke, Inc.*

Grace G. Drayton

Maker: Various companies
Date: 1909 - on
Material: All-cloth, or composition and cloth combination, or all-composition
Size: Various
Designer: Grace G. Drayton
Mark: Usually a cloth label or a stamp

Puppy Pippin: 1911. Horsman Co., New York, N.Y., U.S.A. Composition head with puppy dog face, plush body with jointed legs; all in good condition. Cloth label. (For photograph see *7th Blue Book,* page 135.)

8in (20cm) sitting **$400 - 425****

Campbell Kid: (See page 127.)

**Not enough price samples to compute a reliable range.

Grace G. Drayton continued

Peek-a-Boo: 1913 - 1915. Horsman Co., New York, N.Y., U.S.A. Composition head, arms, legs and lower torso, cloth upper torso; character face with molded hair, painted eyes to the side, watermelon mouth; dressed in striped bathing suit, polka dot dress or ribbons only; cloth label on outfit; all in good condition. (For photograph see *7th Blue Book*, page 136.)

7½in (19cm) **$140 - 160**

Hug-Me-Tight: 1916. Colonial Toy Mfg. Co., New York, N.Y., U.S.A. Mother Goose characters and others in one piece, printed on cloth; all in good condition. (For photograph see *8th Blue Book*, page 149.)

11in (28cm) **$225 - 250****

Chocolate Drop: 1923. Averill Manufacturing Co., New York, N.Y., U.S.A. Brown cloth doll with movable arms and legs; painted features, three yarn pigtails; appropriate clothes; all in good condition. Stamped on front torso and paper label. (For photograph see *6th Blue Book*, page 120.)

11in (28cm) **$400 - 450**
16in (41cm) **550 - 600****

Dolly Dingle: 1923. Averill Manufacturing Co., New York, N.Y., U.S.A. Cloth doll with painted features and movable arms and legs; appropriate clothes; all in good condition. Stamped on front torso and paper label.
DOLLY DINGLE
COPYRIGHT BY
G.G. DRAYTON
11in (28cm) **$350 - 400**
16in (41cm) **500 - 550**

Composition Child: Composition shoulder head, arms and legs, cloth torso; molded bobbed hair, watermelon mouth, painted eyes, round nose; original or appropriate clothes; in fair condition. (For photograph see *8th Blue Book*, page 150.)

Mark: 9 · 9 · DRAYTON

14in (36cm) **$375 - 425****

Kitty-Puss: All-cloth with painted cat face, flexible arms and legs, tail; original clothing; all in good condition. (For photograph see *9th Blue Book*, page 145.)
Mark: Cardboard tag **$400****

**Not enough price samples to compute a reliable range.

Dressel

Maker: Cuno & Otto Dressel verlager & doll factory of Sonneberg, Thüringia, Germany. Heads by Armand Marseille, Simon & Halbig, Ernst Heubach, Gebrüder Heubach.
Date: 1700 - on
Material: Composition wax over or bisque head, kid, cloth body or ball-jointed composition body
Trademarks: Fifth Ave. Dolls (1903), Jutta (1907), Bambina (1909), Poppy Dolls (1912), Holz-Masse (1875)

Marked Holz-Masse Heads: 1875 - on. Composition shoulder head, molded hair or sometimes mohair wig, usually painted eyes, sometimes pierced ears; cloth body with composition arms and legs with molded boots; old clothes; all in good condition. (For photograph see *7th Blue Book*, page 137.)
Mark:

Molded hair:

13 - 15in (33 - 38cm)	**$250 - 300**
23 - 25in (58 - 64cm)	**500 - 550**

Wigged with glass eyes:
(Patent Washable)

16 - 18in (41 - 46cm)	**200 - 250**
22 - 24in (56 - 61cm)	**275 - 325**

Child Doll: 1893 - on. Perfect bisque head, original jointed kid or composition body; good wig, glass eyes, open mouth; suitable clothes; all in good condition. See color photograph on page 106.
Mark:

1915

Made in Germany

Germany

1912 · 5 ·

1896
C.O.D⁷ DEP

13/0

Composition body:

18 - 20in (46 - 57cm)	**$ 375 - 425**
23 - 25in (58 - 64cm)	**475 - 525**
30 - 31in (76 - 79cm)	**750 - 850**
38in (96cm)	**1900 - 2000**

Kid Body:

17 - 20in (43 - 51cm)	**285 - 325***
24in (61cm)	**425***

Character-type face, similar to **K★R 117n**:

18 - 20in (46 - 51cm)	**550 - 600**
26 - 28in (66 - 71cm)	**900 - 1000**

23in (58cm) 1912 child. *H & J Foulke, Inc.*

*Allow extra for fine bisque.

Dressel continued

13in (33cm) Jutta 1349 child. *H & J Foulke, Inc.*

Marked Jutta Child: Ca. 1906 - 1921. Perfect bisque socket head, good wig, sleep eyes, open mouth, pierced ears; ball-jointed composition body; dressed; all in good condition. Head made by Simon & Halbig.
Mold **1348 or 1349**
Mark:

     1349
     Jutta
    S & H
     11

13 - 15in (33 - 38cm)	$ 575 - 625
18 - 21in (46 - 53cm)	650 - 675
24 - 26in (61 - 66cm)	800 - 900
29 - 31in (74 - 79cm)	1200 - 1400
39 - 42in (99 - 105cm)	3000 - 3500

Character Child: 1909 - on. Perfect bisque socket head, ball-jointed composition body; mohair wig, painted eyes, closed mouth; suitable clothes; all in good condition. Glazed inside of head.
Mark:

10 - 12in (25 - 31cm)	**$1650 - 1850****
16 - 18in (41 - 46cm)	**2500 - 2600****

**Not enough price samples to compute a reliable range.

Marked C.O.D. Character Baby: Ca. 1910 - on. Perfect bisque character face with marked wig or molded hair, painted or glass eyes; jointed baby body; dressed; all in good condition. (For photograph see *5th Blue Book*, page 117.)

13 - 15in (33 - 38cm)	**$350 - 400**
18 - 20in (46 - 51cm)	**475 - 525**
22 - 24in (56 - 61cm)	**650 - 750**

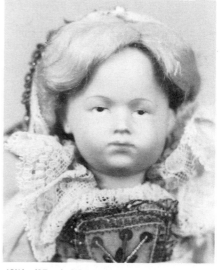

10½in (27cm) COD A2 character child. *H & J Foulke, Inc.*

Dressel continued

Marked Jutta Character Baby: Ca. 1910 - 1922. Perfect bisque socket head, good wig, sleep eyes, open mouth; bent-limb composition baby body; dressed; all in good condition.

Mark:

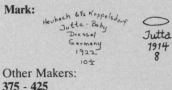

Heubach 6½ Köppelsdorf
Jutta - Baby
Dressel
Germany
1922
10½

Jutta
1914
8

S&H:		
12 - 13in (31 - 33cm)	$ 450 -	500
16 - 18in (41 - 46cm)	600 -	700
23 - 24in (58 - 61cm)	1200 -	1400

Toddler:

7 - 8in (18 - 20cm)	525 -	575
14 - 16in (36 - 41cm)	850 -	900
20 - 22in (51 - 56cm)	1250 -	1450

Other Makers:

375 - 425
450 - 475
650 - 750

Lady Doll: Ca. 1920s. Mold *#1469*. Bisque socket head with young lady face, good wig, sleep eyes, closed mouth; jointed composition body in adult form with molded bust, slim waist and long arms and legs, feet modeled to wear high-heeled shoes; all in good condition. (For photograph see page 386.) Same mold as Simon & Halbig *1469* lady.

Mark:

1469
C.O. Dressel
Germany
2.

14in (36cm)
Naked $2000 - 2200
Original clothes   3000 - 4200

15½in (39cm) Jutta baby 1920. *Jensen's Antique Dolls.*

E. D. Bébé

Maker: Probably Dancl & Cie or Etienne Denamur of Paris, France
Date: 1885 - 1895
Material: Bisque head, wood and composition jointed body
Mark:

E 8 D
DEPOSÉ

Marked E. D. Bébé: Perfect bisque head, wood and composition jointed body; good
   wig, beautiful blown glass eyes, pierced ears; nicely dressed; good condition. Often
   found on a marked Jumeau body.

Closed mouth:

14 - 16in (36 - 41cm)	$2600 - 3000*
21 - 24in (53 - 61cm)	3500 - 3800*
29 - 30in (74 - 75cm)	4500 - 5000*

Open mouth:

22 - 24in (56 - 61cm)	2300 - 2600*

*For a pretty face.

26in (66cm) E 12 D child. Note similarity to Jumeau. See *9th Blue Book*, page 149 for a
face more typical of E.D. *Private Collection.*

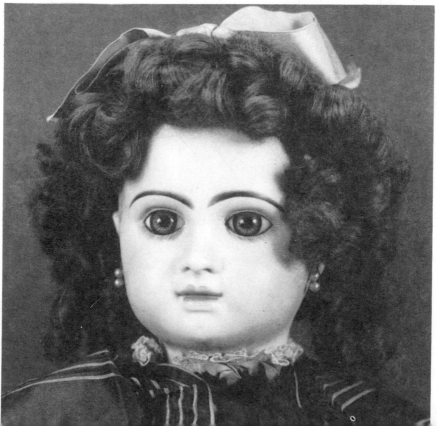

Eden Bébé

Maker: Fleischmann & Bloedel, doll factory, of Fürth, Bavaria, and Paris, France
Date: Founded in Bavaria in 1873. Also in Paris by 1890, then on into S.F.B.J. in 1899.
Material: Bisque head, composition jointed body
Trademark: Eden Bébé (1890), Bébé Triomphe (1898)
Mark: "EDEN BÉBÉ, PARIS"

Marked Eden Bebe: Ca. 1890. Perfect bisque head, fully-jointed or five-piece composition jointed body; beautiful wig, large set paperweight eyes, closed or open/closed mouth, pierced ears; lovely clothes; all in nice condition.

Closed mouth,

14 - 16in (36 - 41cm)	**$2300 - 2500**
21 - 24in (53 - 61cm)	**2900 - 3300**
5-piece body, 12in (31cm)	**1200 - 1500**

Open mouth,

20 - 23in (51 - 58cm)	**2200 - 2500**

Kissing, Walking, Flirting Doll: 1892. Head from mold *1039* by Simon & Halbig, ball-jointed composition body with mechanism for walking, throwing kisses and flirting eyes. (For photograph see *7th Blue Book*, page 142.)

20 - 22in (51 - 56cm)	**$1000 - 1100**

All original with French label,

22in (56cm)	**1500 - 1600**

12in (31cm) *Eden Bébé*, all original. *Joanna Ott Collection.*

EFFanBEE®

Maker: EFFanBEE Doll Co., New York, N.Y., U.S.A.
Date: 1912 - on
Marks: Various, but nearly always marked "EFFanBEE" on torso or head. Sometimes with dolls' name. Wore a metal heart-shaped bracelet; later a gold paper heart label.
Metal Heart Bracelet: **$45 - 50**

Effanbee

Early Characters Composition character face, molded painted hair, closed mouth, painted eyes; cloth stuffed body with metal disk joints at shoulders and hips, composition lower arms, sewn-on shoes; appropriate clothes; in fair condition.

Sizes: 10 - 15in (25 - 38cm)
Baby Grumpy, 1912. Molds *172, 174* or *176.*   **$225 - 275**
Coquette, 1912.   **225 - 275****
Pouting Bess, 1915. Some mold *162* or *166.*
(For photograph see *9th Blue Book,* page 152.)   **175 - 225****

16in (41cm) unmarked composition doll similar to Effanbee's *Coquette. H & J Foulke, Inc.*

**Not enough price samples to compute a reliable range.

12in (31cm) *Baby Grumpy* dressed as Amish and Dunker Pennsylvania Dutch Dolls. *H & J Foulke, Inc.*

EFFanBEE continued

Katie Kroose, 1918. (For photograph see
9th Blue Book, page 152.)
225 - 275**
Buds, 1915 - 1918.   **175 - 185**

**Not enough price samples to compute a
reliable range.

Shoulder Head Dolls: Composition
shoulder head, painted molded hair or
human hair wig, open or closed mouth,
painted tin sleep eyes; cloth torso,
composition arms and legs; original or
appropriate old clothes; all in good
condition. Came with metal heart
bracelet.

Baby Grumpy, 1925 - 1939. (For photograph see *9th Blue Book,* page 151.)
12in (31cm) white   **$200 - 225**
Black   **275 - 300**
Pennsylvania Dutch Dolls: 1936 - 1940,
all original and excellent
175 - 200

14in (36cm) *Rosemary. H & J Foulke, Inc.*

Baby Dainty, 1912 - 1922.
15in (38cm)   **225**
Rosemary, 1925. *Marilee,* 1924.
14in (36cm)   **225 - 250**
17in (43cm)   **265 - 285**
25in (64cm)   **400 - 425**
Mary Ann, 1928.
16in (41cm)   **250 - 275**
Mary Lee, 1928. (For photograph see *8th
Blue Book,* page 158.)
19in (48cm)   **300 - 325**

Mary Jane: 1917 - 1920. Composition
"dolly face" head with metal sleeping
eyes, painted eyebrows and eyelashes,
open mouth with teeth, original human hair or mohair wig; jointed composition body with wood arms;
dressed; all in very good condition.
(For photograph see *7th Blue Book,*
page 144.) *Effanbee*
Mark: *Effanbee* back of
head and torso in raised letters
20 - 24in (51 - 61cm)   **$250 - 275**

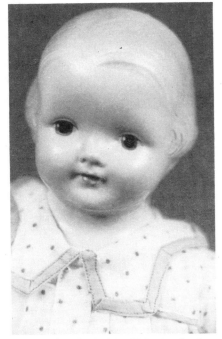

12in (31cm) *Baby Dainty. H & J Foulke, Inc.*

EFFanBEE continued

Babies: Composition head with painted hair or wigged, sleep eyes, open smiling mouth with teeth or closed mouth; cloth body, curved composition arms and legs; original or appropriate old clothes; all in good condition. Came with metal heart bracelet, later with gold heart hang tag.

Bubbles, 1924. (For photograph see *9th Blue Book*, page 153.)

Mark:

19 © 24

(EFFanBEE DOLLS WALK-TALK-SLEEP) MADE IN U.S.A.

EFFANBEE
BUBBLES
COPYR. 1924
MADE IN U.S.A.

16 - 18in (41 - 46cm)	**$275 - 300**
22 - 24in (56 - 61cm)	**400 - 425**
Black: 19in (48cm)	**850****

16in (41cm) *Sweetie Pie* with caracul wig, all original. *Miriam Blankman Collection.*

Lovums, 1928. (For photograph see *8th Blue Book*, page 158.)

EFFANBEE
LOVUMS
©

Mark: PAT. N°. 1,283,558

16 - 18in (41 - 46cm)	**225 - 275**
22 - 24in (56 - 61cm)	**325 - 375**

Mickey, Baby Bright Eyes, Tommy Tucker, 1939 - 1949.

16 - 18in (41 - 46cm)	**250 - 275**
22 - 24in (56 - 51cm)	**325 - 375**

Sweetie Pie, 1942.

16 - 18in (41 - 46cm)	**225 - 250**
22 - 24in (56 - 61cm)	**300 - 350**

Baby Effanbee, 1925.

12in (31cm)	**125 - 150**

Lambkin, 1930s.

16in (41cm)	**350****

Sugar Baby, 1936. Caracul wig.

16 - 18in (41 - 46cm)	**250 - 275**

Pat-O-Pat, 1925. (For photograph see *7th Blue Book*, page 145.)

13 - 15in (33 - 38cm)	**150**

24in (61cm) *Mickey*, all original. See color photograph on page 109. *H & J Foulke, Inc.*

**Not enough price samples to compute a reliable range.

EFFanBEE continued

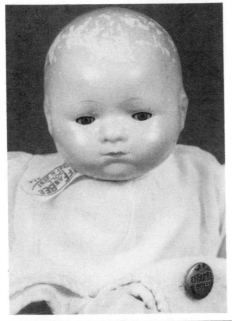

Patsy Family: 1928 - on. All-composition, jointed at neck, shoulders and hips; molded hair (sometimes covered with wig), bent right arm on some members, painted or sleep eyes; original or appropriate old clothes; may have some crazing. Came with metal heart bracelet. (See previous *Blue Books* for *Patsy* dolls not pictured here. See color photographs on page 107.)

Mark:

EFFANBEE
PATSY JR.
DOLL

EFFANBEE
PATSY
DOLL

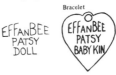
Bracelet

EFFANBEE
PATSY
BABY KIN

12in (31cm) *Baby Effanbee*, all original with label and button. *H & J Foulke, Inc.*

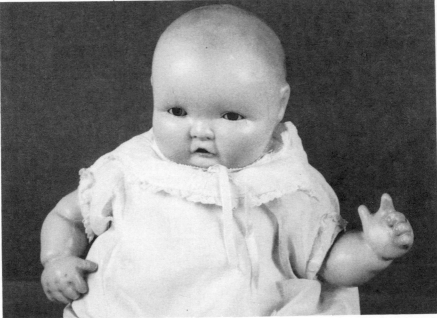

16in (41cm) *Lambkin. Miriam Blankman Collection.*

6in (15cm) *Wee Patsy*, all original	$325
7in (18cm) *Baby Tinyette*	200 - 225
9in (23cm) *Patsy Babyette*	225 - 235
Patsyette	250 - 265
11in (28cm) *Patsy Baby*	235 - 265
Patsy Jr.	275 - 300
Patricia Kin	275 - 300
14in (36cm) *Patsy*	300 - 325
Patricia	350 - 375
16in (41cm) *Patsy Joan*	350 - 375
19in (48cm) *Patsy Ann*	425 - 450
22in (56cm) *Patsy Lou*	450 - 475
26in (66cm) *Patsy Ruth*	700 - 800
30in (76cm) *Patsy Mae*	700 - 800

19in (48cm) *Patsy Ann*, all original. *H & J Foulke, Inc.*

25 - 26in (64 - 66cm) *Patsy Ruth*, all original. *H & J Foulke, Inc.*

EFFanBEE continued

Skippy: 1929. All-composition, jointed at neck, hips and shoulders, (later a cloth torso, still later a cloth torso and upper legs with composition molded boots for lower legs); molded hair, painted eyes to the side; original or appropriate clothes; all in good condition. Came with metal heart bracelet.

Mark:

EFFANBEE
SKIPPY
©
P.L. Crosby

14in (36cm) $375 - 425

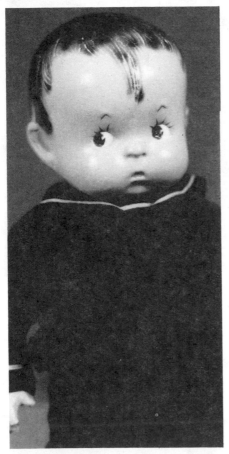

14in (36cm) *Skippy*, all original. *H & J Foulke, Inc.*

Dy-Dee Baby: 1933 - on. First dolls had hard rubber head with soft rubber body, caracul wig or molded hair, open mouth for drinking, soft ears (after 1940). Later dolls had hard plastic heads with rubber bodies. Still later dolls had hard plastic heads with vinyl bodies. Came with paper heart label. Various sizes from 9 - 20in (23 - 51cm). Very good condition. (For photograph see *9th Blue Book*, page 156.)

Mark:
"EFF-AN-BEE
DY-DEE BABY
US PAT.-1-857-485
ENGLAND-880-060
FRANCE-723-980
GERMANY-585-647
OTHER PAT PENDING"
Rubber body:
14 - 16in (36 - 41cm) $150 - 165
24in (61cm)   275 - 300

EFFanBEE continued

All-Composition Children: 1933 - on. All-composition jointed at neck, shoulders and hips; human hair or mohair wigs, sleep eyes, closed mouths; original clothes; all in very good condition. Came with metal heart bracelet.

Anne Shirley, 1935 - 1940. Marked on back.

14 - 15in (36 - 38cm)	**$ 210 - 235**
17 - 18in (43 - 46cm)	**260 - 285**
21in (53cm)	**325 - 350**
27in (69cm)	**450**

American Children, 1936 - 1939. Open mouth, unmarked

15in (38cm)		
Barbara Joan	**550 -**	**650**
17in (43cm)		
Barbara Ann	**650 -**	**750**
21in (53cm)		
Barbara Lou	**750 -**	**850**

Closed mouth, (For photograph see *9th Blue Book*, page 157.)

19 - 21in (48 - 53cm) marked head on **Anne Shirley** body, sleep or painted eyes **1100 - 1300**

17in (43cm) boy, unmarked, painted eyes. (For photograph see *6th Blue Book*, page 131.)

1200 - 1300

21in (53cm) **Barbara Lou** (left) and **Little Lady** (right), both all original. *H & J Foulke, Inc.*

Suzette, 1939. Painted eyes (For photograph see *9th Blue Book*, page 159.)
11½in (29cm)   **210 - 235**
Suzanne, 1940. (For photograph see *8th Blue Book*, page 165.)
14in (36cm)   **235 - 265**
Little Lady, 1940 - 1949. Same prices as **Anne Shirley.**
Little Girl, 1940. (For photograph see *7th Blue Book*, page 148.)
9in (23cm)   **200 - 225**

9in (23cm) 1930s girl with molded hair, all original. *H & J Foulke, Inc.*

12in (31cm) **Candy Kid,** all original with box. *H & J Foulke, Inc.*

Portrait Dolls, 1940. Ballerina, **Bo-Peep, Gibson Girl,** bride, groom, dancing couple, colonial. (For photograph see *7th Blue Book*, page 152.)
11in (28cm)   **225 - 250**
Candy Kid, 1946. Toddler, molded hair.
12in (31cm)   **275 - 300**
Betty Brite, 1933. Caracul wig. (For photograph see *6th Blue Book*, page 130.)
16½in (42cm)   **250 - 275**
Button Nose, 1939. (For photograph see *8th Blue Book*, page 164.)
9in (23cm)   **200 - 225**

EFFanBEE continued

Charlie McCarthy: 1937. Composition head, hands and feet, cloth body; painted hair and eyes; strings at back of head to operate mouth; original clothes; all in very good condition. (For photograph see *8th Blue Book*, page 163.)

MARK:
"EDGAR BERGEN'S CHARLIE McCARTHY,
AN EFFanBEE PRODUCT"

17 - 20in (43 - 51cm)	**$500 - 550**
Mint-in-box with button	**675 - 750**

Historical Dolls: 1939. All-composition, jointed at neck, shoulders and hips. Three each of 30 dolls portraying the history of American fashion, 1492—1939. "American Children" heads used with elaborate human hair wigs and painted eyes; elaborate original costumes using velvets, satins, silks, brocades, and so forth; all in excellent condition. Came with metal heart bracelet. See color photograph on page 108.

Marks: On head:
"EFFANBEE AMERICAN CHILDREN"
On body:
"EFFANBEE ANNE SHIRLEY"

21in (53cm)	**$1300 - 1500**

20in (51cm) *Charlie McCarthy*, all original with pin. *H & J Foulke, Inc.*

End of *Charlie McCarthy's* original box. *H & J Foulke, Inc.*

Historical Doll Replicas: 1939. All-composition, jointed at neck, shoulders and hips. Series of 30 dolls, popular copies of the original historical models (see above). Human hair wigs, painted eyes; original costumes all in cotton, copies of those on the original models. Came with metal heart bracelet. All in excellent condition. See color photograph on page 109.

Mark: On torso:
"EFFanBEE
ANNE SHIRLEY"

14in (36cm)   **$450 - 550**

Howdy Doody: 1949 - 1950. Hard plastic head and hands, molded hair, sleep eyes; cloth body; original clothes; all in excellent condition.

19 - 23in (48 - 58cm)   **$150 - 250**

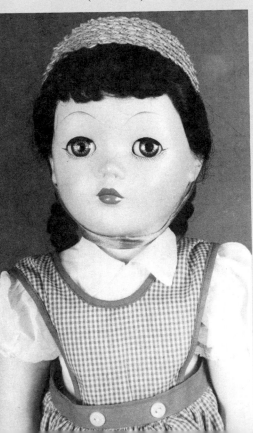

Honey: 1949 - 1955. All-hard plastic, jointed at neck, shoulders and hips; synthetic, mohair or human hair, sleep eyes; original clothes; all in excellent condition.

Mark: EFFANBEE

14in (36cm)	**$225**
18in (46cm)	**250 - 275**
24in (61cm)	**350 - 375**
Prince Charming	**300 - 350***
Cinderella	**300 - 350***
Alice	**275 - 300**

*(For photograph see *6th Blue Book*, page 135.)

Vinyl Dolls: All original and excellent condition.

Mickey, 1956.
10 - 11in (25 - 28cm)   **$100**

Champagne Lady, 1959.
19in (48cm)   **250****

Fluffy Girl Scout, 1957 on.
11in (28cm)   **50 - 65**

Patsy Ann Girl Scout, 1960 - 61. (For photograph see *7th Blue Book*, page 154.)
     100 - 125

Mary Jane Nurse, 1959.
32in (81cm)   **175 - 200****
**Not enough price samples to compute a reliable range.

Effanbee Club Limited Edition Dolls: 1975 - on. All-vinyl jointed doll; original clothes; excellent condition.

1975 *Precious Baby*	**$450**
1976 *Patsy*	**350**
1977 *Dewees Cochran*	**175**
1978 *Crowning Glory*	**150**
1979 *Skippy*	**350**
1980 *Susan B. Anthony*	**150**
1981 *Girl with Watering Can*	**150**
1982 *Princess Diana*	**125**
1983 *Sherlock Holmes*	**125**
1984 *Bubbles*	**125**
1985 *Red Boy*	**125**
1986 *China Head*	**125**

25in (64cm) *Honey Walker*, all original. *H & J Foulke, Inc.*

Maud Tousey Fangel

Maker: Averill Manufacturing Co. and Georgene Novelties, New York, N.Y., U.S.A.
Date: 1938
Material: All-cloth
Size: 10in (25cm) and up
Designer: Maude Tousey Fangel
Mark: "M.T.F. ©" at side of face on hair, but often inside the seam

---

Maud Tousey Fangel Doll: All-cloth with printed face in several variations which came dressed as a baby or child; some bodies are of printed cloth, some plain; soft stuffed, flexible arms and legs; original or appropriate clothes; all in very good condition. *Snooks, Sweets, Peggy-Ann* and possibly other names.

12 - 14in (31 - 36cm)	**$600 - 650**
17in (43cm)	**750**

14in (36cm) Maud Tousey Fangel girl. *H & J Foulke, Inc.*

French Bébé
(Unmarked)

Maker: Numerous French firms
Date: Ca. 1880 - 1925
Material: Bisque head, jointed composition body
Mark: None, except perhaps numbers, Paris, France or DEP

Unmarked French Bébé: Perfect bisque head, swivel neck, lovely wig, set paperweight eyes, closed mouth, pierced ears; jointed French body; pretty costume; all in good condition.

Early, fine quality
(desirable face):
14 - 16in (36 - 41cm)
$4000 - 4400
20 - 22in (51 - 56cm)
5500 - 6000
Standard quality:
17 - 19in (43 - 48cm)
2650 - 2850
22 - 24in (56 - 61cm)
3300 - 3700
Open Mouth:
1890s:
16 - 18in (41 - 46cm)
1900 - 2100
24 - 25in (61 - 64cm)
2650 - 2850
1920s:
16 - 18in (41 - 46cm)
675 - 775
22 - 24in (56 - 61cm)
875 - 925
DEP:
14 - 16in (36 - 41cm)
2300 - 2600
21 - 24in (53 - 61cm)
3400 - 3800

20in (51cm) unmarked French Bébé. *Private Collection.*

French Bébé
(Unknown Manufacturers)

H.

Marked H Bébé: Ca. late 1870s. Possibly by A. Halopeau. Perfect pressed bisque socket head of fine quality, paperweight eyes, pierced ears, closed mouth, cork pate, good wig; French-style wood and composition jointed body with straight wrists; appropriate clothes; all in excellent condition.

Mark:

Size 0 = 16½in (42cm)
    2 = 19in (48cm)
    3 = 21in (56cm)
    4 = 24in (61cm)
21 - 23in (53 - 61cm)

$90,000 - 100,000**

J.M.

Marked J.M. Bébé: Ca. 1880s. Perfect pressed bisque socket head, paperweight eyes, closed mouth, pierced ears, good wig; French-style composition body; appropriate clothes; all in good condition. (For photograph see *9th Blue Book*, page 179.)

Mark:

19 - 21in (48 - 53cm) **$25,000 - 30,000****

**Not enough price samples to compute a reliable range.

16½in (42cm) *H Bébé*, size 0. See color photograph on page 109. *Private Collection.*

French Bébés (Unknown Manufacturers) continued

B.L.

Marked B.L. Bébé: Ca. 1880. Possibly by Lefebvre or perhaps Jumeau for the Louvre department store. Perfect bisque socket head, closed mouth, paperweight eyes, pierced ears, good wig; French-style jointed composition body; appropriate clothes; all in good condition. (For photograph see *Doll Classics*, page 41 or *5th Blue Book*, page 54.)

Mark:

18 - 21in (46 - 53cm) $4200 - 4700

R.R.

Marked R.R. Bébé: Ca. 1880s. Some possibly made by Jumeau. Perfect bisque head, closed mouth, paperweight eyes, pierced ears, good wig; French-style jointed composition body; appropriate clothes; all in good condition. (For photograph see *9th Blue Book*, page 180.)

Mark:

R 10 R

21 - 23in (53 - 58cm) $4900 - 5300**

M.

Marked M. Bébé: Mid 1890s. Perfect bisque socket head, closed mouth, paperweight eyes, pierced ears, good wig; French-style jointed composition body; appropriate clothes; all in good condition. Some dolls with this mark may be *Bébé Mascottes.*

Mark:

M.
4

14 - 16in (36 - 41cm)   **$3000 - 3300**
21 - 23in (53 - 58cm)   **4000 - 4500**

**Not enough price samples to compute a reliable range.

18in (46cm) *M//5 Bébé.* Private Collection.

French Fashion-Type

Maker: Various French firms
Date: Ca. 1860 - 1930
Material: Bisque shoulder head, jointed kid body, some with bisque lower limbs or wood arms; or fully-jointed wood body sometimes covered with kid; or cloth body with kid arms.

(See also *Bru, Jumeau, Gaultier, Gesland, Huret, Rohmer* and *Barrois*)

French Fashion Lady: Perfect unmarked bisque shoulder head, swivel or stationary neck, kid body or cloth body with kid arms -- some with wired fingers; original or old wig, lovely blown glass eyes, closed mouth, earrings; appropriate old clothes; all in good condition. Fine quality bisque.

12 - 13in (31 - 33cm)
$2000 up*
15 - 16in (38 - 41cm)
2400 up*
18 - 19in (46 - 48cm)
3000 up*
21in (53cm) **3500 up***
Fully-jointed wood body,
15 - 17in (38 - 43cm)
4500 up +

*Allow at least $400 additional for kid-over-wood upper and bisque lower arms.
*Greatly depending upon the appeal of the face.
*Allow extra for original clothing.
+Allow extra for joints at ankle and waist.

13in (33cm) French fashion, all original. See color photograph on page 110. *H & J Foulke, Inc.*

French Fashion-Type (continued)

Dainty Oval Face:
   12 - 14in (31 - 36cm)   **$2100 - 2200**
Round face, cobalt eyes (shoulder head)
   13 - 15in (33 - 38cm)   **2100 - 2300**
   21in (53cm)   **2900 - 3100**
Twill-over-wood body (Simon & Halbig-type):
   15 - 17in (38 - 43cm)   **3900 - 4500**
With original trunk, extra clothes and miniature accessories,
   16in (41cm) at auction   **7900**
Period Clothes:
  Fashion Lady Clothing:
    Dress   **500 - 1000**
    Boots   **200 - 300**
    Elaborate wig   **300**
    Nice wig   **150**

See color photographs on pages 110 and 111.

Freundlich

Maker: Freundlich Novelty Corp., New York, N.Y., U.S.A.
Date: 1923 - on
Material: All-composition

Baby Sandy: 1939 - 1942. All-composition with swivel head, jointed shoulders and hips, chubby toddler body; molded hair, smiling face, larger sizes have sleep eyes, smaller ones painted eyes; appropriate clothes; all in good condition.
   Mark: On head: "Baby Sandy"
8in (20cm)   **$125 - 135**
12in (31cm)   **165 - 185**
14 - 15in (36 - 38cm)   **275 - 300**

General Douglas Mac-Arthur: Ca. 1942. All-composition portrait doll, molded hat, painted features, one arm to salute if desired; jointed shoulders and hips; original khaki uniform; all in good condition. (For photograph see *9th Blue Book*, page 183.) **Mark:** Cardboard tag: "General MacArthur"
18in (46cm) **$275**

Military Dolls: Ca. 1942. All-composition with molded hats, jointed shoulders and hips, character face, painted features; original clothes. *Soldier, Sailor, WAAC,* and *WAVE,* all in good condition. (For photograph see *7th Blue Book*, page 161.) **Mark:** Cardboard tag
15in (38cm) **$150 - 175**

15in (38cm) *Baby Sandy* with original button. *H & J Foulke, Inc.*

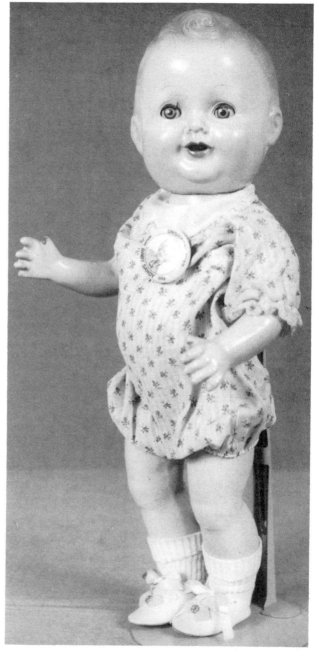

Frozen Charlotte
(Bathing Doll)

Maker: Various German firms
Date: Ca. 1850s - early 1900s
Material: Glazed china; sometimes bisque
Size: 1 - 18in (3 - 46cm)
Mark: None, except for "Germany," or numbers or both

Frozen Charlotte: All-china doll, black or blonde molded hair parted down the middle, painted features; hands extended, legs separated but not jointed; no clothes; perfect condition. Good quality.

2 - 3in (5 - 8cm)	$ 40 - 50*
4 - 5in (10 - 13cm)	90 - 110*
6 - 7in (15 - 18cm)	135 - 165*
9 - 10in (23 - 25cm)	225 - 250*
14 - 15in (36 - 38cm)	375 - 400*

5½in (14cm) Frozen Charlotte with molded bow. *H & J Foulke, Inc.*

Pink tint, early hairdo	
2½ - 3½in (6 - 9cm)	140 - 165
5in (13cm)	225 - 250
Pink tint with bonnet,	
5in (13cm)	350 - 375
Black china, 5in (13cm)	150
Black boy, molded turban and pants,	
3in (8cm)	250
Blonde hair, molded bow,	
5½in (14cm)	165
Wig, lovely boots,	
5in (13cm)	175 - 185
Tinted bisque, blonde hair,	
5in (13cm)	$135 - 160
Parian-type (untinted bisque 1860s style)	
5in (13cm)	160 - 185
Alice style with pink boots (bisque),	
5in (13cm)	300

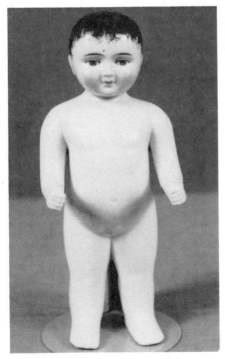

10in (25cm) Frozen "Charlie" with pink tint head. *H & J Foulke, Inc.*

*Allow extra for pink tint, fine decoration and modeling, unusual hairdo.

Fulper

Maker: Heads by Fulper Pottery Co. of Flemington, N.J., U.S.A. for other companies, often Amberg or Horsman
Date: 1918 - 1921
Material: Bisque heads; composition ball-jointed or jointed kid bodies
Mark: "Fulper - Made in U.S.A."

Fulper Child Doll: Perfect bisque head, good wig; kid jointed or composition ball-jointed body; set or sleep eyes, open mouth; suitably dressed; all in good condition. Good quality bisque.
Kid body,
  16 - 19in (41 - 48cm)
      $350 - 400*
Composition body,
  18 - 22in (46 - 56cm)
      500 - 600*

Fulper Baby or Toddler: Same as above, but with bent-limb or jointed toddler body.
14 - 16in (36 - 41cm)
      $450 - 550*
20 - 22in (51 - 56cm)
      650 - 750*

*Allow more for an especially pretty or cute doll.

15in (38cm) Fulper character baby. *H & J Foulke, Inc.*

Gaultier

Maker: Francois Gauthier (name changed to Gaultier in 1875); St. Maurice, Charenton, Seine, Paris, France (This company made only porcelain parts, not bodies.)
Date: 1860 to 1899 (then joined S.F.B.J.)
Material: Bisque head for kid or composition body; all-bisque

---

Marked F. G. Fashion Lady: 1860 to 1930. Bisque swivel head on bisque shoulder plate, original kid body, kid arms with wired fingers or bisque lower arms and hands; original or good French wig, lovely large stationary eyes, closed mouth, ears pierced; dressed; all in good condition.

Mark: "F.G." on side of shoulder

10½ - 11½in (27 - 29cm)
$1600 - 1800*
13 - 14in (33 - 36cm)
2000 - 2400*
16 - 18in (41 - 46cm)
2500 - 2700*
21 - 23in (53 - 58cm)
3000 - 3300*
26 - 27in (66 - 69cm)
3700 - 4000*
Wood body, 16 - 18in (41 - 46cm)
3800 - 4200*
Late doll in ethnic costume:
8 - 9in (20 - 23cm)
600 - 700

*Allow extra for original clothes.

See color photograph on page 112.

Approximate size chart:
Size 3/0	10½in (27cm)
2/0	11½in (29cm)
1	13½in (34cm)
2	15in (38cm)
3	17in (43cm)
5	20in (51cm)

13½in (34cm) French fashion lady "1." See color photograph on page 111. *H & J Foulke, Inc.*

Gaultier continued

16in (41cm) F. G. in scroll Bébé. *Private Collection.*

Marked F. G. Bébé: Ca. 1879 - 1887. Bisque swivel head on shoulder plate and gusseted kid body with bisque lower arms or chunky jointed composition body; good wig, large bulgy paperweight eyes, closed mouth, pierced ears; dressed; all in good condition. "So-called "Block letters" mark. See color photograph on page 145.

Mark:

F . 7.G

11 - 13in (28 - 33cm)	**$3850 - 4250**
16 - 18in (41 - 46cm)	**4500 - 4700**
21 - 23in (53 - 58cm)	**4900 - 5200**
26 - 28in (66 - 71cm)	**5500 - 6000**
Early style, kid body,	
15in (38cm)	**4800**
Gutta-percha-type body,	
17in (43cm)	**5250**

Marked F. G. Bébé: Ca. 1887 - 1900 and probably later. Bisque head, composition jointed body; good French wig, beautiful large set eyes, closed mouth, pierced ears; well dressed; all in good condition. So-called "Scroll" mark.

Mark:

5 - 6in (13 - 15cm)	**$ 650 - 750**
15 - 17in (38 - 43cm)	**2500 - 2800***
21 - 23in (53 - 58cm)	**3200 - 3500***
28 - 29in (71 - 74cm)	**4100 - 4400***
Open mouth:	
8in (20cm)	**550 - 600**
15 - 17in (38 - 43cm)	**1650 - 1850**
20 - 22in (51 - 56cm)	**2000 - 2300**
27 - 29in (69 - 74cm)	**2800 - 3000**

*Allow more for an especially pretty doll.

German Bisque
(Unmarked or Unidentified Marks)

Maker: Various German firms
Date: 1860s - on
Material: Bisque head, composition, kid or cloth body
Mark: Some numbered, some "Germany," some both

Molded Hair Doll: Ca. 1880. Tinted bisque shoulder head with beautifully molded hair (usually blonde), painted eyes (sometimes glass), closed mouth; original kid or cloth body; bisque lower arms; appropriate clothes; all in good condition. See color photograph on page 145.

5 - 7in (13 - 18cm)	**$ 115 - 140**
11 - 13in (28 - 33cm)	**225 - 250**
15 - 18in (38 - 46cm)	**325 - 375**
23 - 25in (38 - 64cm)	**550 - 625**

9¾in (25cm) shoulder head with molded blonde hair, glass eyes, all original. *Private Collection.*

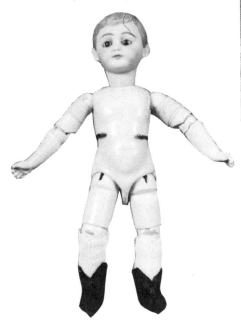

With glass eyes		
10 - 12in (25 - 31cm)	**450 -**	**550**
18 - 22in (46 - 56cm)	**800 -**	**900**
Unusual hairdo,		
18 - 22in (46 - 56cm)	**600 up**	
With glass eyes,	**1000 up**	
With glass eyes and		
decorated bodice	**1200 up**	
American Schoolboy:		
cloth or kid body,		
10 - 12in (25 - 31cm)	**325 -**	**375**
15in (38cm)	**500 -**	**525**
20in (51cm)	**700 -**	**725**
Composition body,		
9 - 11in (23 - 28cm)	**400 -**	**500**

11in (28cm) so-called *American Schoolboy.* H & J Foulke, Inc.

German Bisque continued

Hatted or Bonnet Doll: Ca. 1880 - 1920. Bisque head with painted molded hair and molded fancy bonnet with bows, ribbons, flowers, feathers, and so forth; painted eyes and facial features; original cloth body with bisque arms and legs; good old clothes or nicely dressed; all in good condition.

8 - 9in (20 - 23cm)   **$ 135 - 175**

12 - 15in (31 - 38cm)

   "Marqueritas" stone bisque (Hertwig & Co.)   **200 - 250***

18 - 22in (46 - 56cm)

   fine quality (A.B.G.)   **900 - 1000***

26in (66cm) blonde hair, molded orange bonnet, glass eyes A.B.G. ***#1024***
       3200

All bisque, 4½in (12cm)   **165 - 185***

   7in (18cm) molded baby hat
       85

*Allow extra for unusual style.

8in (20cm) shoulder head with molded whimsical butterfly bonnet. *H & J Foulke, Inc.*

German Bisque continued

Child Doll with closed mouth: Ca. 1880 - 1890. Perfect bisque head; kid or cloth body, gusseted at hips and knees with good bisque hands or jointed composition body; good wig; nicely dressed; all in good condition. See color photograph on page 146.

Kid or cloth body:

12 - 13in (31 - 33cm)	**$ 600 - 650**
17 - 19in (38 - 48cm)	**800 - 900**
21 - 23in (53 - 58cm)	**1050 - 1250**
26in (66cm)	**1450 - 1550**

19in (48cm) unmarked Bébé with swivel neck on kid body, unknown German or French manufacturer, fine quality. *H & J Foulke, Inc.*

13in (33cm) 60/2 German fashion-type doll, all original. *H & J Foulke, Inc.*

German fashion, swivel neck:

20in (51cm)	**1300 - 1400***

Shoulder head, painted eyes:

22in (56cm)	**1350**

#50

18 - 20in (46 - 51cm)	**1300 - 1500**

#132, Bru-type face

19in (48cm)	**2200**

#51, 13 - 14in (33 - 36cm) **1100 - 1200**

Composition body:

13 - 15in (33 - 38cm)	**1600 - 1800***
19 - 21in (48 - 53cm)	**2200 - 2500***
24 - 25in (61 - 64cm)	**2750 - 3000***

#136, 12 - 15in (31 - 38cm)

	2150 - 2250
19 - 21in (48 - 53cm)	**2600 - 3000**

*Allow extra for French look.

Child Doll with open mouth "Dolly Face:" 1888 - on. Perfect bisque head, ball-jointed composition body or kid body with bisque lower arms; good wig, glass eyes, open mouth; dressed; all in good condition.

Very good quality:

12in (31cm)	**$ 375 - 400**
14 - 16in (36 - 41cm)	**475 - 500**
18 - 20in (46 - 51cm)	**550 - 600**

14in (36cm) LHK dolly face, unknown manufacturer. *Jensen's Antique Dolls.*

23 - 24in (48 - 51cm)	**675 -**	**725**
28 - 30in (71 - 76cm)	**1000 -**	**1100**
#50, 16 - 18in (41 - 46cm)		
	700 -	**900**
#51, 14 - 15in (36 - 38cm)		
	1000 -	**1100**
Standard quality:		
12 - 14in (31 - 36cm)	**275 -**	**300**
16 - 18in (41 - 46cm)	**350 -**	**400**
22 - 24in (56 - 61cm)	**500 -**	**550**
28 - 30in (71 - 76cm)	**775 -**	**875**

Tiny child doll: 1890 to World War I. Perfect bisque socket head of good quality, five-piece composition body of good quality with molded and painted shoes and stockings; good wig, set or sleep eyes, open mouth; cute clothes; all in good condition.

Very good quality:		
5 - 6in (13 - 15cm)	**$225 -**	**250**
8 - 10in (20 - 25cm)	**300 -**	**350**
Fully-jointed body,		
7 - 8in (18 - 20cm)	**400 -**	**450**
Closed mouth:		
4½ - 5½in	**275 -**	**325**
8in (20cm)	**550 -**	**650**

4½in (12cm) 4/0 tiny girl with closed mouth. *H & J Foulke, Inc.*

#39-13, five-piece mediocre body,		
glass eyes, 5in (13cm)	**200**	
painted eyes	**85 -**	**95**
Standard quality:		
5 - 6in (13 - 15cm)	**85 -**	**95**
8 - 10in (20 - 25cm)	**125 -**	**140**

Character Baby: 1910 - on. Perfect bisque head, good wig or solid dome with painted hair, sleep eyes, open mouth; composition bent-limb baby body; suitably dressed; all in good condition.

8 - 9in (20 - 23cm)	**$250 -**	**275***
13 - 15in (33 - 38cm)	**450 -**	**525***
18 - 20in (46 - 51cm)	**550 -**	**650***
22 - 24in (56 - 61cm)	**750 -**	**850***

13in (33cm) 199 character baby, unknown manufacturer. *H & J Foulke, Inc.*

*Allow more for open/closed mouth, closed mouth or unusual face.

(Continued on page 208.)

German Bisque continued

Painted eyes:
7 - 8in (18 - 20cm)	**225 - 275***
12in (31cm)	**425 - 475***

*Allow more for open/closed mouth, closed mouth or unusual face.

Character Child: 1910 - on. Bisque head with good wig or solid dome head with painted hair, sleep or painted eyes, open or closed mouth, expressive character face; jointed composition body; dressed; all in good condition.
15 - 19in (38 - 48cm)   **$ 1000 up***
#111, 128 See color photograph on page 147.
   18 - 20in (45 - 51cm) glass eyes
             $25,000**
   16in (41cm) painted eyes
             15,000**
#163
   12 - 14in (31 - 36cm)
             850

*Depending upon individual face.

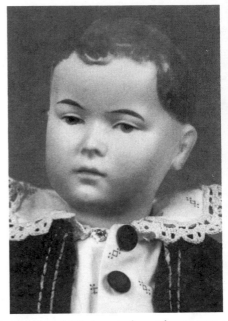

14in (36cm) 163 character boy, unknown manufacturer. *H & J Foulke, Inc.*

23in (58cm) character child "1," unknown manufacturer. *Esther Schwartz Collection.*

Infant, unmarked or unidentified maker: 1924 - on. Perfect bisque head with molded and painted hair, glass sleep eyes; cloth body, celluloid or composition hands; dressed; all in good condition.
10 - 12in (25 - 31cm) long
             $ 325 - 375*
15 - 18in (38 - 46cm) long
             525 - 625*

*More depending upon appeal and rarity of face.

#926 See color photograph on page 148.
   18in (46cm) toddler
             $2000**

**Not enough price samples to compute a reliable range.

Gesland

Maker: Heads: François Gaultier, Paris, France
Bodies: E. Gesland, Paris, France
Date: 1860 - 1928
Material: Bisque head, stockinette stuffed body on metal frame, bisque or composition lower arms and legs. (For photograph see *7th Blue Book*, page 175.)
Mark: Head:

F. G   Body: Sometimes stamped E. Gesland

Fashion lady: Perfect bisque swivel head, good wig, paperweight eyes, closed mouth, pierced ears; stockinette body with bisque hands and legs; dressed; all in good condition.
Early face:
16 - 20in (41 - 51cm)
$5000 - 6000
F.G. face:
14 - 16in (36 - 41cm)
3300 - 3600
19 - 20in (48 - 51cm)
3800 - 4000

Bébé: Perfect bisque swivel head; composition shoulder plate, good wig, paperweight eyes, closed mouth, pierced ears; stockinette body with composition lower arms and legs; dressed; all in good condition. (For photograph see *8th Blue Book*, page 183.)
Beautiful early face:
16 - 18in (41 - 46cm)
$4800 - 5200
21 - 24in (53 - 61cm)
5500 - 6000
Scroll Mark face:
22 - 24in (56 - 61cm)
4000 - 4500

30in (76cm) F.G. on Gesland body. *Esther Schwartz Collection.*

Gladdie

Maker: Heads made in Ohrdruf area, Germany for George Borgfeldt, New York, N.Y., U.S.A. Bisque heads by ABG.
Date: 1929
Material: Ceramic or bisque head, cloth torso, composition arms and legs
Designer: Helen W. Jensen
Mark:
[sic]

*Gladdie
Copyriht By
Helen W. Jensen*

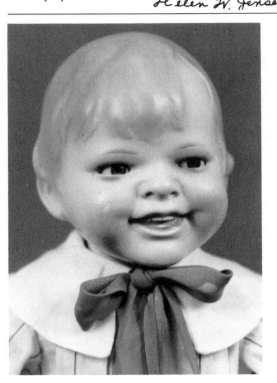

Marked Gladdie: Biscaloid or ceramic head, molded and painted hair, glass eyes, open/closed mouth with molded teeth, laughing face; cloth torso, composition arms and legs; dressed; all in good condition.
16 - 19in (41 - 48cm)
$ 900 - 1000
Bisque head *#1410* (For photograph see *8th Blue Book*, page 201.)

17in (43cm)	**4000****
28in (71cm)	**7000****

**Not enough price samples to compute a reliable range.

16½in (42cm) *Gladdie.* See color photograph on page 149. *H & J Foulke, Inc.*

Godey's Little Lady Dolls

Maker: Ruth Gibbs, Flemington, N.J., U.S.A.
Date: 1946
Material: China head and limbs, cloth body
Size: Most 7in (18cm); a few 9, 10, 12 or 13in (23, 25, 31 or 33cm)
Designer: Herbert Johnson
Mark: Paper label inside skirt "Godey's Little Lady Dolls;" "R. G." incised on back plate.

Godey's Little Lady Dolls continued

Ruth Gibbs Doll: China head with painted black, brown, blonde or auburn hair and features; pink cloth body with china limbs and painted slippers which often matched the hair color; original clothes, usually in an old-fashioned style.

7in (18cm)	$ 65 - 75
12 or 13in (31 or 33cm)	165 - 185
Boxed	200 - 225

Miss Moppet Gift Set, 10in (25cm) hard plastic doll with wardrobe **175****

**Not enough price samples to compute a reliable range.

Label on *Miss Moppet* box.

10in (25cm) hard plastic *Miss Moppet* all original and boxed with wardrobe. *H & J Foulke, Inc.*

Goebel

Maker: F. & W. Goebel porcelain factory, near Coburg, Thüringia, Germany. Made heads for Max Handwerck and others.
Date: 1879 - on
Material: Bisque heads, composition bodies; also all-bisque
Mark:

"B" + number; "Germany"
sometimes A, C, G, H, K, S, SA & T

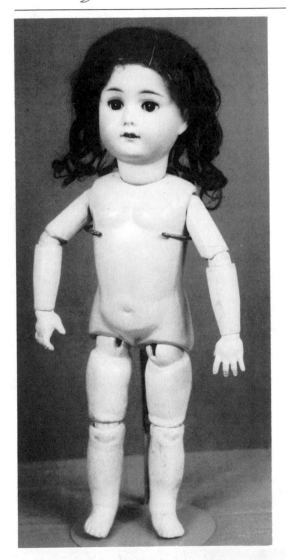

Goebel Child Doll: 1895 - on. Perfect bisque socket head, good wig, sleep eyes, open mouth; composition jointed body; dressed; all in good condition. Some mold **#120** or B.
Mark:

120 5/0
Germany

4½ - 5in (12 - 13cm)
$165 - 175
14 - 16in (36 - 41cm)
325 - 375
22 - 24in (56 - 61cm)
475 - 550
Socket head, open/closed mouth with molded teeth, gusseted kid body, bisque hands. (For photograph see *8th Blue Book*, page 203.)
18 - 20in (46 - 51cm)
850 - 900**

**Not enough price samples to compute a reliable range.

20in (51cm) Goebel child. *H & J Foulke, Inc.*

Pincushion Half Doll: Ca. 1915. Perfect china half figure usually of a lady with molded hair and painted features, sometimes with molded clothing, hats or accessories; lovely modeling and painting. Most desirable have fancy clothing or hair ornamentation and extended arms.

Mark:

2½in (6cm)	$100 up*
4in (10cm)	150 up*

Half-bisque child, (For photograph see *9th Blue Book*, page 197.)

3½in (9cm)	100 - 125

*Depending upon rarity.

Goebel Character Baby: Ca. 1910. Perfect bisque socket head, good wig, sleep eyes, open mouth with teeth; composition jointed baby body; dressed; all in good condition.

13 - 15in (33 - 38cm)	$400 - 425
19 - 21in (48 - 53cm)	500 - 600
14 - 16in (36 - 41cm) Toddler	575 - 700

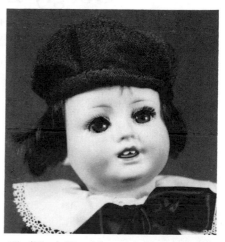

15in (38cm) 4B toddler, probably by Goebel. See color photograph on page 149. *H & J Foulke, Inc.*

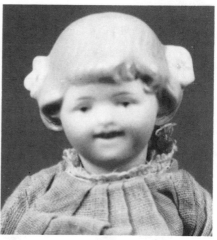

7in (18cm) Goebel character girl, all original. *H & J Foulke, Inc.*

Goebel *Jenny Lind* pincushion doll. *H & J Foulke, Inc.*

Goebel Character Doll: Ca. 1910. Perfect bisque head with molded hair in various styles, some with hats, character face smiling or somber with painted features; papier-mâché five-piece body; all in excellent condition.

6½in (17cm)	$275 - 325

Googly-Eyed Dolls

Maker: J. D. Kestner, Armand Marseille, Hertel, Schwab & Co., Heubach, H. Steiner, Goebel and other German and French firms
Date: Ca. 1911 - on
Material: Bisque heads and composition or papier-mâché bodies or all-bisque

---

All-Bisque Googly: Jointed at shoulders and hips, molded shoes and socks; mohair wig, glass eyes, impish mouth; undressed; in perfect condition.

4½in (12cm)	$ 450 - 475
6in (15cm)	550 - 600
Swivel neck,	
5in (13cm)	600 - 650
6in (15cm)	700 - 750

Jointed elbows and knees (Kestner), swivel neck,

5in (13cm)	**1800**
7in (18cm)	**2900**
Stiff neck, 5in (13cm)	**1400 - 1500**
Painted eyes,	
4½in (12cm)	**350**
6in (15cm)	**500**
Baby, 4½in (12cm)	

K&R 131, 7in (18cm)   **2500 - 2800****
See color photograph on page 149.

**Not enough price samples to compute a reliable range.

6½in (17cm) A.M. 253 and 7in (18cm) Gebrüder Heubach 9573 googlies. *H & J Foulke, Inc.*

Painted eyes, composition body: Perfect bisque swivel head with molded hair, painted eyes to the side, impish mouth; five-piece composition toddler or baby body jointed at shoulders and hips, some with molded and painted shoes and socks; cute clothes; all in good condition. See color photograph on page 148.
A.M., E. Heubach, Goebel, R.A.
6 - 7in (15 - 18cm)
$350 - 375*
10in (25cm)   625 - 675*
Gebrüder Heubach
6 - 7in (15 - 18cm)
450 - 500*

*Allow extra for unusual models.

Googly-Eyed Dolls continued

Glass eyes, composition body: Perfect bisque head, mohair wig or molded hair, sleep or set large googly eyes, impish mouth closed; original composition body jointed at neck, shoulders and hips, sometimes with molded and painted shoes and socks; cute clothes; all in nice condition.

JDK 221: See color photograph on page 150.

13 - 15in (33 - 38cm) Toddler
$4500 - 5500

AM #323 and other similar models by H. Steiner, E. Heubach,
Goebel and Recknagle:

6½ - 7in (17 - 18cm)	**600 - 650**
9 - 10in (23 - 25cm)	**1000 - 1100**
12 - 14in (31 - 36cm)	**1500 - 1600**

Baby body,
10 - 11in (25 - 28cm)	**800 - 900**

AM #253: Watermelon mouth:
6½ - 7½in (17 - 19cm)	**700 - 750**
9in (23cm)	**1100**

SFBJ #245:
8in (20cm), five-piece body
1300
11in (28cm) jointed body
2500
15in (38cm) **4200 - 4600****

K★R 131:
8in (20cm), five-piece body
2200 - 2500**
15 - 16in (38 - 41cm) **7500 - 8500****

AM #200, 240, 241:
11 - 12in (28 - 31cm) **2400 - 2500**

G. Heubach Einco:
14 - 15in (36 - 38cm)
Elizabeth: 9in (23cm) **1650 - 1850**

G. Heubach 8678, 9573
7in (18cm)	**750**
9in (23cm)	**1000**

Schieler, 12in (31cm), at auction
4000

**Not enough price samples to compute a reliable range.

Gebrüder Heubach Einco googly. *Lesley Hurford Collection. Photograph by Norman Hurford.*

11½in (29cm) A.M. 200 googly. *Ruth West Antique Dolls.*

Googly-Eyed Dolls continued

Hertel, Schwab & Co. See page 239.
Demalcol (Dennis, Malley, & Co. London, England):
9 - 11in (23 - 28cm)   **$ 650**
Kley & Hahn 180:
16½in (43cm)   **3100****
P.M. 950:
6½in (17cm)   **1150****
Disc Eyes, shoulder head, girl with molded bow, *223* DRGM 954642
11 - 13in (28 - 33cm)   **1200 - 1300**

**Not enough price samples to compute a reliable range.

Composition face: 1911 - 1914. Made by various companies in 9½ - 14in (24 - 36cm) sizes; marked with paper label on clothing. Called "Hug Me Kiddies," "Little Bright Eyes," as well as other trade names. Round all-composition or composition mask face, wig, round glass eyes looking to the side, water- melon mouth; felt body; original clothes; all in very good condition. See color photograph on page 151.
10in (25cm)   **$650**
12 - 14in (31 - 36cm)   **750 - 850**

Googly with molded hat: 1915. Perfect bisque head with glass side-glancing eyes, watermelon mouth, molded hat; jointed composition body. Made for Max Handwerck, possibly by Hertel, Schwab & Co. All were soldiers: "U.S." (Uncle Sam hat); "E," (English Bellhop-type hat); "D," (German); "T," (Austrian/Turk - two faces) and Japanese.
Mark:

"Dep
Elite"

12 - 13in (31 - 33cm)   **$2000 - 2200**
Japanese Soldier, at auction **3400**

Composition mask face googly, all original. *H & J Foulke, Inc.*

30in (76cm) Jullien. For further information see page 259. *H & J Foulke, Inc.*

BELOW RIGHT: 26in (66cm) Jumeau fashion lady with kid body and bisque hands, all original. For further information see page 260. *Kay & Wayne Jensen Collection.*

BELOW: Italian hard plastic *Fata*, all original. For further information see page 257. *H & J Foulke, Inc.*

219

34in (86cm) Jumeau Triste (so-called Long-Face). For further information see page 261. *Mary Barnes Kelley Collection.*

21in (53cm) early Jumeau (so-called Portrait) with almond eyes. For further information see page 261. *Private Collection.*

LEFT: 29in (74cm) Jumeau Fashion Portrait with rarely found face. For further information see page 260. *Private Collection.*

22in (56cm) Tête Jumeau with open mouth. For further information see page 263. *H & J Foulke, Inc.*

18in (46cm) *Kamkins*. For further information see page 266. *H & J Foulke, Inc.*

LEFT: 23in (58cm) Jumeau character 208, size 10. For further information see page 264. *Private Collection.*

16in (41cm) Kämmer & Reinhardt 128 character baby, all original. For further information see page 270. *H & J Foulke, Inc.*

8½in (22cm) Kämmer & Reinhardt 192 child with closed mouth, all original. For further information see page 267. *H & J Foulke, Inc.*

23½in (60cm) Kämmer & Reinhardt 114 character child, rare version with glass eyes. For further information see page 271. *Mary Barnes Kelley Collection.*

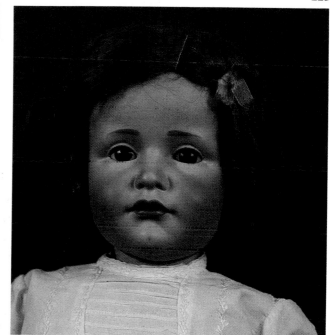

11½in (29cm) Kämmer & Reinhardt 101 character child. For further information see page 271. *H & J Foulke, Inc.*

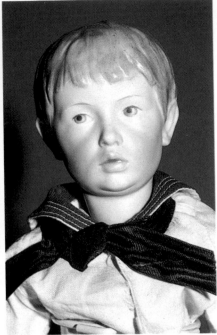

ABOVE LEFT: 15½in (39cm) Kämmer & Reinhardt 115 character child. For further information see page 271. *Mary Barnes Kelley Collection.*

ABOVE RIGHT: 12in (30cm) Kämmer & Reinhardt 102 character child. For further information see page 271. *Richard Wright Antiques.*

LEFT: 21in (53cm) Kestner 154 child. For further information see page 274. *Jensen's Antique Dolls.*

27in (69cm) J. D. Kestner 220 character child, size Q 20 on toddler body. For further information see page 277. *Mary Barnes Kelley Collection.*

26in (66cm) J. D. Kestner 241 character child. For further information see page 276. *Mary Barnes Kelley Collection.*

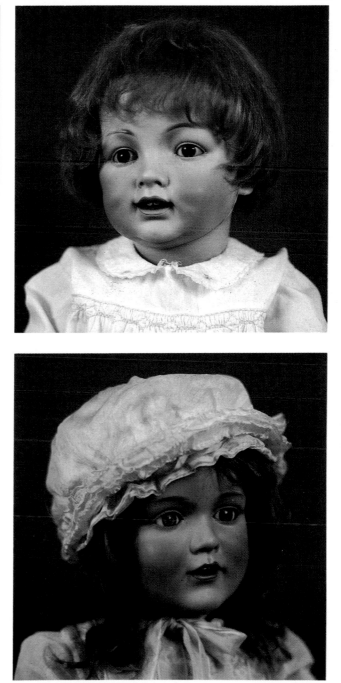

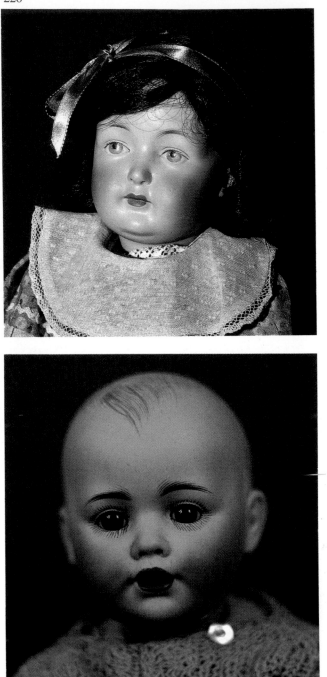

14in (36cm) Kestner 182 character child. For further information see page 276. *Jackie Kaner.*

BELOW LEFT: 13in (33cm) J. D. Kestner character baby with fat-cheeked look. For further information see page 277. *H & J Foulke, Inc.*

25in (64cm) J.D. Kestner *Hilda* toddler, size 0 18. For further information see page 278. *Mary Barnes Kelley Collection.*

INSET: 16in (41cm) J.D. Kestner *Hilda* with solid dome head. For further information see page 278. *Ruth West Antique Dolls.*

18½in (47cm) Kley & Hahn Walküre child. For further information see page 284. *H & J Foulke, Inc.*

11 and 12in (28 and 31cm) composition *Kewpies*. For further information see page 282. *H & J Foulke, Inc.*

23in (58cm) Kley & Hahn 526 character child. For further information see page 285. *H & J Foulke, Inc.*

11in (28cm) German bisque shoulder head boy, probably by Kling & Co. For further information see page 286. *H & J Foulke, Inc.*

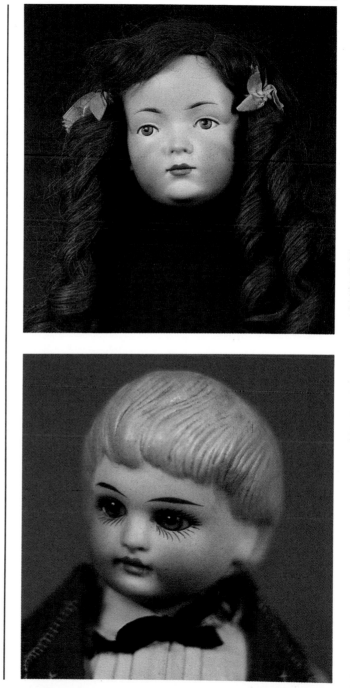

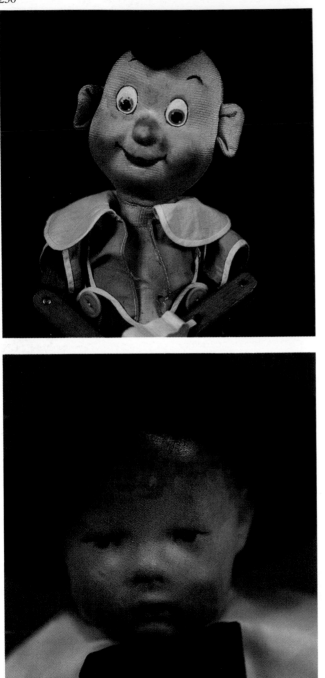

230

11in (28cm) Krueger *Pinocchio*. For further information see page 290. *H & J Foulke, Inc.*

BELOW LEFT: 16½in (42cm) early cloth Käthe Kruse Doll I. For further information see page 291. *H & J Foulke, Inc.*

18in (46cm) unmarked French character of the type made by Lanternier. For further information see page 296. *H & J Foulke, Inc.*

INSET: 10in (25cm) vinyl Käthe Kruse *Doggi*, all original. For further information see page 293. *H & J Foulke, Inc.*

14in (36cm) Lenci boudoir doll, all original. For further information see page 314. *H & J Foulke, Inc.*

INSET: 10in (25cm) Lenci character, all original. For further information see page 313. *H & J Foulke, Inc.*

Greiner

Maker: Ludwig Greiner of Philadelphia, Pa., U.S.A.
Date: 1858 - 1883, but probably as early as 1840s
Material: Heads of papier-mâché, cloth bodies, homemade in most cases, but later some Lacmann bodies were used.
Size: Various, 13 - over 35in (33 - over 89cm), Sizes "0" to "13"
Mark: Paper label on back shoulder:

GREINER'S
IMPROVED
PATENTHEADS
Pat. March 30TH'58

or

GREINER'S
PATENT DOLL HEADS
No7
Pat. Mar. 30'58. Ext.'72

Greiner: Blonde or black molded hair, painted features; homemade cloth body, leather arms; nice old clothes; entire doll in good condition.

'58 label: See color photograph on page 151.

20 - 23in (51 - 58cm)	**$ 900 - 1200**
28 - 30in (71 - 76cm)	**1500 - 1700**

Much worn:

20 - 23in (51 - 58cm)	**650 - 750**
28 - 30in (71 - 76cm)	**850 - 950**

Glass eyes,

20 - 23in (51 - 58cm)	**2000****

'72 label:

19 - 22in (48 - 56cm)	**475 - 525**
29 - 31in (71 - 79cm)	**750 - 850**
35in (89cm)	**1000 - 1100**

**Not enough price samples to compute a reliable range.

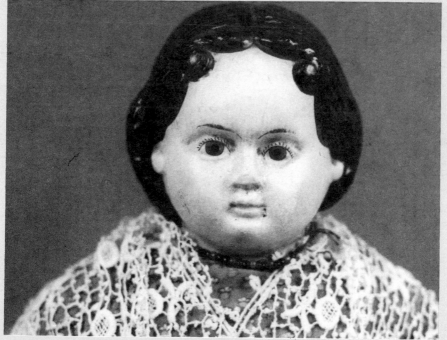

24in (61cm) Greiner with '58 label. *H & J Foulke, Inc.*

Heinrich Handwerck

Maker: Heinrich Handwerck, doll factory, Waltershausen, Thüringia, Germany. Heads by Simon & Halbig.
Date: 1855 - on
Material: Bisque head, composition ball-jointed body or kid body
Trademarks: Bébé Cosmopolite, Bébé de Réclame, Bébé Superior
Mark:

Germany   XANDWERCK

HEINRICK HANDWERCK   109-11
SIMON & HALBIG

Germany

Marked Handwerck Child Doll: Ca. 1885 - on. Perfect bisque socket head, original or good wig, sleep or set eyes, open mouth, pierced ears; ball-jointed body; dressed; entire doll in good condition.

No mold number:

14 - 16in (36 - 41cm)	$ 400 - 450*
19 - 21in (43 - 53cm)	500 - 550
23 - 25in (58 - 64cm)	600 - 700
28 - 30in (71 - 76cm)	900 - 1100
33 - 35in (84 - 89cm)	1350 - 1550
42in (107cm)	2600 - 2800

Mint-in-box with factory dress,
24in (64cm), at auction   **1250**

#69, 79, 89, 99, 109, 119:
10 - 12in (25 - 31cm)
     500 - 550*
14 - 16in (36 - 41cm)
     500 - 550*
19 - 21in (43 - 53cm)
     625 - 725
23 - 25in (58 - 64cm)
     750 - 850
28 - 30in (71 - 76cm)
     1100 - 1300
33 - 35in (84 - 89cm)
     1700 - 2000
42in (107cm)   3500
#79, 89 closed mouth:
12in (31cm)   1500
18 - 20in (46 - 51cm)
     2000 - 2200
24in (61cm)   2600 - 2800
#189, open mouth:
18 - 20in (46 - 51cm)
     850

*Allow extra for mint condition with original clothes.

16in (41cm) Handwerck/Simon & Halbig girl, all original. See color photograph on page 152. *Esther Schwartz Collection.*

Max Handwerck

Maker: Max Handwerck, doll factory, Waltershausen, Thüringia, Germany. Some heads by Goebel.

Date: 1900 - on

Material: Bisque head, ball-jointed composition or kid body

Trademarks: Bébé Elite, Triumph-Bébé

Mark:

23½in (60cm) Max Handwerck 297 girl. *H & J Foulke, Inc.*

Marked Max Handwerck Child Doll: Perfect bisque socket head, original or good wig, set or sleep eyes, open mouth, pierced ears; original ball-jointed body; well dressed; all in good condition. Some mold #283 or 297.

15 - 17in (38 - 43cm)	$ 350 - 375
22 - 24in (56 - 61cm)	500 - 550
29 - 31in (74 - 79cm)	850 - 950
38in (97cm)	2000 - 2100

Marked Bébé Elite Character: Perfect bisque socket head with sleep eyes, open mouth with upper teeth, smiling character face; bent-limb composition baby body; appropriate clothes; all in good condition. (For photograph see *6th Blue Book,* page 171.)

14 - 16in (36 - 41cm)	$400 - 450
19 - 21in (48 - 53cm)	500 - 600
25in (64cm)	750 - 850

Karl Hartmann

Maker: Karl Hartmann, doll factory, Stockheim/Upper Franconia, Germany
Date: 1911 - 1926
Material: Bisque head, jointed composition body
Mark:

Marked Karl Hartmann Doll: Perfect bisque head, good wig, glass eyes, open mouth; jointed composition body; suitable clothing; all in good condition.
22 - 24in (56 - 61cm)
$550 - 650
28 - 30in (71 - 76cm)
900 - 1000

23in (58cm) Karl Hartmann girl. See color photograph on page 152. *H & J Foulke, Inc.*

Heine & Schneider

Maker: Heine & Schneider, Bad-Kosen, Germany
Date: 1920 - 1922
Material: Pressed cardboard covered with cloth or all-cloth. Some with cloth covered composition arms and hands.
Size: 17 - 19in (43 - 48cm)
Mark: Stamped on foot

Schneider's Kunstpuppen-Atelier
Karl Schneider
Bad-Kosen

Puppenkunst Elizabeth
* Heine & Schneider *
Bad-Kosen, Saale

Heine & Schneider Art Doll: Cloth covered head with molded hair, painted eyes, closed mouth, oil painted features. Cloth body with jointed shoulders and hips. Appropriate clothes, all in good condition. See color photograph on page 152.
$1300 - 1500

Hertel, Schwab & Co.

Maker: Stutzhauser Porzellanfabrik, Hertel Schwab & Co., Stutzhaus, near Ohrdruf, Thüringia, Germany

Date: 1910 on

Material: Bisque heads to be used on composition, cloth or leather bodies, all-bisque dolls, pincushion dolls

Mark:

Made
in
Germany
151/2

152
4

Made
in
Germany
136/10

152
LWBC·
3

Marked Character Baby: Perfect bisque head, molded and painted hair or good wig, sleep or painted eyes, open or open/closed mouth with molded tongue; bent limb baby body; dressed; all in good condition.

#130, 142, 150, 151, 152:

10 - 11in (25 - 28cm)	**$ 400 - 425**
14 - 16in (36 - 41cm)	**500 - 550**
20 - 22in (51 - 56cm)	**725 - 800**
25 - 26in (64 - 71cm)	**950 - 1100**

#152 head only, 11½in (29cm) head circumference, original box

400

#142 All-Bisque, 11in (28cm) painted eyes

750

#125 (so-called "Patsy Baby"):

11 - 12in (28 - 31cm)	**700 - 850****

#126 (so-called "Skippy"):

10in (25cm)	**700 - 900****

#127 (so-called "Patsy"):

16in (41cm)	**1000 - 1200****

**Not enough price samples to compute a reliable range.

20in (51cm) 151 character baby. See color photograph on page 153. *H & J Foulke, Inc.*

Hertel, Schwab & Co. continued

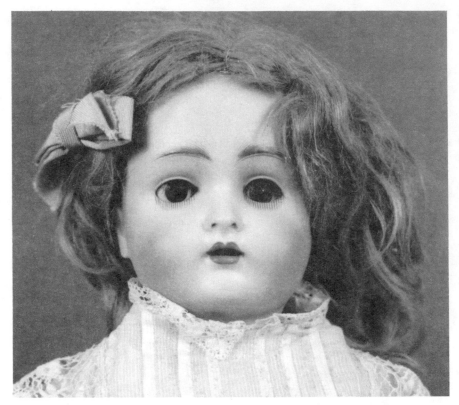

23in (58cm) 136 child. *H & J Foulke, Inc.*

Child Doll: Ca. 1910. Perfect bisque head, mohair or human hair wig, sleep eyes, open mouth with upper teeth; good quality jointed composition body (some marked K & W); dressed; all in good condition. Mold *#136*. See color photograph on page 153.

16 - 18in (41 - 46cm)   **$450 - 500**
22 - 24in (56 - 61cm)   **550 - 650**

Marked Character Child: Perfect bisque head, painted or sleeping eyes, closed mouth; jointed composition body; dressed; all in good condition. See color photograph on page 154.

#134, 149, 141:
16 - 18in (41 - 46cm)   **$4700 - 5700***
#154 (closed mouth):
16 - 17in (41 - 43cm)   **2200 - 2300**
#154 (open mouth):
17 - 18in (43 - 46cm)   **1200 - 1300**
25in (64cm)   **1850**
#169 (closed mouth):
19 - 21in (48 - 53cm) toddler
  3500 - 4000
24 - 26in (61 - 66cm) toddler
  4500 - 5500
#169 (open mouth):
23in (58cm) baby   **1500***

*Glass eyes are more popular.
**Not enough price samples to compute a reliable range.

Hertel, Schwab & Co. continued

All-Bisque Doll: Jointed shoulders and hips; good wig, glass eyes, closed or open mouth; molded and painted shoes and stockings; undressed; all in good condition. Mold *#208*, often with *Prize Baby* label.

4 - 5in (10 - 13cm)	**$225 - 275**
7in (18cm)	**375 - 400**
8in (20cm)	**500 - 550**
Swivel neck,	
6in (15cm)	**450 - 475**

Marked Googly: Perfect bisque head, large glass side-glancing sleeping eyes, wig or molded hair, impish closed mouth; composition body; cute clothes; all in good condition.

#173, 165: (For photograph see *8th Blue Book*, page 207.) Toddler:
   11in (28cm)   **$3000**
   14 - 15in (36 - 38cm)
               4000 - 4500
#163: (For photograph see *8th Blue Book*, page 217.)
   16in (41cm)   **5000****
#172 (See color photograph on page 150.):
   15 - 16in (38 - 41cm)
               6500**
#222 Our Fairy,
   11in (28cm)   **2200**

**Not enough price samples to compute a reliable range.

8½in (22cm) 208 all-bisque child, size 7. *H & J Foulke, Inc.*

Ernst Heubach

Maker: Ernst Heubach, porcelain factory, Köppelsdorf, Thüringia, Germany
Date: 1887 - on
Material: Bisque head; kid, cloth or composition bodies
Mark: D.E.P. 1902 Heubach · Kopplesdorf. ─────

300 · 14/0

2/0 Germany

Heubach Child Doll: Ca. 1888 - on. Perfect bisque head, good wig, sleep eyes, open mouth; kid, cloth or jointed composition body; dressed; all in good condition.

#275 or horseshoe, kid or cloth body:

12 - 13in (31 - 33cm)	**$185 - 210**
16 - 18in (41 - 46cm)	**250 - 275**
21 - 23in (53 - 58cm)	**350 - 400**

#250, composition body:

8 - 9in (20 - 23cm)	**185 - 210**
13 - 15in (33 - 38cm)	**275 - 325**
18 - 20in (46 - 51cm)	**375 - 425**
23 - 24in (58 - 61cm)	**475 - 550**
28in (71cm)	

Painted bisque, *#250, 407*

7 - 8in (18 - 20cm)	**95 - 110**

#312 SUR,

14in (36cm)	**350 - 375**
28in (71cm)	**700 - 750**

25in (64cm) 250 child. *H & J Foulke, Inc.*

Ernst Heubach continued

15in (38cm) 320 character baby. See color photograph on page 155. *H & J Foulke, Inc.*

Character Baby: 1910 - on. Perfect bisque head, good wig, sleep eyes, open mouth (sometimes also wobbly tongue and pierced nostrils); composition bent-limb baby or toddler body; dressed; all in good condition.

#300, 320, 342 and others:

6in (15cm)	**$250**
8 - 10in (20 - 25cm)	**275 - 325**
14 - 17in (36 - 43cm)	**425 - 475**
19 - 21in (48 - 53cm)	**500 - 550**
24 - 25in (61 - 64cm)	**800 - 850**

#300, 320, jointed composition body,

17in (43cm)	**450**
24in (61cm)	**650**

Toddler:

9in (23cm) five-piece body:

	350 - 375
13 - 14in (33 - 36cm)	**500 - 550**
23 - 25in (58 - 64cm)	**850 - 950**

Character Children: 1910 - on. Perfect bisque shoulder head with molded hair in various styles, some with hair bows, painted eyes, open/closed mouth; cloth body with composition lower arms. (For photograph see *8th Blue Book*, page 221.)

#262 and others,

12in (31cm)	**$400 - 450******

**Not enough price samples to compute a reliable range.

Ernst Heubach continued

Infant: Ca. 1925. Perfect bisque head, molded and painted hair, sleep eyes, closed mouth; cloth body, composition or celluloid hands, appropriate clothes; all in good condition. (For photograph see *9th Blue Book*, page 229.)

#349, 339, 350:
 10 - 12in (25 - 31cm)   **$475 - 575****

#338, 340:
 14 - 16in (36 - 41cm)   **725 - 825****

Googly: Perfect bisque character head, molded hair, painted eyes, impish mouth; five-piece composition body; dressed; all in good condition. Mold *#260, 261, 263, 264.* (For photograph see *9th Blue Book*, page 229.)
 6 - 8in (15 - 20cm)   **$350 - 450**

**Not enough price samples to compute a reliable range.

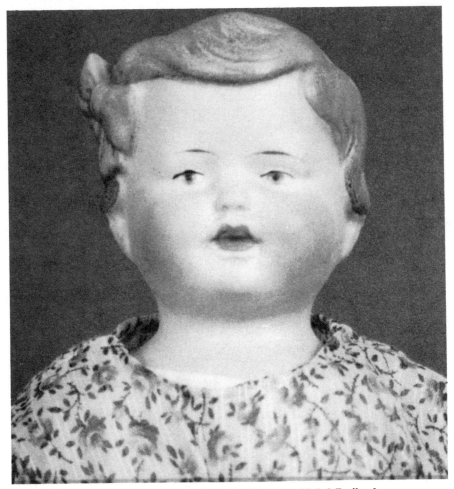

13in (33cm) character girl with molded hair bow. *H & J Foulke, Inc.*

Gebrüder Heubach

Maker: Gebrüder Heubach, porcelain factory, Licht and Sonneberg, Thüringia, Germany

Date: 1820 - on; doll heads 1910 - on

Material: Bisque head, kid, cloth or jointed composition body or composition bent-limb body, all bisque

Mark:

Heubach Character Child: Ca. 1910. Perfect bisque head, molded hair, glass or intaglio eyes, closed or open/closed mouth, character face; jointed composition or kid body; dressed; all in good condition. (For photographs of Heubach dolls see *Focusing On Dolls*, pages 30-68.)

#5636 laughing child, glass eyes,
15 - 16in (38 - 41cm)   **$ 2000 - 2200**

#5689 smiling child (For photograph see *6th Blue Book*, page 197),
23 - 27in (58 - 69cm)   **2300 - 2800**

#5730 Santa,
19 - 21in (48 - 53cm)   **2200 - 2500**

#5777 Dolly Dimple,
19 - 22in (48 - 56cm)   **3000 - 3500**

#6969, 6970, 7246, 7347, 7407, 8017, 8420
(pouty child, must have glass eyes)
12 - 13in (31 - 33cm)   **2000 - 2500**
16 - 19in (41 - 48cm)   **3000 - 3500**
24in (61cm)   **4200 - 4500**

#7684 Screamer,
12in (31cm)   **850**

#7622 and other socket head pouties (intaglio eyes)
14 - 17in (36 - 43cm)   **950 - 1150**

#7679 Whistler socket head,
14in (36cm)   **1000 - 1100**

#7665, Smiling,
16in (41cm)   **1800**

#7788 Coquette, JCB,
14in (36cm)   **950**

#7852 molded coiled braids shoulder head,
19in (48cm)   **2600**

Character girl 5636. *Esther Schwartz Collection.*

#7911, 8191 grinning,
15in (38cm)   **1100 - 1200**

#7925, 7926 (For photograph see *9th Blue Book*, page 167.)   **2500****

#8192
9 - 11in (23 - 28cm)   **450 - 550**
14 - 16in (36 - 41cm)   **700 - 775**
18 - 22in (46 - 56cm)   **950 - 1050**

#7602 and other socket head pouties,
14 - 16in (36 - 41cm)   **650 - 750**

#7661, squinting eyes, crooked mouth,
16in (41cm)   **3000 - 4000**

#8556. See color photograph on page 157.
   11,500

**Not enough price samples to compute a reliable range.

Gebrüder Heubach continued

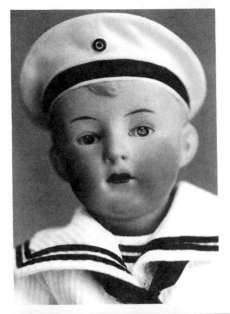

Smiling girl with hair bow. See color photograph on page 157.

18in (46cm)	**8000**

#9141 Winker,

9in (23cm) glass eyes	**1500**
7in (18cm) painted eye	**850 - 950**

Socket heads smiling with two teeth. See color photograph on page 156.

16in (41cm)	**750**

Shoulder heads, pouty or smiling, intaglio eyes. See color photograph on page 155.

14 - 16in (36 - 41cm)	**$ 600 - 650**
20in (51cm)	**850**

#10532,

20 - 22in (51 - 56cm)	**1200 - 1300**

12in (31cm) 9891 character with molded sailor cap "S.M.S. Emden," (famous German warship). *Ingrid Liebers Collection. Photograph by Norman Hurford.*

9in (23cm) trio of all-bisque girls with different hair styles, the left one being a rare version with swivel neck. *Lesley Hurford Collection. Photograph by Norman Hurford.*

#10586, 10633, JCB,
18 - 20in (46 - 51cm)   **650 - 750**
#11173 Tiss Me, 8in (20cm) (For photograph see *8th Blue Book*, page 224.)
1400 - 1600**
Baby Bo Kaye,
6½in (17cm)   **800 - 850**
#1907 Jumeau. See color photograph on page 156.
20 - 22in (51 - 56cm)   **2400 - 2600**

**Not enough price samples to compute a reliable range.

All-Bisque: (For photographs see *Focusing On Dolls*, pages 71—77.)
Position Babies,
5in (13cm)   **$ 350 - 450**
Boy or Girl with bows or hair band:
7 - 8in (18 - 20cm)   **800 - 900**
9in (23cm)   **1000**
Bunny Boy or Girl,
5½in (14cm)   **300 - 350**
9in (23cm)   **600**
All-bisque boy or girl,
4in (10cm)   **275 - 300**
5 - 6in (13 - 15cm)   **450 - 550**
Chin-Chin character,
4in (10cm)   **250 - 275**
Action figures:
6in (15cm)   **350 - 450**
4in (10cm)   **200 - 250**

See color photograph on page 158.

Heubach Babies: Ca. 1910. Perfect bisque head, molded hair, intaglio eyes, open or closed mouth, character face; composition bent-limb body; dressed; all in nice condition.
#6894, 7602, 6898, 7759 and other pouty babies:
4½in (12cm)   **$ 200 - 225**
6in (15cm)   **250 - 275**
10in (25cm)   **400 - 425**
14in (36cm)   **550**
#7604 laughing,
13 - 14in (33 - 36cm)   **650 - 750**

10in (25cm) baby with pink molded cap (illegible mold number.) *Lesley Hurford Collection. Photograph by Norman Hurford.*

13in (33cm) 7977, so-called *Stuart Baby* with molded cap. *Esther Schwartz Collection.*

#7877, 7977 Baby Stuart,
10in (25cm)   **1100 - 1200**
12in (31cm) glass eyes   **2100**
#7745 or **7746** laughing baby, at auction
4100
Molded pink cap,
10in (25cm)   **1800**

Horsman

Maker: E. I. Horsman Co., New York, N.Y., U.S.A. Also distributed dolls as a *verlager* for other manufacturers and imported French and German dolls.
Date: 1878 - on

Billiken: 1909. Composition head with peak of hair at top of head, slanted slits for eyes, watermelon mouth; velvet or plush body; in very good condition. (For photograph see *9th Blue Book*, page 234.)
    Mark: Cloth label on body; "Billiken" on right foot
12in (31cm)   **$325 - 350**

Baby Bumps: 1910. Composition head with molded hair and painted features; stuffed cloth body. Good condition with some wear. (For photograph see *8th Blue Book*, page 226.)
    Mark: None
12 - 14in (31 - 36cm)   **$175 - 200**
Black   **250**

13in (33cm) *Blink*, redressed and refinished. *H & J Foulke, Inc.*

Horsman continued

Can't Break 'Em Characters: Ca. 1910. Heads and hands of "Can't Break 'Em" composition, hard stuffed cloth bodies with swivel joints at shoulders and hips; molded hair, painted eyes, character faces; appropriate clothes; all in good condition. (For photograph see *8th Blue Book*, page 226.)

Mark: "E.I.H.1911"

10 - 12in (25 - 31cm)   **$135 - 165**

Peterkin: 1914 - 1930. All-composition with character face, molded hair, painted eyes to side, watermelon mouth; various boy and girl clothing or simply a large bow; all in good condition. (For photograph see *9th Blue Book*, page 234.)

11in (28cm)   **$250 - 300****

**Not enough price samples to compute a reliable range.

Gene Carr Character: 1916. Composition head with molded and painted hair, eyes painted open or closed, wide smiling mouth with teeth; cloth body with composition hands; original or appropriate clothes; all in good condition. Names such as: *"Snowball"* (Black Boy); *"Mike"* and *"Jane"* (eyes open); *"Blink"* and *"Skinney"* (eyes closed). Designed by Bernard Lipfert from Gene Carr's cartoon characters.

Mark: None

13 - 14in (33 - 36cm)   **$250 - 300**
Black *Snowball*   **450 - 550**

20in (51cm) *Rosebud*, all original. *H & J Foulke, Inc.*

Mama Dolls: Ca. 1920 - on. Composition head, cloth body, composition arms and lower legs; mohair wig or molded hair; sleep eyes; original clothes; all in very good condition.

Mark: "E. I. H. Co." or "HORS-MAN"

Babies:	
12 - 14in (31 - 36cm)	**$135 - 175**
18 - 20in (46 - 51cm)	**225 - 250**
Girls including *Rosebud*:	
14 - 16in (36 - 41cm)	**225 - 250**
22 - 24in (56 - 61cm)	**300 - 350**

9½in (24cm) all-bisque *Tynie Baby*. *H & J Foulke, Inc.*

Jackie Coogan: 1921. Composition head with molded hair, painted eyes, closed mouth; cloth torso with composition hands; appropriate clothes; all in good condition. (For photograph see *8th Blue Book*, page 228.)
Mark: "E. I. H. Co. 19 © 21"
14in (36cm)   **$450 - 500**

Marked Tynie Baby: 1924. Solid dome infant head with sleep eyes, closed mouth, slightly frowning face; cloth body with composition arms; appropriate clothes; all in good condition. Designed by Bernard Lipfert.
Mark: © 1924
          E.I. Horsman Inc.
          Made in
Bisque head,   Germany
12in (31cm) h.c.
                    $ 650 - 675
Composition head. (For photograph see *9th Blue Book*, page 237.)
15in (38cm) long **250 - 275**
All-bisque with swivel neck, glass eyes, wigged or solid dome head,
9 - 10in (23 - 25cm)
                    1650

12in (31cm) baby, all original. *H & J Foulke, Inc.*

HEbee-SHEbee: 1925. All-composition, jointed at shoulders and hips, painted eyes, molded white chemise and real ribbon or wool ties in molded shoes; all in good condition. Blue shoes indicate a *HEbee,* pink ones a *SHEbee.* (For photograph see *7th Blue Book,* page 212.)

11in (28cm)   **$450 - 500**
Fair condition
  (some peeling)   **275 - 300**

Ella Cinders: 1925. Composition head with molded hair, painted eyes; cloth body with composition arms and lower legs; original clothes; all in fair condition. From the comic strip by Bill Conselman and Charlie Plumb, for the Metropolitan Newspaper Service. (For photograph see *8th Blue Book,* page 229.)

Mark: "1925 © MNS"
18in (46cm)   **$500 - 550**

Baby Dimples: 1928. Composition head with molded and painted hair, tin sleep eyes, open mouth, smiling face; soft cloth body with composition arms and legs; original or appropriate old clothes; all in good condition.

Mark: " ©
          E. I. H. CO. INC."
16 - 18in (41 - 46cm)   **$200 - 225**
22 - 24in (56 - 61cm)   **275 - 325**

Child Dolls: Ca. 1930s and 1940s. All-composition with swivel neck, shoulders and hips; mohair wig, sleep eyes; original clothes; all in good condition. (For photograph see *8th Blue Book,* page 229.)

Mark: "HORSMAN"
13 - 14in (33 - 36cm)   **$160 - 185**
16 - 18in (41 - 46cm)   **225 - 250**

Chubby Toddler,
  16 - 18in (41 - 46cm)   **225 - 250**
Jo-Jo, 1937. 12in (31cm) toddler, mint-in-box, at auction   **375**

Cindy: Ca. 1950. All-hard plastic, sleep eyes, open mouth with upper teeth and tongue, synthetic wig with braids.
Mark: "170 made in USA." Walker.
16in (41cm)   **$125**

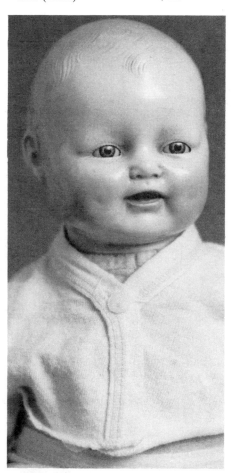

Dimples. See color photograph on page 158. *H & J Foulke, Inc.*

Mary Hoyer

Maker: The Mary Hoyer Doll Mfg. Co., Reading, Pa., U.S.A.
Date: Ca. 1925 - on
Material: First all-composition, later all-hard plastic
Size: 14 and 18in (36 and 46cm)
Mark: Embossed on torso:

"The
Mary Hoyer
Doll"

or in a circle:

"ORIGINAL
Mary Hoyer
Doll"

Marked Mary Hoyer: Material as above; swivel neck; jointed shoulders and hips, original wig, sleep eyes with eyelashes, closed mouth; all in excellent condition. Original tagged factory clothes or garments made at home from Mary Hoyer patterns.
Composition,
14in (36cm)
$350 - 400
Hard plastic,
14in (36cm) **425 - 475**
14in (36cm) boy with caracul wig **475 - 525**
18in (46cm), *Gigi*
500 - 600

14in (36cm) hard plastic, all original Mary Hoyer. *H & J Foulke, Inc.*

Hülss

Maker: Adolf Hülss, doll factory, Waltershausen, Thüringia, Germany; heads by Simon & Halbig
Date: 1913 - on
Material: Bisque socket heads, composition bodies (later heads of painted bisque)
Size: Various
Mark:

Marked Hülss Character Baby: 1925 - on. Mold number **156**. Perfect bisque head with good wig, sleep eyes, open mouth with teeth and tongue, smiling face; composition bent-limb body; nicely dressed; all in good condition.

15 - 17in (38 - 43cm)	**$ 525 - 575**

Toddler:

11in (28cm)	**650**
15 - 16in (38 - 41cm)	**700 - 750**
22 - 24in (56 - 61cm)	**1200 - 1500**

Marked Hülss Child: 1920s. Mold number **176**. Perfect bisque head with good wig, flirty sleep eyes, open mouth with teeth and tongue. Jointed composition body with high knee joint; dressed; all in good condition.

18in (46cm)	**$ 750****
30in (76cm)	**1400 - 1500****

**Not enough price samples to compute a reliable range.

15in (38cm) 156 character baby. *H & J Foulke, Inc.*

Huret

17in (43cm) signed Huret lady on wood body. See color photograph on page 158. *Private Collection.*

Maker: Maison Huret, Paris, France
Date: 1850 - on
Material: China or bisque heads; kid or wood jointed bodies, sometimes with pewter hands and feet
Mark: "Huret" or "Maison Huret" stamped on body

Marked Huret Doll: China or bisque shoulder head, good wig, painted or glass eyes, closed mouth; kid body; beautifully dressed; all in good condition.
16 - 19in (41 - 48cm)
$ 5000 - 6000
Wood body,
16 - 19in (41 - 48cm)
8000 - 9000
Gutta-percha body,
16 - 19in (41 - 48cm)
10,000 up

Ideal

Maker: Ideal Novelty and Toy Co., Brooklyn, N.Y., U.S.A.
Date: 1907 - on

Uneeda Kid: 1914 - 1919. Composition head with molded brown hair, blue painted eyes, closed mouth; cloth body with composition arms and legs with molded black boots; original bloomer suit, yellow slicker and rain hat; carrying a box of Uneeda Biscuits; all in good condition, showing some wear. (For photograph see *9th Blue Book*, page 241.)
16in (41cm) $425 - 450

Snoozie: 1933. Composition head, character expression with yawning mouth, sleeping eyes, molded hair, composition arms and legs or rubber arms, cloth body; baby clothes; all in good condition. 13, 16 and 20in (33, 41 and 51cm). (For photograph see *7th Blue Book*, page 216.)
Mark:
©
By B. LIPFERT
16 - 20in (41 - 51cm) $200 - 225

Ideal continued

Shirley Temple: 1935. For detailed information see pages 380 and 381.

Mama Doll: Ca. 1920 - on. Composition head, cloth body, composition arms and lower legs; mohair wig or molded hair, sleep eyes; appropriate old clothes; all in very good condition.

Mark:

14 - 16in (36 - 41cm)   **$175 - 200**

Flossie Flirt, See color photograph on page 159.
  20in (51cm)   **250 - 275**

Betsy Wetsy: 1937 - on. Composition head with molded hair, sleep eyes; soft rubber body jointed at neck, shoulders and hips; drinks, wets; appropriate clothes; all in good condition. This doll went through many changes including hard plastic head on rubber body, later vinyl body, later completely vinyl. Various sizes.
  Mark: "IDEAL"
14 - 16in (36 - 41cm) rubber body   **$90 - 110**

Snow White: 1937. All-composition, jointed at neck, shoulders and hips; black mohair wig, lashed sleep eyes, open mouth; original dress with velvet bodice and cape, and rayon skirt with figures of seven dwarfs; in good condition. 11in (28cm), 13in (33cm) and 18in (46cm) sizes. (For photograph see *Doll Classics*, page 190.)
  Mark: On body: "SHIRLEY TEMPLE/18"
    On dress: "An Ideal Doll"
11 - 13in (28 - 33cm)
                  $425 - 450
18in (46cm)   **475 - 525**
Molded black hair, painted blue bow, painted eyes,
    13 - 14in (33 - 36cm)
                  160 - 185

16in (41cm) mama doll, all original. *H & J Foulke, Inc.*

Ideal continued

Betty Jane: 1943. All-composition *Shirley Temple*-type doll with jointed neck, shoulders and hips; lashed sleeping eyes (sometimes flirty), open mouth with teeth; all original; very good condition. (For photograph see *7th Blue Book*, page 217.)

Mark: IDEAL
18

18in (46cm)   **$250 - 275**

16in (41cm) baby with flirty eyes, all original. *H & J Foulke, Inc.*

Flirty-eyed Baby: 1938. Composition head, lower arms and legs, cloth body; flirty eyes, closed mouth, molded hair; original clothing; all in good condition.

Mark: "IDEAL DOLL"

16 - 18in (41 - 46cm)   **$200 - 225**

Deanna Durbin: 1938. All-composition, jointed at neck, shoulders and hips; original human hair or mohair wig, sleep eyes, smiling mouth with teeth; original clothing; all in good condition. Various sizes.

Mark: Metal button with picture:
"DEANNA DURBIN,
IDEAL DOLL, U.S.A."

14in (36cm)	**$425 - 475**
20 - 21in (51 - 53cm)	**575 - 625**
24 - 25in (61 - 64cm)	**700 - 750**

21in (53cm) **Deanna Durbin**, all original. *Maxine Salaman Collection.*

Ideal continued

Judy Garland as Dorothy of the Wizard of Oz: 1939. All-composition, jointed at neck, shoulders and hips; dark human hair wig, dark sleep eyes, open mouth with teeth; original dress; all in good condition.

Mark: On head:
"IDEAL DOLL"
MADE IN U.S.A.
Body:
U.S.A.
16

16in (41cm)	**$1000 up**
Replaced dress	**850**

Flexy Dolls: 1938 - on. Head, hands and feet of composition; arms and legs of flexible metal cable, torso of wire mesh; in original clothes; all in good condition. See previous Blue Books for photographs.
Mark: On head: "Ideal Doll"
12in (31cm)

Baby Snooks (Fanny Brice)

	$235 - 265
Mortimer Snerd	**235 - 265**
Soldier	**175 - 200**
Children	**175 - 200**

Composition and wood segmented characters: 1940. Molded composition heads with painted features, wood segmented bodies. Label on front torso gives name of character. See color photograph on page 160.

Pinocchio, 10½in (27cm)	**$235 - 265**
King-Little, 14in (36cm)	**210 - 235**
Jiminy Cricket, 9in (23cm)	**265 - 285**

Magic Skin Baby and Plassie: 1940 - on. Composition or hard plastic head with molded hair, sleep eyes, closed mouth; stuffed latex rubber body; appropriate clothes; all in good condition. See color photograph on page 160.
Mark: On head: "IDEAL"

14 - 15in (36 - 38cm)	**$ 75 - 95**
22in (56cm)	**125 - 135**

Toni and P-90 and P-91 Family: 1948 - on. Series of girl dolls. Most were completely of hard plastic with jointed neck, shoulders and hips, nylon wig, sleep eyes, closed mouth; original clothes; all in excellent condition. Various sizes, but most are 14in (36cm).

Mark: On head: "IDEAL DOLL"
On body: "IDEAL DOLL
P-90
Made in USA"

Toni,

14 - 15in (36 - 38cm) P-90	**$160 - 185**
21in (53cm) P-93	**350 - 400**
22½in (57cm) P-94	**450****

Mary Hartline,

14in (36cm) P-90	**225**
22in (56cm) P-94	**550****

Betsy McCall, vinyl head,

14in (36cm)	**160 - 185**

Harriet Hubbard Ayer, vinyl head,

14in (36cm)	**160 - 185**

**Not enough price samples to compute a reliable range.

16in (41cm) ***Judy Garland***, replaced dress. See color photograph on page 159. *H & J Foulke, Inc.*

Ideal continued

21in (53cm) P-93 *Toni*, original dress. *H & J Foulke, Inc.*

***Miss Curity*,**
   14in (36cm)   **225**
***Sara Ann*,**
   14in (36cm)   **225**

Saralee: 1950. Black vinyl head, painted hair, sleep eyes, open/ closed mouth; cloth body, vinyl limbs; original clothes; all in excellent condition. Designed by Sarah Lee Creech; modeled by Sheila Burlingame. (For photograph see *9th Blue Book*, page 246.)
17 - 18in (43 - 46cm)   **$250 - 275**
Undressed   **125**

Saucy Walker: 1951. All-hard plastic, jointed at neck, shoulders and hips with walking mechanism; synthetic wig, flirty eyes, open mouth with tongue and teeth; original clothes; all in excellent condition. (For photograph see *8th Blue Book*, page 238.)
Mark: "IDEAL DOLL"
16 - 17in (41 - 43cm)   **$ 90 - 115**
20 - 22in (51 - 56cm)   **135 - 165**

Miss Revlon: 1955. Vinyl head with rooted hair, sleep eyes, closed mouth, earrings; hard plastic body with jointed waist and knees, high-heeled feet, vinyl arms with polished nails; original clothes; all in excellent condition. (For photograph see *6th Blue Book*, page 213.)
Mark: On head and body: "IDEAL DOLL"
18in (46cm)   **$125 - 135**
20in (51cm)   **135 - 165**
***Little Miss Revlon*,**
   10½in (27cm)   **75 - 95**

Peter and Patti Playpal: 1960. Vinyl heads with rooted hair, sleep eyes; hard vinyl body, jointed at shoulders and hips; appropriate clothes; all in excellent condition. (For photograph see *7th Blue Book*, page 221.)
Mark: Peter: "IDEAL TOY CORP.
                  BE—35—38"
           Patty: "IDEAL DOLL
                  G-35"
35 - 36in (89 - 91cm):
   Peter   **$300 - 325**
   Patti   **250 - 275**
18in (46cm)
   Patti   **125 - 150**
42in (107cm)
   Daddy's Girl   **800 up**
29in (74cm)
   Miss Ideal   **325 - 375**
Bye-Bye Baby, complete set, at auction
                         625

Italian Hard Plastic

Maker: Bonomi, Ottolini, Ratti, Furga and other Italian firms
Date: Later 1940s and 1950s
Material: Heavy hard plastic, sometimes painted, or plastic coated papier-mâché
Mark: Usually a wrist tag; company name on head
Ottolini - Lion head trademark

Italian Hard Plastic:
Heavy, fine quality
material jointed at
shoulders and hips;
human hair wig, sleep
eyes, sometimes flirty,
often a character face;
original clothes; all in
excellent condition.
See color photograph
on page 217.
15 - 17in (38 - 43cm)
$110 - 135
19 - 21in (48 - 53cm)
165 - 185

17in (43cm) Ottolini girl, all
original. *H & J Foulke, Inc.*

Japanese Bisque Caucasian Dolls

Maker: Various Japanese firms; heads were imported by New York importers, such as Morimura Brothers, Yamato Importing Co. and others.

Date: 1915 - on

Material: Bisque head, composition body

Mark: Morimura Brothers

Various other marks with Japan or Nippon, such as J. W., F. Y., and others

$\mathcal{F}$ $\mathcal{Y}$

NIPPON
501

Character Baby: Perfect bisque socket head with solid dome or wig, glass eyes, open mouth with teeth, dimples; composition bent-limb baby body; dressed; all in good condition.

9 - 10in (23 - 25cm)	**$135 - 165***
14 - 15in (36 - 38cm)	**225 - 275***
20 - 22in (51 - 56cm)	**425 - 475***
Hilda look-alike, 19in (48cm)	**650 - 750***

Child Doll: Perfect bisque head, mohair wig, glass sleep eyes, open mouth; jointed composition or kid body; dressed; all in good condition.

14 - 16in (36 - 41cm)	**$250 - 275***
20 - 22in (51 - 56cm)	**325 - 375***

*Do not pay as much for doll with inferior bisque head.

14in (36cm) Nippon character baby. *H & J Foulke, Inc.*

Jullien

Maker: Jullien, Jeune of Paris, France
Date: 1875 - 1904 when joined with S.F.B.J.
Material: Bisque head, composition and wood body
Mark: "JULLIEN" with size number

JuLLiEN
1

Marked Jullien Bébé:
Bisque head, lovely wig, paperweight eyes, closed mouth, pierced ears; jointed wood and composition body; pretty old clothes; all in good condition.
16 - 17in (41 - 43cm)
$3650 - 3850
23 - 25in (58 - 64cm)
4750 - 5000
Open mouth,
23 - 24in (58 - 61cm)
2200 - 2500
30in (76cm)
3250 - 3350

30in (76cm) Jullien Bébé. See color photograph on page 217. *H & J Foulke, Inc.*

Jumeau

Maker: Maison Jumeau, Paris, France
Date: 1842 - on
Material: Bisque head, kid or composition body
Trademark: Bébé Jumeau (1886)
Bébé Prodige (1886)
Bébé Francais (1896)

Fashion Lady: Late 1860s - on. Usually marked with number only on head, blue stamp on body. Perfect bisque swivel head on shoulder plate, old wig, paperweight eyes, closed mouth, pierced ears; all-kid body or kid with bisque lower arms and legs; appropriate old clothes; all in good condition.
Mark: JUMEAU
MEDAILLE D'OR
PARIS

Standard Face:
12 - 13in (31 - 33cm)
$ 2200 - 2500
18 - 20in (46 - 51cm)
3000 - 3300
Wood body with bisque limbs, 18in (46cm)
5000**
Later face with large eyes:
10 - 12in (25 - 31cm)
1800 - 2000
14 - 15in (36 - 38cm)
2400 - 2500
Portrait face. See color photograph, page 217.
19 - 21in (48 - 53cm)
6300 - 6800
25in (64cm)
7500
30in (76cm)
9000 - 11,000
Wood body,
27in (69cm)
18,000**
Rare Portrait Face. See color photograph on page 218.
24in (61cm)
22,000**

**Not enough price samples to compute a reliable range.

18in (46cm) Jumeau lady, standard face. *H & J Foulke, Inc.*

Jumeau continued

17in (43cm) almond-eyed portrait Jumeau incised "1," on wood jointed body incised "Jumeau." *H & J Foulke, Inc.*

Period Clothes:
Bébé Clothing:

Jumeau shift	**$225 - 250**
Jumeau shoes	**300 - 400**
Jumeau dress	**550 up**

Long-Face Triste Bébé: Ca. 1870s. Usually marked with number only on head, blue stamp on body. Perfect bisque socket head with beautiful wig, blown glass eyes, closed mouth, applied pierced ears; jointed composition body with straight wrists; lovely clothes; all in good condition. See color photograph on page 219.

22 - 24in (56 - 61cm)	**$22,000 - 25,000**
28 - 30in (71 - 76cm)	**28,000 - 32,000**
34in (86cm)	**35,000 - 38,000**
Size 11 = 24in (61cm)	
14 = 29in (74cm)	

Portrait Jumeau: Ca. 1870s. Usually marked with size number only on head, blue stamp on body; skin or other good wig; unusually large paperweight eyes, closed mouth, pierced ears; jointed composition body with straight wrists; nicely dressed; all in good condition. See color photograph on page 219.

Standard Faces (See *9th Blue Book*, page 251.)

13 - 14in (33 - 36cm)	**$ 5500 - 6000**
19 - 21in (48 - 53cm)	**7500 - 8500**
24 - 25in (61 - 64cm)	**9500 - 11,000**

Almond-Eyed

12in (31cm)	**6000 - 6500**
15in (38cm)	**7500 - 8500**
17 - 19in (43 - 48cm)	**9000 - 10,000**
23in (58cm)	**15,000**

Extreme Almond-Eyed

17in (43cm)	**11,000**
22in (56cm), at auction	**23,800**

Jumeau continued

E. J. Bébé: Ca. 1880. Head incised as below, blue stamp on body. Perfect bisque socket head with good wig, paperweight eyes, closed mouth, pierced ears; jointed composition body with straight wrists, early models with separate ball joints; lovely clothes; all in good condition.

Mark:

E. 8 J.

10in (25cm)	**$ 5500**
14 - 16in (36 - 41cm)	**5700 - 6200**
19 - 21in (48 - 53cm)	**6500 - 7200**
25 - 26in (64 - 66cm)	**9000 - 10,000**
Later Tête-style face:	
18 - 19in (46 - 48cm)	**5000 - 5500**
25 - 26in (64 - 66cm)	**6800 - 7500**
33in (84cm)	**10,000**

Early mark:

7

E.J.

19 - 21in (48 - 53cm)	**11,000 - 13,000**
23in (58cm)	**15,000 - 18,000**
EJA, 26in (66cm) only	**24,000 - 26,000**

Incised Jumeau Déposé Bébé: Ca. 1880. Head incised as below, blue stamp on body. Perfect bisque socket head with good wig, paperweight eyes, closed mouth, pierced ears; jointed composition body with straight wrists; lovely clothes; all in good condition.

Mark: Incised on head:

DÉPOSÉ
JUMEAU
8

15 - 17in (38 - 43cm)	**$5500 - 6000**
20 - 21in (51 - 53cm)	**6700 - 7000**
24 - 26in (61 - 66cm)	**7500 - 8500**

20in (51cm) E.J. with standard face, eight-loose-ball-joint body. *Richard Wright Antiques.*

Tête Jumeau Bébé: 1879 - 1899, then through S.F.B.J. Red stamp on head as indicated below, blue stamp or "Bebe Jumeau" oval sticker on body. Perfect bisque head, original or good French wig, beautiful stationary eyes, closed mouth, pierced ears; jointed composition body with jointed or straight wrists; original or lovely clothes; all in good condition.

Mark:

DÉPOSÉ
TETE JUMEAU
Bᵀᴱ SGDG
6

10in (25cm) #1	**$4500 - 5200**
12 - 13in (31 - 33cm)	**3300 - 3600**
15 - 16in (38 - 41cm)	**4100 - 4300**
18 - 20in (46 - 51cm)	**4500 - 4800**
21 - 23in (53 - 58cm)	**5000 - 5500**
25 - 27in (64 - 69cm)	**5800 - 6500**
31 - 33in (79 - 84cm)	**7500 - 8500**
Lady body, 20in (51cm)	**5500 - 6000**
Open mouth:	
14 - 16in (36 - 41cm)	**2200 - 2500**
20 - 22in (51 - 56cm)	**2800 - 3000**
24 - 25in (61 - 64cm)	**3200 - 3500**
27 - 29in (69 - 74cm)	**3800 - 4000**
32 - 34in (81 - 86cm)	**4200 - 4500**

(See page 264 for photograph.)

20in (51cm) incised "DEPOSE JUMEAU." *Kay & Wayne Jensen Collection.*

Jumeau continued

Approximate sizes for E.J.s and Têtes:

1 = 10in (25cm)
2 = 11in (28cm)
3 = 12in (31cm)
4 = 13in (33cm)
5 = 14 - 15in (36 - 38cm)
6 = 16in (41cm)
7 = 17in (43cm)
8 = 19in (48cm)
9 = 20in (51cm)
10 = 21 - 22in (53 - 56cm)
11 = 24 - 25in (61 - 64cm)
12 = 26 - 27in (66 - 69cm)
13 = 29 - 30in (74 - 76cm)

See color photograph on page 221.

#230 Character Child: Ca. 1910. Perfect bisque socket head, open mouth, set or sleep eyes, good wig; jointed composition body: dressed; all in good condition. (For face see photograph on page 369. Same mold as S.F.B.J. *230*.)

16in (41cm)   **$1450**
21 - 23in (53 - 58cm)   **1800 - 2000**

#1907 Jumeau Child: Ca. 1900. Sometimes red-stamped "Tête Jumeau." Perfect bisque head, good quality wig, set or sleep eyes, open mouth, pierced ears; jointed composition body; nicely dressed; all in good condition. (For photograph see *9th Blue Book*, page 254.)

16 - 18in (41 - 46cm)   **$2300 - 2500**
24 - 25in (61 - 64cm)   **3000 - 3200**
33 - 34in (84 - 87cm)   **4000 - 4200**

Jumeau Characters: Ca. 1900. Tête Jumeau mark. Perfect bisque head with glass eyes, character expression; jointed composition body; appropriately dressed; all in good condition. See color photograph on page 220.

#203, 208 and others:
                 $75,000 - 85,000**
Two-face,   **12,000 - 15,000**
#221 Great Ladies,
  10 - 11in (25 - 28cm) all original
                    550 -   600

Princess Elizabeth Jumeau: 1938 through S.F.B.J. Perfect bisque socket head highly colored, good wig, glass flirty eyes, closed mouth; jointed composition body; dressed; all in good condition. (For photograph see *9th Blue Book*, page 254.)

Mark:

71   UNIS
        FRANCE   149
          306   Body Incised:
        JUMEAU   JUMEAU
          1938   PARIS
         PARIS   Princess

18 - 19in (46 - 48cm)   **$1200 - 1400**
32 - 33in (81 - 84cm)   **2400**

**Not enough price samples to compute a reliable range.

20in (51cm) Tête Jumeau, size 8. *H & J Foulke, Inc.*

K & K

Maker: K & K Toy Co., New York, N.Y., U.S.A.
Date: 1915 - on
Material: Bisque or composition head; cloth and composition body
Mark:

Germany
K & K
60
Thuringia

K.&K.
39
Made in Germany.

K & K Character Child: Perfect bisque shoulder head, mohair wig, sleep eyes, open mouth with teeth; cloth body with composition arms and legs or cloth or leather legs; appropriate clothes; all in good condition.
19 - 22in (48 - 56cm)   **$450 - 500**
Composition head, some marked "Fiberoid"
   20 - 24in (51 - 61cm)   **225 - 275**

24in (61cm) K & K "Fiberoid" mama doll. *H & J Foulke, Inc.*

Kamkins

Maker: Louise R. Kampes Studios, Atlantic City, N.J., U.S.A.
Date: 1919 - on
Material: Molded mask face, cloth stuffed torso and limbs
Size: About 16 - 19in (41 - 48cm)
Mark:

Red paper heart on
left side of chest:

Also sometimes stamped with
black on foot or back of head:

KAMKINS
A DOLLY MADE TO LOVE
PATENTED
FROM
L.R. KAMPES
ATLANTIC CITY
N.J.

KAMKINS
A DOLLY MADE TO LOVE
PATENTED BY L.R. KAMPES
ATLANTIC CITY, N.J.

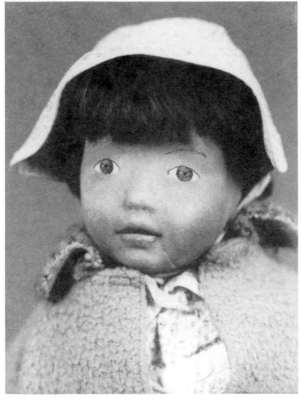

Marked Kamkins: Molded mask face with painted features, wig; cloth body and limbs; original clothing; all in excellent condition.
18 - 20in (46 - 51cm)
$1300 - 1600
Fair to good condition
750 - 850

Kamkins child, all original. See color photograph on page 221. *H & J Foulke, Inc.*

Kämmer & Reinhardt

Maker: Kämmer & Reinhardt of Waltershausen, Thüringia, Germany
Heads often by Simon & Halbig
Date: 1886 - on
Material: Bisque socket head, composition body, later papier-mâché, rubber or celluloid heads, composition bodies
Size: 5½ to 42in (14 to 107cm)
Trademarks: Magestic Doll, Mein Liebling (My Darling), Der Schelm (The Flirt), Die Kokette (The Coquette)
Mark: In 1895 began using K(star)R, sometimes with "S & H." Mold number for bisque socket head begins with a 1; for papier-mâché, 9; for celluloid, 7. Size number is height in centimeters.

K ⬡ R

SIMON & HALBIG
116/A
50

Child Doll: 1886 - 1895. Perfect bisque head, original or good wig, sleep or set eyes, open or closed mouth, pierced ears; ball-jointed composition body; dressed; all in good condition.

#192:
Closed mouth:
6 - 7in (15 - 18cm)
$ 500 - 575*
16 - 18in (41 - 46cm)
2200 - 2500
23 - 25in (58 - 64cm)
2800 - 3200
Open mouth:
7 - 8in (18 - 20cm)
450 - 500*
14 - 16in (36 - 41cm)
675 - 750
20 - 22in (51 - 56cm)
1000 - 1100
25 - 27in (64 - 69cm)
1400 - 1700

*Allow more for a fully-jointed body.

8½in (22cm) 192 child, all original. See color photograph on page 222. *H & J Foulke, Inc.*

Kämmer & Reinhardt continued

Child Doll: 1895 - 1930s. Perfect bisque head, original or good wig, sleep eyes, open mouth, pierced ears; dressed; ball-jointed composition body; all in good condition. Numbers 15-100 low on neck are centimeter sizes, not mold numbers.

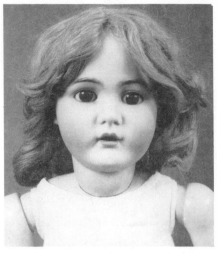

33in (84cm) K & R child. *H & J Foulke, Inc.*

#191, 290, 403 or size number only:

12 - 14in (31 - 36cm)	**$ 550 -**	**650* +**
16 - 17in (41 - 43cm)	**650 -**	**700* +**
19 - 21in (48 - 53cm)	**750 -**	**800***
23 - 25in (58 - 64cm)	**900 -**	**1000***
29 - 31in (74 - 79cm)	**1200 -**	**1400***
35 - 36in (89 - 91cm)	**1900 -**	**2100 +**
39 - 42in (99 - 107cm)	**3200 -**	**3500**

*Allow $50 additional for flirty eyes.
+ Allow 50% additional for fantastic totally original clothes, wig and shoes in pristine condition.

Tiny Child Doll: Perfect bisque head, mohair wig, sleep eyes, open mouth; five-piece composition body with molded and painted shoes and socks.

6 - 7in (15 - 18cm)	**$ 375 - 425**
8 - 9in (20 - 23cm)	**450 - 500**
Walker,	
6 - 7in (15 - 18cm)	**425 - 475**
Closed mouth,	
6in (15cm)	**450 - 500**
Jointed body,	
8 - 10in (20 - 25cm)	**525 - 550**

8in (20cm) in original trunk with wardrobe, at auction **2337**

6in (15cm) K & R tiny child with closed mouth, all original. *H & J Foulke, Inc.*

Kämmer & Reinhardt continued

Character Babies or Toddlers: 1909 - on. Perfect bisque head, original or good wig, sleep eyes, open mouth; composition bent-limb or jointed toddler body; nicely dressed; may have voice box or spring tongue; all in good condition. (See *Simon & Halbig Dolls, The Artful Aspect* for photographs of mold numbers not pictured here.)

#100 Baby, painted eyes:

12in (31cm)	**$ 550 - 575**
14 - 15in (36 - 38cm)	**625 - 675**
18 - 20in (46 - 51cm)	**900 - 1100**

Glass eyes

14in (36cm)	**1800**
19in (48cm) brown bisque	**1600**

#126, 22, 26 Baby Body:

10 - 12in (25 - 31cm)	**425 - 450***
15 - 18in (38 - 46cm)	**575 - 675***
22 - 24in (56 - 61cm)	**900 - 1000***
30 - 33in (76 - 84cm)	**1800 - 2200**

#126, 22 Toddler Body:

6 - 7in (15 - 18cm)	**600 - 650***
9 - 10in (23 - 25cm)	**650 - 750***
15 - 17in (38 - 43cm)	**800 - 900***
23 - 25in (58 - 64cm)	**1300 - 1600***
28 - 30in (71 - 76cm)	**1900 - 2300**

#126 All-Bisque Toddler,

7in (18cm), at auction	**1400**

*Allow $50 extra for flirty eyes.

15in (38cm) **Baby** 100, all original and boxed. *Roberts Collection.*

Kämmer & Reinhardt continued

#126 Child Body:
  24in (61cm)   **$ 850**
  38in (96cm), at auction
                   3800
#121 Baby Body:
  12in (31cm)   **525**
  15 - 17in (38 - 43cm)
                   675 - 775
  24 - 25in (61 - 64cm)
                   1200 - 1500
#122, 128 Baby Body:
  11 - 12in (28 - 31cm)
                   550 - 575
  15in (38cm)   **750 - 800**
  18 - 20in (46 - 51cm)
                   1200 - 1300
  30in (76cm)   **2600 - 2800**
#121, 122, 128 Toddler Body:
  12 - 14in (31 - 36cm)
                   1000 - 1200
  23 - 25in (58 - 64cm)
                   1800 - 1900
#118A Baby Body:
  18 - 20in (46 - 51cm)
                   2200**
#119 Baby Body:
  24in (61cm)   **5000****
#135 Baby Body:
  20in (51cm)   **2200****

16in (41cm) 128 character baby, all original. See color photograph on page 222. *H & J Foulke, Inc.*

Composition Head **#926**, five-piece toddler body:
  17in (43cm)   **325 - 375**
  23in (58cm)   **550 - 600**

*Allow $50 additional for flirty eyes.
**Not enough price samples to compute a reliable range.

11½in (29cm) 101 character **Marie.** See color photograph on page 223. *H & J Foulke, Inc.*

Kämmer & Reinhardt continued

Character Children: 1909 - on. Perfect bisque socket head, good wig, painted or glass eyes, closed mouth; composition ball-jointed body; nicely dressed; all in good condition. (See *Simon & Halbig, The Artful Aspect* for photographs of mold numbers not pictured here.)

#101 (Peter or Marie):
9in (12cm) five-piece body

$	1800 -	2000
11 - 12in (28 - 31cm)	2500	
15 - 16in (38 - 41cm)	3200 -	3700
19 - 20in (48 - 51cm)	5200 -	6200

Glass eyes:
14in (36cm)	7500**
20in (51cm)	12,000**

#102: See color photograph on page 224.
| 12in (31cm) | 32,000** |

#103, 104:
| 20 - 22in (51 - 56cm) | 60,000 up** |

#105:
| 21½in (55cm), at auction | |
| | 170,000 |

#106:
| 22in (56cm) | 60,000 up** |

#107 (Carl):
12in (30cm)	12,000**
22in (55cm), at auction	
	40,700**

#109 (Elise):
| 16in (41cm) | 8500 |
| 19 - 21in (48 - 53cm) | 12,000 - 13,000 |

#112, 112x:
14in (36cm)	8500
23in (58cm)	25,000
Glass eyes, 12in (31cm)	
	6500**

#114 (Hans or Gretchen):
8in (20cm)	1800	
12in (31cm)	3000 -	3300
15 - 16in (38 - 41cm)	4200 -	4500
19 - 20in (48 - 51cm)	5500 -	6500
24in (61cm)	8500**	

Glass eyes, See color photograph on page 223.
| 23in (58cm) | 15,000** |

#115, 115A: See color photograph on page 224.
Toddler, 15 - 16in (38 - 41cm)		
	4450 -	4950
20 - 21in (51 - 53cm)	5000 -	5500

#116, 116A, open/closed mouth:
Baby, 13 - 15in (33 - 38cm)		
	2200 -	2500
Toddler, 16 - 17in (36 - 41cm)		
	2900 -	3200

**Not enough price samples to compute a reliable range.

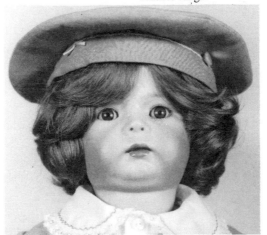

21in (53cm) 115A character child. *Kay & Wayne Jensen Collection.*

Kämmer & Reinhardt continued

#116A, open mouth:
Baby, 15 - 17in (38 - 43cm)
$ 1900 - 2200
Toddler, 18 - 21in (46 - 53cm)
2500 - 2700

#117, 117A, closed mouth:
12 - 14in (31 - 36cm)	**3500 - 4000**
18 - 20in (46 - 51cm)	**5000 - 5500**
23 - 25in (59 - 64cm)	**6800 - 7800**
28 - 31in (71 - 79cm)	**8500 - 10,500**

#117n, sleep eyes:
14 - 16in (36 - 41cm)	**950 - 1050**
30in (76cm)	**2100**

#117n, flirty eyes:
14 - 16in (36 - 41cm)	**1100 - 1300**
20 - 22in (51 - 56cm)	**1700 - 1900**
28 - 30in (71 - 76cm)	**2500 - 2700**

#117, open mouth:
27in (69cm) **4700****

#123, 124:
17in (43cm) **18,000 - 20,000****

#127:
Baby, 10in (25cm)	**750**
14 - 15in (36 - 38cm)	**1100 - 1200**
23 - 25in (59 - 64cm)	**1900 - 2200**
Toddler or child, 15in (38cm)	**1100 - 1300**
Toddler, 27in (69cm)	**2300 - 2500**

#135 Child, 15in (38cm)
1100 - 1200**

Infant: 1924 - on. Perfect bisque head, molded and painted hair, glass eyes; cloth body, composition hands; nicely dressed; all in good condition.
14in (36cm) **$3400****

**Not enough price samples to compute a reliable range.

17in (43cm) 117n character child with naughty eyes. *H & J Foulke, Inc.*

Kestner

Maker: J. D. Kestner, Jr., doll factory, Waltershausen, Thüringia, Germany.
Kestner & Co., porcelain factory, Ohrdruf.
Date: 1816 - on
Material: Bisque heads, kid or composition bodies, bodies on tiny dolls are jointed at the knee, but not the elbow, all bisque
Size: Up to 42in (107cm), size Q 20.

Child doll, early socket head: Ca. 1880. Perfect bisque head, plaster dome, good wig, paperweight or sleep eyes; composition ball-jointed body, some with straight wrists and elbows; well dressed; all in good condition. Marked with size number only.

#169, 128, and unmarked pouty face, closed mouth:

6½in (17cm) five-piece body	**$ 900 - 1000**
7½in - 8in (19 - 20cm)	**1100 - 1300**
9 - 10in (23 -2 5cm)	**2100 - 2300**
12in (31cm)	**2400**
14 - 16in (36 - 41cm)	**2500 - 2600**
19 - 21in (48 - 53cm)	**2800 - 3000**
24 - 25in (61 - 64cm)	**3200 - 3500**

28in (71cm) closed mouth child "16." *Esther Schwartz Collection.*

#XI, 103 and very pouty face, closed mouth:

10 - 12in (25 - 31cm)	**$ 2800 - 3000 +**
14 - 16in (36 - 41cm)	**3200 - 3500 +**
19 - 21in (48 - 53cm)	**3800 - 4000 +**
24 - 25in (61 - 64cm)	**4200 - 4300 +**
27in (69cm)	**4500 +**
32in (81cm)	**5000 +**

A.T.-type: Closed mouth,

Any size	**18,000 up +**
Open mouth, 19in (48cm)	**2400 + ** **

Bru-type, molded teeth, jointed ankles: (For photograph see *8th Blue Book,* page 258.)

20in (51cm)	**5000**
Kid body, 15 - 17in (38 - 43cm)	**2300 - 2400**

Open mouth, square cut teeth:

10 - 11in (25 - 28cm)	**675 - 725**
14 - 16in (36 - 41cm)	**800 - 850**
28in (71cm)	**1750** **

7in (18cm) closed mouth child on composition body with jointed knees and stiff elbows. *H & J Foulke, Inc.*

+ Allow less for a kid body.
**Not enough price samples to compute a reliable range.

Child doll, early shoulder head: Ca. 1880s. Perfect bisque head, plaster dome, good wig, set or sleep eyes; sometimes head is slightly turned; kid body with bisque lower arms; marked with size letters or numbers. (No mold numbers.)

Closed mouth:
14 - 16in (36 - 41cm)	$ 750 - 850*
20 - 22in (51 - 56cm)	950 - 1150*
26in (66cm)	1500*

Open/closed mouth:
16 - 18in (41 - 46cm)	725 - 825

Open mouth:
14 - 16in (36 - 41cm)	500 - 550
20 - 22in (51 - 56cm)	650 - 725
25in (64cm)	800 - 850

*Allow $100 - 200 extra for a very pouty face or swivel neck.

Child doll, bisque shoulder head, open mouth: Ca. 1892. Kid body, some with rivet joints. Plaster dome, good wig, sleep eyes, open mouth; dressed, all in good condition. (See *Kestner, King of Dollmakers* for photographs of mold numbers not pictured here.)

HEAD MARK: 154. 8 dep.
D made in Germany

BODY MARK:

#145, 154, 147, 148, 166, 195:
8in (20cm)	$250 - 275
12 - 13in (31 - 33cm)	325 - 375*
16 - 18in (41 - 46cm)	425 - 475*
20 - 22in (51 - 56cm)	550 - 600
26 - 28in (66 - 71cm)	800 - 900*

*Allow additional for a rivet jointed body.

13in (33cm) closed-mouth turned shoulder head child "E." *Edna Black Collection.*

Child doll, open mouth: Bisque socket head on ball-jointed body; plaster dome, good wig, sleep eyes, open mouth; dressed; all in good condition. (See *Kestner, King of Dollmakers* for photographs of mold numbers not pictured here.)

HEAD MARK:

made in
D *Germany.* 8.
162..

BODY MARK:

Excelsior
DRP N. 70686
Germany

Mold numbers 142, 144, 146, 164, 167, 168, 171, 196, 214:

10in (25cm)	**$ 700 -**	**800**
12 - 14in (31 - 36cm)		
	600 -	**700**
18 - 21in (46 - 53cm)		
	750 -	**850**
24 - 26in (61 - 66cm)		
	900 -	**1000**
30in (76cm)	**1200 -**	**1400**
36in (91cm)	**1800 -**	**2200**
42in (107cm)	**3500 -**	**3800**

18in (46cm) 171 *Daisy* with original blonde mohair wig. This is the only size 171 mold which is truly *Daisy. H & J Foulke, Inc.*

16in (41cm) 168 child. *H & J Foulke, Inc.*

#155:
8in (20cm) five-piece body
500 - 525
8in (20cm) fully-jointed body
725 - 775

#171: *Daisy,* blonde mohair wig,
18in (46cm) only **825 - 875**

See color photograph on page 224.

#129, 149, 152, 156, 160, 174:

10in (25cm)	**700 -**	**800**
15in (38cm)	**775 -**	**825**
19in (48cm)	**850 -**	**900**
24in (61cm)	**1000 -**	**1100**

Kestner continued

18in (46cm) 180 character child. *Richard Wright Collection.*

15½in (39cm) 189 character child. *Jane Alton Collection.*

Character Child: 1909 - on. Perfect bisque head character face, plaster pate, wig, painted or glass eyes, closed, open or open/closed mouth; good jointed composition body; dressed; all in good condition. (See *Kestner, King of Dollmakers* for photographs of mold numbers not pictured here.)

#143 (Pre 1897):

7in (18cm)	**$ 625 - 675**
9 - 9½in (23 - 24cm)	
	725 - 775
12 - 14in (31 - 36cm)	
	850 - 950
18 - 20in (46 - 51cm)	
	1200 - 1400

#178-190,

Painted Eyes:

12in (31cm)	**1800 - 2000**
15in (38cm)	**2800 - 3200**
18in (46cm)	**3800 - 4300**

Glass Eyes:

12in (31cm)	**2800 - 3200**
15in (38cm)	**3800 - 4300**
18in (46cm)	**4800 - 5300**

Boxed set,

15in (38cm)	**7500 up****

#206,

19in (48cm), at auction	
	12,700**
12in (31cm)	**4000****

#208,

Painted Eyes,

23 - 24in (58 - 61cm)	
	12,000**

#239 Toddler,

15 - 17in (38 - 43cm)	
	3500 - 3700**

#241:

22in (56cm)	**5500 - 6000****
30in (76cm)	**9000****

#249:

20 - 22in (51 - 56cm)	
	1400 - 1800

**Not enough price samples to compute a reliable range.

Kestner continued

#260:
8in (20cm) Toddler
          600 - 650
12 - 14in (31 - 36cm)
          725 - 800
18 - 20in (46 - 51cm)
          800 - 1000
41in (103cm), at auction
          4800

#220 Toddler:
16in (41cm)   **6000 - 6500****
24in (61cm)   **7500 - 8000****

**Not enough price samples to compute a reliable range.

See color photographs on pages 225 and 226.

Character Baby: 1910 - on. Perfect bisque head, molded and/or painted hair or good wig, sleep or set eyes, open or open/closed mouth; bent-limb body; well dressed; nice condition. (See *Kestner, King of Dollmakers* for photographs of mold numbers not pictured here.)
Mark:

made in
F. Germany. 10
     211
J.D.K.

#211, 226, 262, 263, JDK solid dome:
11 - 13in (28 - 33cm)
        $ 500 - 600
16 - 18in (41 - 46cm)
        675 - 775
20 - 22in (51 - 56cm)
        900 - 1000
25in (64cm)   **1400 - 1600**
Rare model, solid dome, o/c mouth, molded forehead curl:
16in (41cm), at auction
        8750

8in (20cm) 260 character toddler. *H & J Foulke, Inc.*

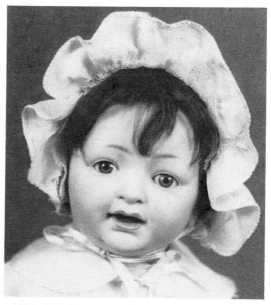

14½in (37cm) 211 character baby. *H & J Foulke, Inc.*

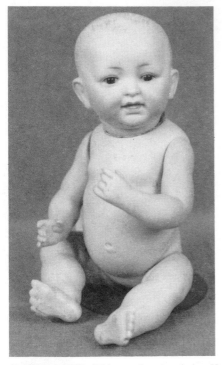

9in (23cm) JDK all-bisque character baby. *H & J Foulke, Inc.*

#234, 235, 238 shoulder heads:

13 - 14in (33 - 36cm)	$ 650 - 750

Hilda, #237, 245, Solid Dome Baby:

11 - 13in (28 - 33cm)	2750 - 2950
16 - 17in (41 - 43cm)	3800 - 4400
20 - 22in (51 - 56cm)	5000 - 5300
24in (61cm)	6000 - 7000

Toddler:

16in (41cm)	5000 - 5500
24in (61cm)	6500 - 7000
27in (69cm)	7500 - 8000

#247:

12 - 13in (31 - 33cm)	1150 - 1250
14 - 16in (36 - 41cm)	1750 - 1950

#257:

9 - 10in (23 - 25cm)	475 - 525
17 - 20in (43 - 51cm)	850 - 950
Toddler 17in (43cm)	900
22in (56cm)	1350

Solid dome, fat-cheeked: See color photograph on page .

11 - 12in (28 - 31cm)	850 - 950
18 - 20in (46 - 51cm)	1300 - 1500

All-bisque:

Painted eyes, stiff neck

4½ - 5¼in (12 - 14cm)	175 - 225
7in (18cm)	275

Glass eyes, swivel neck

9 - 10in (23 - 25cm)	850 - 950

See color photograph on pages 226 and 227.

All-Bisque Child: Perfect all-bisque child jointed at shoulders and hips; mohair wig, sleeping eyes, open mouth with upper teeth; blue or pink painted stockings, black strap shoes. Naked or with appropriate clothes. Very good quality.

#130, 150, 160, 184 and 208:

4 - 5in (10 - 13cm)	$ 225 - 275*
6in (15cm)	300 - 350*
7in (18cm)	375 - 425*
8in (20cm)	500 - 550*
9in (23cm)	700 - 750
11in (28cm)	1000
12in (31cm)	1200

*Allow 30 - 40% extra for a swivel neck.
Allow $25 - 50 extra for yellow boots.

Gibson Girl: Ca. 1910. Perfect bisque shoulder head with good wig, glass eyes, closed mouth, up-lifted chin; kid body with bisque lower arms (cloth body with bisque lower limbs on small dolls); beautifully dressed; all in good condition; sometimes marked "Gibson Girl" on body.

#172:

10in (25cm)	$1100 - 1200
15in (38cm)	1900 - 2200
20 - 21in (51 - 53cm)	3600 - 4100

Lady Doll: Perfect bisque socket head, plaster dome, wig with lady hairdo, sleep eyes, open mouth with upper teeth; jointed composition body with molded breasts, nipped-in waist, slender arms and legs; appropriate lady clothes; all in good condition.

Mark:
#162:

made in
D germany. 8.
162.

16 - 18in (41 - 46cm)   **$1300 - 1500**

16in (41cm) 162 lady. *Dolly Valk Collection.*

7½in (19cm) all-bisque girl. *H & J Foulke, Inc.*

Kewpie

Maker: Various
Date: 1913 - on
Size: 2in (5cm) up
Designer: Rose O'Neill, U.S.A. U.S. Agent: George Borgfeldt & Co., New York, N.Y., U.S.A.
Mark: Red and gold paper heart or shield on chest and round label on back

All-Bisque: Made by J. D. Kestner and other German firms. Often have imperfections in making. Sometimes signed on foot "O'Neil ". Standing, legs together, arms jointed, blue wings, painted features, eyes to side.

2½in (5 - 6cm)	$ 85 - 95
4 - 5in (10 - 13cm)	100 - 125
6in (15cm)	150 - 165
7in (18cm)	200 - 250
8 - 9in (20 - 23cm)	350 - 400
10in (25cm)	650
12 - 13in (31 - 33cm)	1200 - 1500
Jointed hips, 4in (10cm)	425 - 475
Shoulder head, 3in (8cm)	425

Black Hottentot, 5in (13cm)	450
Button hole, 2in (5cm)	150 - 165
Pincushion, 2 - 3in (5 - 8cm)	225 - 250
Painted shoes and socks, 5in (13cm)	425 - 450

13in (33cm) standing *Kewpie*. *Richard Wright Antiques.*

9in (23cm) Hottentot *Kewpie*. *Richard Wright Antiques.*

Kewpie continued

Action Kewpies (sometimes
stamped: ©):
  Thinker, 4in (10cm)
                $ 250 - 275
  6in (15cm)   **425**
  Kewpie with cat,
  3½in (9cm)   **400 - 450**
  Kewpie holding pen,
  3in (8cm)   **375 - 425**
  Reclining or sitting
  3 - 4in (8 - 10cm)
                375 - 425
  Gardener, Sweeper, Farmer,
  4in (10cm)   **450 - 475**
  Kewpie 2in (5cm) with rabbit,
    rose, turkey, pumpkin,
    shamrock, etc.
                275 - 325
  Doodledog:
  3in (9cm)   **1300 - 1500**
  1½in (4cm)   **650 - 750**
  Huggers,
  3½in (9cm)   **175 - 200**
  Guitar player,
  3½in (9cm)   **300 - 350**
  Traveler,
  3½in (9cm)   **300 - 325**
  Governor,
  3½in (9cm)   **350 - 375**
  Kewpie and *Doodledog* on
  bench,
  3½in (9cm) **2800**
  Kewpie sitting on inkwell,
  3½in (9cm)   **650**
  Kewpie Traveler with
    Doodledog,
  3½in (9cm) **1000**
  Kewpie Soldiers
  5 - 6in (13 - 15cm)
             650 - 750
  Kewpie at tea table
             1800
  Kewpie driving chariot
             3000
  Kewpie Mountain with 17
  figures   **17,000**

3in (8cm) action ***Kewpie*** with pen. *H & J Foulke, Inc.*

3in (8cm) action ***Kewpie*** with cat. *H & J Foulke, Inc.*

Kewpie continued

Bisque head on chubby jointed composition toddler body, glass eyes: Made by J. D. Kestner. (For photograph see *9th Blue Book*, page 276.)
Mark:
"Ges. gesch.
O'Neill J.D.K."
10in (25cm) five-piece body **$3500 - 4000**
12 - 14in (31 - 36cm)   **4500 - 5500**

Bisque head on cloth body
Mold *#1377* made by Alt, Beck & Gottschalck
12in (31cm) Glass eyes   **$2600 - 2800***
Painted eyes   **1600 - 2000***

**Not enough price samples to compute a reliable range.

12in (31cm) bisque head *Kewpie* with flange neck, cloth body, all original with label. *Carole Stoessel Zvonar Collection.*

11in (28cm) and 12in (31cm) composition *Kewpies.* See color photograph on page 228. *H & J Foulke, Inc.*

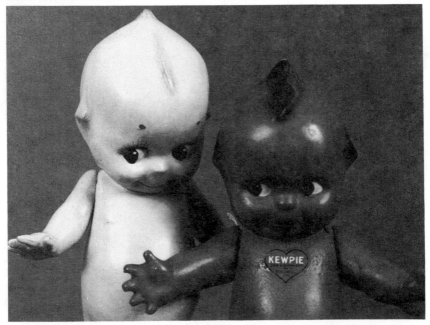

Kewpie continued

Celluloid: Made by Karl Standfuss, Deuben near Dresden,
Saxony, Germany. Straight
standing, arms jointed, blue
wings; very good condition.

2½in (6cm)	$ 35
5in (13cm)	75
8in (20cm)	125 - 150
Black, 2½in (6cm)	65 - 75

All-Composition: Made by
Cameo Doll Co., Rex Doll
Co., and Mutual Doll Co.,
all of New York, N.Y.,
U.S.A. All-composition,
jointed at shoulders, some at
hips; good condition.

8in (20cm)	$135 - 150
11 - 13in (28 - 33cm)	185 - 225
Black, 12 - 13in (31 - 33cm)	275 - 325
Talcum container, 7in (18cm)	160 - 185
13in (33cm) mint and all original with wrist tag	300
Composition head, cloth body: 12in (31cm)	150 - 165

12in (31cm) composition head *Kewpie* with flange neck, cloth body. *H & J Foulke, Inc.*

All-Cloth: Made by Richard G. Kreuger, Inc., New York, N.Y., U.S.A. Patent number 1785800. Mask face with fat-shaped cloth body, including tiny wings and peak on head. Cloth label sewn in side seam. (For photograph see *9th Blue Book*, page 278.)

10 - 12in (25 - 31cm)	$160 - 185
18in (46cm) with tagged dress and bonnet	350

Hard Plastic: Ca. 1950s.

Standing Kewpie, one piece with jointed arms, 8in (20cm)	$ 85 - 95
Fully jointed with sleep eyes; all original clothes, 13in (33cm)	325 - 375**

**Not enough price samples to compute a reliable range.

Vinyl: Ca. 1960s.

Kewpie Baby with hinged body 16in (41cm)	$165 - 185

Kley & Hahn

Maker: Kley & Hahn, doll factory, Ohrdruf, Thüringia, Germany. Heads by Hertel, Schwab & Co. (100 series), Bähr & Pröschild (500 series) and J. D. Kestner (250, 680 and Walkure).
Date: 1902 - on
Material: Bisque head, composition body
Trademarks: Walküre, Meine Einzige, Special, Dollar Princess
Mark:

> ⟩K&H⟨
> Germany   *K H*
>   *Walküre*

Child Doll: Perfect bisque head, wig, glass eyes, open mouth; jointed composition child body; fully dressed; all in good condition.

#250 or *Walküre:*

7½in (19cm)	$ 325 - 350
16 - 18in (41 - 46cm)	450 - 500
22 - 24in (56 - 61cm)	550 - 650
30 - 31in (76 - 79cm)	1000 - 1100
35 - 36in (89 - 91cm)	1500 - 1600

Special   Dollar Princess:

23 - 25in (58 - 64cm)	525 - 575

18½in (47cm) Walküre flapper. See color photograph on page 228. *H & J Foulke, Inc.*

Character Child: Perfect bisque head, wig, glass or painted eyes, closed mouth; jointed composition child or toddler body; fully dressed; all in good condition. See color photograph on page 229.

#520, 526, 536, 546, 549:
15 - 16in (36 - 38cm)
$3000 - 3200*
19 - 21in (48 - 53cm)
4000 - 4500*
#154, 166, closed mouth,
16 - 17in (41 - 43cm) jointed body
2200 - 2300
15in (38cm) baby
1250 - 1350
#154, 166, open mouth:
17 - 18in (43 - 46cm) jointed body
1200 - 1300
25in (64cm)
1850
20in (51cm) baby
1100 - 1200

*Allow $500 extra for glass-eyed models.

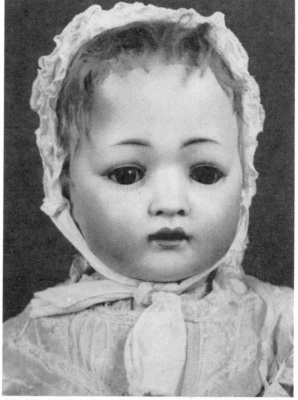

23in (58cm) 169 character baby with open mouth. *H & J Foulke, Inc.*

#169, closed mouth:
13in (33cm) toddler **$2000 - 2100**
19 - 21in (48 - 53cm) toddler
3400 - 3800
20in (51cm) baby **3100****
#169, open mouth:
23in (58cm) baby **1500 - 1600****

Character Baby: Perfect bisque head with molded hair or good wig, sleep or painted eyes, open or closed mouth; bent-limb baby body; nicely dressed; all in good condition.

#138, 158, 160, 167, 176, 458, 525, 531, 680 and others:
11 - 13in (28 - 33cm) **$ 450 - 500***
18 - 20in (46 - 51cm) **650 - 750***
24in (61cm) **1000***
28in (71cm) **1400 - 1500**
26 - 27in (66 - 69cm) toddler
1950 - 2250

*Allow $100 - 150 extra for a toddler or jointed body.
*Allow extra for mold *#568.*

Two-Face Baby, 13in (33cm)
2000 - 2200**

**Not enough price samples to compute a reliable range.

Kling

Maker: Kling & Co., porcelain factory, Ohrdruf, Thüringia, Germany
Date: 1836 - on (1870 - on for dolls)
Material: Bisque or china shoulder head, cloth body, bisque lower limbs; bisque socket head, composition body, all-bisque
Mark:

China shoulder head: Ca. 1880. Black- or blonde-haired china head with bangs, sometimes with a pink tint; cloth body with china limbs or kid body; dressed; all in good condition.
#188, 189, 200 and others:

13 - 15in (33 - 38cm)	**$250 - 300**
18 - 20in (46 - 51cm)	**350 - 400**
24 - 25in (61 - 64cm)	**475 - 525**

Bisque shoulder head: Ca. 1880. Molded hair or mohair wig, painted eyes, closed mouth; cloth body with bisque lower limbs; dressed; in all good condition. Mold numbers such as *140* and *186*.

12 - 14in (31 - 36cm)	**$ 275 - 350***
18 - 20in (46 - 51cm)	**475 - 525***
23 - 25in (58 - 64cm)	**575 - 625***

Glass eyes and molded hair: See color photograph on page 229.

11in (28cm)	**425 - 475**

Boy styles

11in (28cm)	**550 - 600**
16 - 18in (41 - 46cm)	**800 - 850**

Girl styles, such as *#186*

15in (38cm)	**625 - 650**

Lady styles with decorated bodice, such as *#135, 170*
1500 up

*Allow extra for unusual or elaborate hairdo.

11in (28cm) unmarked boy, probably Kling. See color photograph on page 229. *H & J Foulke, Inc.*

Kling continued

Bisque head: Ca. 1890. Mohair or human hair wig, glass sleep eyes, open mouth; kid or cloth body with bisque lower arms or jointed composition body; dressed; all in good condition.

#373 or *377* shoulder head:
13 - 15in (33 - 38cm)	$375 - 425**
19 - 22in (48 - 56cm)	475 - 525**

#370 or *372* socket head:
14 - 16in (36 - 41cm)	425 - 475**
22 - 24in (56 - 61cm)	575 - 675**
#123 shoulder head, cloth body, 9 - 10in (23 - 25cm)	225

All-bisque Child: Jointed shoulders and hips; wig, glass eyes, closed mouth; molded footwear (usually two-strap boots with heels, blue shirred hose with brown strap shoes or black hose with green shoes).

Mark: on back or in leg joint

#36 or *69:*
4in (10cm)
> **$200 - 225**

5½in (14cm)
> **300**

#99 baby with bare feet
4in (10cm)
> **225****

**Not enough price samples to compute a reliable range.

10in (25cm) Kling shoulder head girl, original costume. *H & J Foulke, Inc.*

Knickerbocker

Maker: Knickerbocker Doll & Toy Co., New York, N.Y., U.S.A.
Date: 1937
Material: All-composition
Mark: (Embossed on dwarfs)

"WALT DISNEY
KNICKERBOCKER TOY CO."

Composition Seven Dwarfs: All-composition jointed at shoulders, stiff hips, molded shoes, individual character faces, painted features; mohair wigs or beards; jointed shoulders, molded and painted shoes; original velvet costumes and caps with identifying names: "Sneezy," "Dopey," "Grumpy," "Doc," "Happy," "Sleepy" and "Bashful." Very good condition.

9in (23cm)	**$175 - 200**
Mint-in-box, at auction	**275 each**

Composition Snow White: All-composition jointed at neck, shoulders and hips; black mohair wig with hair ribbon, brown lashed sleep eyes, open mouth; original clothing; all in very good condition.

20in (51cm)	**$ 425 - 475**
With molded black hair and blue ribbon, 13in (33cm)	**275 - 300**

Cloth Seven Dwarfs;

14in (36cm) excellent	**250 each**

Cloth Donald Duck in band uniform

16in (41cm), at auction	**1760**

Complete set of composition Knickerbocker *Seven Dwarfs* with composition Alexander *Snow White. H & J Foulke, Inc.*

König & Wernicke

Maker: König & Wernicke, doll factory, Waltershausen, Thüringia, Germany. Heads
by Hertel, Schwab & Co. and Bähr & Pröschild
Date: 1912 - on
Material: Bisque heads, composition bodies or all-composition
Trademarks: Meine Stolz, My Playmate
Mark:

$$K \& W$$
$$1070$$

Body Mark: K&W

K & W Character: Bisque
head with good wig,
sleep eyes, open
mouth; composition
baby or toddler body;
appropriate clothes;
all in good condition.

#98, 99, 100, 1070:
10 - 11in (25 - 28cm)
$425*
15 - 17in (38 - 43cm)
550 - 650*
21in (53cm)
800 - 825*
24 - 26in (61 - 66cm)
950 - 1100*

*Allow $50 extra for flirty
eyes.
*Allow $100 - 150 extra for
toddler body.

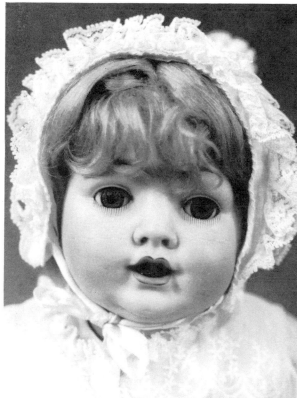

21in (53cm) 99 character
body. *H & J Foulke, Inc.*

Richard G. Krueger, Inc.

Maker: Richard G. Krueger, Inc., New York, N.Y., U.S.A.
Date: 1917 - on
Material: All-cloth, mask face
Mark: Cloth tag or label

All-Cloth Doll: Ca. 1930. Mask face with painted features, rosy cheeks, yarn hair or curly mohair wig on cloth cap; oil cloth body with hinged shoulders and hips; original clothes; in excellent condition.

Label:

Krueger, N.Y.
Reg. U.S. Pat Off.
Made in U.S.A.

16in (41cm)   **$100 - 115**
20in (51cm)   **135 - 165**

Pinocchio: Ca. 1940. Mask character face with black yarn hair, attached ears, round nose, large oval eyes, curved mouth; cloth torso, wood jointed arms and legs; original clothes, all in good condition. See color photograph on page 230.

15in (38cm)   **$250 - 275**

Kewpie: See page 283.

16in (41cm) Krueger girl, all original. *H & J Foulke, Inc.*

Käthe Kruse

Maker: Käthe Kruse, Bad Kösen, Germany
Date: 1910 - on
Material: Molded muslin head (hand-painted), jointed cloth body, later of hard plastic material.
Mark: On cloth: "Käthe Kruse" on sole of foot, sometimes also "Germany" and a number
Hard plastic on back: Turtle mark and "Käthe Kruse"

Käthe Kruse
81971

Made in Germany

Cloth Käthe Kruse: Molded muslin head, hand-painted; jointed at shoulders and hips: See color photograph on page 230.

Doll I (1910), painted hair, wide hips, 16 - 17in (41 - 43cm):
Mint, all original	**$3200 - 3700**
Good condition, suitably dressed	**2200 - 2400**
With jointed knees (1911)	**4200 up****

Doll IH (after 1929), wigged, 16 - 17in (41 - 43cm): (For photograph see *Doll Classics*, page 174.)
Mint, all original	**2200 - 2300**
Good condition, suitably dressed	**1300 - 1600**

**Not enough price samples to compute a reliable range.

17in (43cm) Doll I, 1928. *Private Collection.*

Käthe Kruse continued

Doll II "Schlenkerchen" Smiling Baby (1922 - on).
   13in (33cm)   **$2000**
Doll V & VI Babies *"Traumerchen"* (closed eyes) and *"Du Mein"* (open eyes), some heads of Magnesit, 1925 - on. (For photograph see *9th Blue Book*, page 287.)
   19½ - 23½in (50 - 60cm)
                 3300 - 3700
Doll VII (1927 - on) & *Doll X* (1935 - on):
   14in (36cm)   **1200**
   with *Du Mein* head
     (1928 - 1930)   **1800 - 2000**

Doll II, **Schlenkerchen**, all original. *H & J Foulke, Inc.*

Doll VIII (1929 - on) "German Child" 20½in (52cm) wigged, turning head: (For photograph see *9th Blue Book*, page 287.)
   Mint, all original   **2000 - 2200**
   Good condition, suitably
     dressed   **1200 - 1400**
Doll IX "Little German Child" (1929 - on) wigged, turning head:
   14in (36cm)   **1200**

U.S. Zone Germany: Dolls IX or *X* with cloth or Magnesit heads, very thick paint finish: all original, very good condition. (1945 - 1951)
   14in (36cm)   **$650 - 750**

14in (36cm) **Punktchen**, U.S. Zone Germany, hard plastic head, all original. *H & J Foulke, Inc.*

Käthe Kruse continued

Hard Plastic Head: Ca. 1950s - on. Hard plastic head with lovely wig, painted eyes; pink muslin body; original clothes; all in excellent condition.
U.S. Zone Germany
14in (36cm)   **$500 - 550**
Ca. 1952 - 1975:
14in (36cm)   **425 - 475**
18 - 20in (46 - 51cm)
    575
1975 - on:
14in (36cm)   **350 - 400**
18 - 20in (46 - 51cm)
    450 - 500
20in (51cm) *Du Mein*
    550 - 650

Hanna Kruse Dolls:
10in (25cm) *Däumlinchen* with foam rubber stuffing
(1957 - on)   **175 - 225**
13in (32cm) *Rumpumpel Baby* or *Toddler* (1959 - on)
    350 - 400
10in (25cm) *Doggi*
(1964 - 1967)   **150 - 175****

16in (41cm) *Toni*, all-celluloid or hard plastic, all original. *H & J Foulke, Inc.*

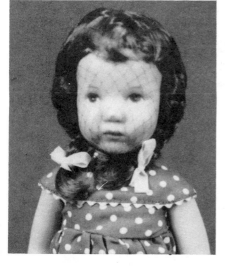

All-Hard Plastic (Celluloid) Käthe Kruse: Wig or molded hair and sleep or painted eyes; jointed neck, shoulders and hips; original clothes; all in excellent condition. Turtle mark. (1955 - 1961).
16in (41cm)   **$375 - 425**

**Not enough price samples to compute a reliable range.

10in (25cm) Hanna Kruse vinyl *Doggi* 1964 - 1967, all original with protective hair net. *H & J Foulke, Inc.*

Gebrüder Kuhnlenz

Maker: Gebrüder Kuhnlenz, porcelain factory, Kronach, Bavaria
Date: 1884 - on
Material: Bisque head, composition or kid body
Size: Various
Mark: " G.K. "

G^{br} 165 K
9
Germany

44-31

and/or numbers, such as:
41-28   56-18   44-15

The first two digits are mold number; second two are size number.

G. K. doll with closed mouth: Ca. 1885 - on. Perfect bisque socket head, inset glass eyes, closed mouth, round cheeks; jointed composition body; dressed; all in good condition.

#32, 31:

10in (25cm)	**$ 675 - 725***
16 - 18in (41 - 46cm)	**1200 - 1500**
22 - 24in (56 - 61cm)	**1800 - 2100**

#34, Bru-type, French JCB

16 - 18in (41 - 46cm)	**2800 - 3000****

#38 shoulder head, kid body:

14 - 16in (36 - 41cm)	**650 - 750**
22 - 23in (56 - 58cm)	**1000 - 1100**

*Allow more for a very pretty doll.
**Not enough price samples to compute a reliable range.

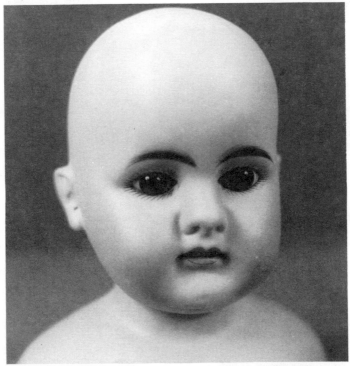

23in (58cm) 61-29.5 shoulder head. *H & J Foulke, Inc.*

Gebrüder Kuhnlenz continued

G. K. child doll: Ca. 1890 - on. Perfect bisque socket head with distinctive face, almost a character look, long cheeks, sleep or paper-weight-type eyes, open mouth, molded teeth; jointed composition body, sometimes French; dressed; all in good condition.

#41, 44, 56:
18 - 20in (46 - 51cm)
$ 800 - 900
24 - 26in (61 - 66cm)
1100 - 1300

#165:
18in (46cm)   425 - 450
22 - 24in (56 - 61cm)
500 - 550
34in (86cm)   1200 - 1300

#61 shoulder head:
19 - 22in (48 - 56cm)
650 - 750

G. K. Tiny Dolls: Perfect bisque socket head, wig, stationary glass eyes, open mouth with molded teeth; five-piece composition body with molded shoes and socks; all in good condition. Usually mold *#44.*

7 - 8in (18 - 20cm)
crude body   **$175 - 200**
better body   **225 - 250**

All-Bisque child: 1895 - on. Socket head with glass eyes, open mouth, nice mohair wig; pegged shoulders and hips, white painted stockings, light blue boots, black straps. Usually mold *#44.* (For photograph see *9th Blue Book,* page 291.)

7½in (19cm)   **$ 800***
8½in (22cm)   **1100***

**Not enough price samples to compute a reliable range.

7in (18cm) 44-17 child, all original. *H & J Foulke, Inc.*

Lanternier

Maker: A Lanternier & Cie. porcelain factory of Limoges, France
Date: 1915 - 1924
Material: Bisque head, papier-mâché body
Mark:

FABRICATION
FRANÇAISE

AL ε Cie
LIMOGES
A   1

Marked Lanternier Child: Ca. 1915. Perfect bisque head, good or original wig, large stationary eyes, open mouth, pierced ears; papier-mâché jointed body; pretty clothes; all in good condition.

Cherie, Favorite or *La Georgienne*
16 - 18in (41 - 46cm) $ 675 - 775*
22 - 24in (56 - 61cm)   900 - 1000*
28in (71cm)   1400 - 1600*

*Allow extra for lovely face and bisque.

26in (66cm) *Favorite. Carole Stoessel Zvonar Collection.*

Lanternier Lady: Ca. 1915. Perfect bisque head with adult look, good wig, stationary glass eyes, open/closed mouth with molded teeth; composition lady body; dressed; all in good condition. (For photograph see *7th Blue Book*, page 271.)
Lorraine
16 - 18in (41 - 46cm)
$850 - 1250*

*Depending upon costume and quality.

Characters, "Toto" and others: Ca. 1915. Perfect bisque smiling character face, good wig, glass eyes, open/closed mouth with molded teeth, pierced ears; jointed French composition body; dressed; all in good condition. See color photograph on page 231.
17 - 19in (43 - 48cm)
$900 - 1000

23in (58cm) Lenci 109 Skier, all original. For further information see page 313. *H & J Foulke, Inc.*

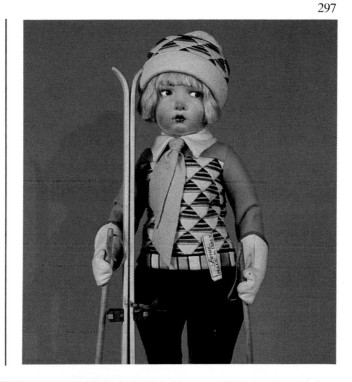

17in (43cm) Lenci Dutch Children #300, all original. For further information see page 313. *H & J Foulke, Inc.*

ABOVE: 8in (20cm) Lenci girl, all original. For further information see page 313. *H & J Foulke, Inc.*

ABOVE LEFT: 16in (41cm) Armand Marseille *Florodora*, all original. For further information see page 319. *H & J Foulke, Inc.*

LEFT: 26in (66cm) Armand Marseille 1894 child. For further information see page 319. *H & J Foulke, Inc.*

24in (61cm) Armand Marseille *Queen Louise.* For further information see page 320. *H & J Foulke, Inc.*

19in (48cm) Armand Marseille 372 *Kiddiejoy* character child. For further information see page 320. *Margaret Benike.*

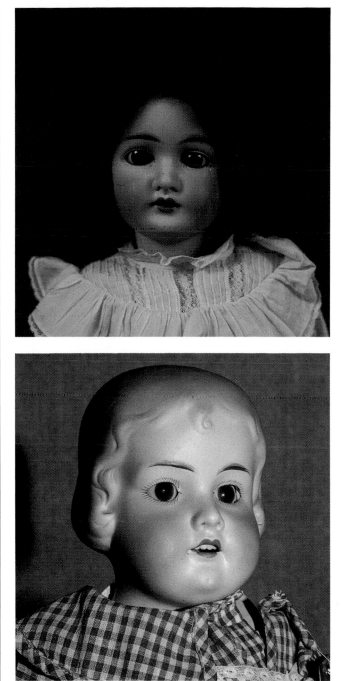

15in (38cm) Armand Marseille 971a character baby. For further information see page 321. *H & J Foulke, Inc.*

INSET: 10in (25cm) painted bisque *Just Me*, A.M. 310, all original. For further information see page 322. *H & J Foulke, Inc.*

16in (41cm) Armand Marseille character child. For further information see page 320. *Richard Wright Antiques.*

31in (79cm) Bébé Mascotte "M." For further information see page 324. *Kay & Wayne Jensen Collection.*

ABOVE: Group of German metal head dolls, all with Minerva trademark. For further information see page 329. *H & J Foulke, Inc.*

17in (43cm) Revalo child by Ohlhaver. For further information see page 333. *H & J Foulke, Inc.*

28in (71cm) B 10 M, Bébé Mothereau. For further information see page 331. *Private Collection*.

13in (33cm) Simon & Halbig 1329 Oriental lady. For further information see page 336. *H & J Foulke, Inc.*

14in (36cm) Simon & Halbig 1129 Oriental lady. For further information see page 337. *C. C. Collection.*

RIGHT: 16in (41cm) J. D. Kestner 243 Oriental baby. For further information see page 336. *Private Collection.*

INSET: 11in (28cm) *Ming Ming* composition baby. For further information see page 337. *H & J Foulke, Inc.*

LEFT: 8in (20cm) German Parian-type lady with molded hat. For further information see page 342. *Private Collection.*

BELOW LEFT: 9½in (24cm) German molded hair papier-mâché lady. For further information see page 340. *H & J Foulke, Inc.*

BELOW: 7in (18cm) German molded hair papier-mâché lady, all original. For further information see page 340. *H & J Foulke, Inc.*

22in (56cm) German Parian-type lady with molded hat and necklace. For further information see page 342. *Becky & Jay Lowe.*

Pair of German Parian-type 5¼in (13cm) dolls with squeeker torsos, parian limbs. For further information see page 342. *Private Collection.*

20in (51cm) German Parian-type lady with molded blue scarf and applied flowers. For further information see page 342. *Private Collection.*

RIGHT: 22in (56cm) *Philadelphia Baby.* For further information see page 344. *Elizabeth McIntyre.*

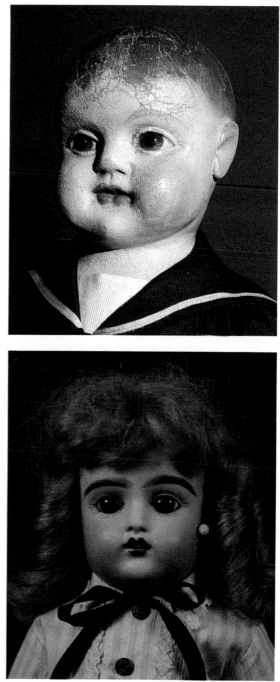

BELOW RIGHT: 18in (46cm) Pintel & Godchaux child. For further information see page 362. *H & J Foulke, Inc.*

BELOW: 2½in (6cm) unusual German pincushion with full figure. For further information see page 361. *H & J Foulke, Inc.*

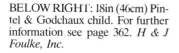

23in (58cm) papier-mâché with glass eyes, so-called Pre-Greiner. For further information see page 362. *Elizabeth McIntyre.*

BELOW: *Raggedy Ann & Andy* dolls by Georgene Novelties. For further information see page 364. *H & J Foulke, Inc.*

20½in (52cm) French fashion lady by Rohmer with cup and saucer neck on a kid body, large bisque arms and wood upper arms. For further information see page 368. *Kay & Wayne Jensen Collection.*

16in (41cm) Rollinson toddler. For further information see page 368. *H & J Foulke, Inc.*

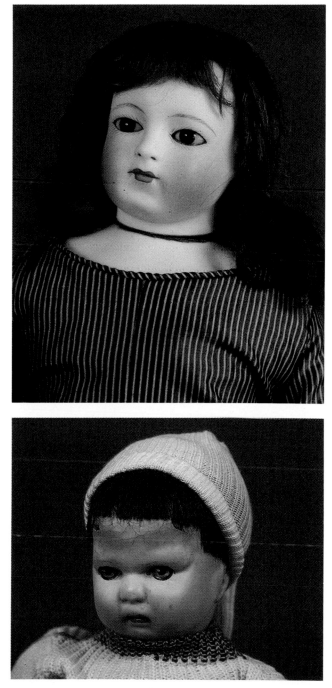

16in (41cm) S.F.B.J. 301 child. For further information see page 369. *H & J Foulke, Inc.*

22in (56cm) S.F.B.J. 230 character child. For further information see page 370. *H & J Foulke, Inc.*

Lenci

Maker: Enrico & Elenadi Scavini, Turin, Italy
Date: 1920 - on
Material: Pressed felt head with painted features, jointed felt bodies
Size: 5 - 45in (13 - 114cm)
Mark: "LENCI" on cloth and various paper tags; sometimes stamped on bottom of foot

> *Lenci* di E. SCAVINI
> TURIN (Italy)
> **Made in ITALY**
> **N. 159G**
> Pat. Sept. 8, 1921 . Pat N. 142433
> Bre SGDG. X 87395. Brevetta 501.178

Lenci: All-felt (sometimes cloth torso) with swivel head, jointed shoulders and hips; painted features, eyes usually side-glancing; original clothes, often of felt or organdy; in excellent condition.

Lenci girl with pouty face, all original. *Esther Schwartz Collection.*

Miniatures and Mascottes:
8 - 9in (20 - 23cm) Regionals
$ 275 - 325
Children or unusual costumes
375 - 425

Children #300, 109, 149, 159, 111:
13in (33cm)   **850 up**
16 - 18in (41 - 46cm)   **1200 up**
20 - 22in (51 - 56cm)   **1800 up**

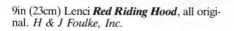

9in (23cm) Lenci *Red Riding Hood*, all original. *H & J Foulke, Inc.*

Lenci continued

"Lucia" face, 14in (36cm)
          $ 700 - 800
Ladies and long-limbed novelty dolls,
    24 - 28in (61 - 71cm)   **1600 up**
Glass eyes, 20in (51cm)   **2800 - 3000**
Celluloid-type, 6in (15cm)   **45 - 55**
"Surprised Eye" (round painted eyes)
    fancy clothes, 20in (51cm) **2200 - 2600**
#1500, scowling face,
    17 - 19in (43 - 48cm)   **1600 - 1800**
Baby, 14 - 18in (36 - 46cm) **1800 - 2200**
Teenager, long legs, 17in (43cm)
          1000 up
Orientals, 18in (46cm)   **3500 - 4000**
Sports Series, 17in (43cm)   **2000 up**
Golfer, 23in (58cm)   **3000**

8in (20cm) Lenci *Pan*, all original and boxed. *Esther Schwartz Collection.*

Benedetta, 18in (46cm)   **2000 up**
Catalogs   **1200 up**
Felt Banner   **950**
Facist Boy, 13in (33cm)   **1200**
Brown South Seas, 16in (41cm)
          1800 - 2000
Mask face, disc eyes, 23in (58cm)
          600 - 700

Collector's Note: Mint examples of rare dolls will bring higher prices. To bring the prices quoted, Lenci dolls must be clean and have good color. Faded and dirty dolls bring only about one-third to one-half these prices.

See color photographs on pages 232, 297 and 298.

Lenci-Type

Maker: Various Italian, French and English firms such as Marguerin, Messina-Vat and others
Date: 1920 - 1940
Material: Felt and cloth
Size: 6in (15cm) up
Mark: Various paper labels, if any

Felt or Cloth Doll: Mohair wig, painted features; stuffed cloth body; original clothes or costume; excellent condition.
Child dolls, 16 - 18in (41 - 46cm) up to **$750** depending upon quality
Foreign costume,
 7½—8½in (19 - 22cm)
                              $35 - 45
 12in (31cm)   **80 - 90**

Alma, Turin, Italy:
 16in (41cm)   **$600 - 700**
(For photograph see *9th Blue Book* page 53.)

Dean's Rag Book Company, England:
 14 - 16in (36 - 41cm)
                     $500 - 600
 Printed Cloth, 10in (25cm)
                     85 - 95
 16 - 18in (41 - 46cm)
                     160 - 185

Farnell's Alpha Toys, London, England: 14in (36cm)
                     $400 - 450
 Coronation Doll of King George VI, 1937.
 16in (41cm)   **375 - 425**
(For photograph see *7th Blue Book*, page 157.)

Eugenie Poir, Gre-Poir French Doll Makers, Paris and New York:
(For photograph see *8th Blue Book*, page 336.)
 17 - 21in (43 - 46cm)
 mint condition **$600 - 700**
 good condition **400 - 500**

14in (36cm) Lenci-type boy, all original. *H & J Foulke, Inc.*

Raynal, Paris, France: (For photograph see *9th Blue Book*, page 339.)
 17 - 18in (43 - 46cm)   **$600 - 700**

Liberty of London

Maker: Liberty & Co. of London, England
Date: 1906 - on
Material: All-fabric
Size: 5½ - 10in (14 - 25cm)
Mark: Cloth label or paper tag "Liberty of London"

British Coronation Dolls: 1939. All-cloth with painted and needle-sculpted faces; original clothes; excellent condition. The Royal Family and Coronation Participants.
5½ - 9½in (14 - 24cm)　　**$85 - 95**

Other English Historical and Ceremonial Characters: All-cloth with painted and needle-sculpted faces; original clothes; excellent condition.
9 - 10in (23 - 25cm)　　**$95 - 100**

10in (25cm) ***Jane Seymour***, all original. *Private Collection.*

Limbach

Maker: Limbach Porzellanfabrik, Limbach, Thüringia, Germany (porcelain factory)
Date: Factory started in 1772
Material: Bisque head, composition body; all bisque
Mark:

MADE IN GERMANY

All-Bisque Child: Ca. 1900. Child all of
bisque (sometimes pink bisque) with
wire jointed shoulders and hips;
molded hair (often with a blue molded
bow) or bald head with mohair wig,
painted eyes, closed mouth, white
stockings, blue garters, brown slippers
or strap shoes.
Mark: P.23

GERMANY

6in (15cm) P.607 girl. *H & J Foulke, Inc.*

4 - 5in (10 - 13cm)	$ 75 - 85
Glass eyes,	
5in (13cm)	150 - 175
8in (20cm)	265 - 285
Character, jointed arms only,	
4 - 5in (10 - 13cm)	75 - 85

All-Bisque Baby: Ca. 1910. Baby with
painted hair and facial features; wire
jointed shoulders and hips, bent arms
and legs; bare feet. (For photograph
see *8th Blue Book*, page 299.)
Mark: Clover and number with P.

4 - 5in (10 - 13cm)	$ 75 - 95*
8½in (22cm)	250 - 275
11 - 12in (28 - 31cm)	500 - 550

*Allow more for fine quality.

4½in (12cm) all-bisque Limbach girl. *H & J Foulke, Inc.*

Limbach continued

Limbach Child Doll: 1893 - 1899; 1919 - on. Perfect bisque head, good wig, glass eyes, open mouth with teeth; composition jointed body; dressed; all in good condition. (For photograph see *9th Blue Book*, page 297.)

Wally, Rita, or *Norma* after 1919.

17 - 19in (43 - 48cm)	**$ 500 - 550***
23 - 24in (58 - 61cm)	**650 - 700***

Incised with clover (1893 - 1899):
14 - 17in (36 - 43cm) open mouth
900 - 1200**
27in (69cm) closed mouth, at auction
2100

*Allow 30 - 40% more for fine quality.
**Not enough price samples to compute a reliable range.

Albert Marque

Maker: Unknown, possibly artist produced
Date: 1916
Material: Bisque head, jointed composition body with bisque lower arms
Size: 22in (56cm) one size only
Designer: Albert Marque, French sculptor
Mark: a Marque

A. Marque Doll: Bisque head with wistful character face, mohair wig, paperweight eyes, closed mouth; jointed composition body of special design with bisque lower arms and hands, fixed wrists; appropriate clothes (some original ones from Paris designer Margaines-Lacroix).

22in (56cm)	**$43,000**

22in (56cm) A. Marque child. *Courtesy of Richard W. Withington, Inc.*

Armand Marseille
(A.M.)

Maker: Armand Marseille of Köppelsdorf, Thüringia, Germany (porcelain and doll factory)
Date: 1885 - on
Material: Bisque socket and shoulder head, composition, cloth or kid body
Marks:

A.M.-DEP
N°. 3600.
3.
Made in Germany.

A0½M
Florodora
Armand Marseille
Made in Germany

1894
A M 5/0 DEP
Germany

18" Made in Germany
A. (Baby 2½ Betty) M.
D.R.G.M.

Child Doll: 1890 - on. Perfect bisque head, nice wig, set or sleep eyes, open mouth; composition ball-jointed body or jointed kid body with bisque lower arms; pretty clothes; all in good condition.

#390, (larger sizes marked only "A. [size] M."), *Florodora* (composition body): See color photograph on page 298.

9 - 10in (23 - 25cm)	$ 235 - 265
12 - 14in (31 - 36cm)	235 - 285
16 - 18in (41 - 46cm)	325 - 350
20in (51cm)	400
23 - 24in (58 - 61cm)	475 - 500
28 - 29in (71 - 74cm)	650 - 700
30 - 32in (76 - 81cm)	800 - 950
35 - 36in (89 - 91cm)	1200 - 1500
40 - 42in (102 - 107cm)	2000 - 2300

Five-piece composition body,

6 - 7in (15 - 18cm)	165 - 185
9 - 10in (23 - 25cm)	235 - 265

Closed mouth,

5 - 5½in (12 - 14cm)	250

#1894 (composition body): See color photograph on page 298.

10in (25cm)	350 - 375
14 - 16in (36 - 41cm)	400 - 450
21 - 23in (53 - 58cm)	675 - 750

#370, 3200, 1894, Florodora, Anchor 2015, Rosebud shoulder heads:

11 - 12in (28 - 31cm)	160 - 185
14 - 16in (36 - 41cm)	215 - 265
22 - 24in (56 - 61cm)	375 - 400

19in (48cm) *Baby Betty* shoulder head. *H & J Foulke, Inc.*

Armand Marseille (A.M.) continued

13½in (34cm) 230 *Fany* with flocked hair. *H & J Foulke, Inc.*

Name shoulder head child: 1898 to World War I. Perfect bisque shoulder head marked with doll's name, jointed kid or cloth body, bisque lower arms; good wig, glass eyes, open mouth; well dressed; all in good condition. Names include *Rosebud, Lilly, Alma, Mabel, Darling, Beauty* and *Princess.*

Marks:

12 - 14in (31 - 36cm)	**$185 - 215**
20 - 22in (51 - 56cm)	**325 - 375**
25in (64cm)	**425 - 475**

Character Children: 1910 - on. Perfect bisque head, molded hair or wig, glass or painted eyes, open or closed mouth; composition body; dressed; all in good condition.

#230 Fany (molded hair):

15 - 16in (38 - 41cm)	**$4500 - 5500**
19in (48cm)	**7500 - 8500**

#231 Fany (wigged):

15 - 16in (38 - 41cm)	**4000 - 4500**

#400 (child body):

20in (51cm)	**3400****

#500, 600:

10in (25cm)	**400 - 425**
15in (38cm)	**600 - 650**

#550 (glass eyes):

18 - 20in (46 - 51cm)	**3450 - 3750****

A.M. (intaglio eyes): See color photograph on page 301.

16 - 17in (41 - 43cm)	**4500 up**

#620 shoulder head,

16in (41cm)	**1250****

#372 Kiddiejoy shoulder head, "Mama" body. See color photograph on page 299.

19in (48cm)	**850 - 900**

#640 shoulder head (same face as *550* socket)

20in (51cm)	**1500 - 1650****
#340 13in (33cm)	**2600****
#700 14in (36cm) child	**3000 - 3500****

**Not enough price samples to compute a reliable range.

Queen Louise, Rosebud (composition body): See color photograph on page 299.

12in (31cm)	**325 - 350**
23 - 25in (58 - 64cm)	**500 - 550**
28 - 29in (71 - 74cm)	**650 - 750**

Baby Betty:

14 - 16in (36 - 41cm) composition body

	475 - 525

19 - 21in (48 - 53cm) kid body

	400 - 450

#1894, 1892, 1896, 1897 shoulder heads (excellent quality):

19 - 22in (48 - 56cm)	**425 - 475**

Armand Marseille (A.M.) continued

Character Babies and Toddlers: 1910 - on.
Perfect bisque head, good wig, sleep
eyes, open mouth some with teeth;
composition bent-limb body; suitably
dressed; all in nice condition.

Marks:

Armand Marseille
Germany
990
A 9/0 M

Germany
326

A 11 M

*Mold #990, 985, 971, 996, 1330, 326 (solid
dome), 980, 991, 327, 329 and others:* See
color photograph on page 300.

10 - 11in (25 - 28cm)	$ 325 -	350
13 - 15in (33 - 38cm)	375 -	425
18 - 20in (46 - 51cm)	500 -	550
22in (56cm)	650	
24 - 25in (61 - 64cm)	750 -	850

#233:

13 - 15in (33 - 38cm)	475 -	525
20in (51cm)	675 -	725

#251/248 (open/closed mouth):

12 - 15in (31 - 38cm)	1400 -	1600

#251/248 (open mouth):

12 - 15in (31 - 38cm)	750 -	850

21in (53cm) 920 shoulder head character
mama doll body. *Courtesy of Judy Newell.*

#410 (2 rows teeth):

15 - 16in (38 - 41cm)	900 - 1000**	

#518:

16 - 18in (41 - 46cm)	550 -	600
25in (64cm)	950	

#560A:

12in (31cm)	525	
15 - 17in (38 - 43cm)	600 -	650

#580, 590 (open/closed mouth):

14 - 15in (31 - 38cm)	1100 -	1300
18 - 20in (46 - 51cm)	1600 -	1800

#590 (open mouth):

12in (31cm)	600	
16 - 18in (41 - 46cm)	850 -	950

#700, closed mouth, glass eyes, wig

10½in (27cm)	1500**

#920 shoulder head, "mama" body

21in (53cm)	900**

Melitta, 19in (48cm) toddler

	650 - 750

11in (28cm) 700 character baby. *Lesley Hurford Collection. Photograph by Norman Hurford.*

**Not enough price samples to compute a
reliable range.

Armand Marseille (A.M.) continued

Infant: 1924 - on. Solid-dome bisque head with molded and/or painted hair, sleep eyes; composition body or hard-stuffed jointed cloth body or soft-stuffed cloth body; dressed; all in good condition.

Mark:

A. M.
Germany.
351. 14K

#351, 341 Kiddiejoy and Our Pet:

Head circumference:

8 - 9in (20 - 23cm)	$225 - 250
10in (25cm)	275 - 300
12 - 13in (31 - 33cm)	350 - 425
15in (38cm)	600 - 650
6in (15cm) compo body	225 - 250
24in (61cm) wigged toddler	
	950

#352:

17 - 20in (43 - 51cm) long **575 - 625**

#347:

Head circumference:
12 - 13in (31 - 33cm) **475 - 525**

Baby Phyllis:

Head circumference:

9in (23cm) black	500
12 - 13in (31 - 33cm)	425 - 475

Baby Gloria

15 - 16in (38 - 41cm) **700 - 800**

Marked "Just Me" Character: Ca. 1925. Perfect bisque socket head, curly wig, glass eyes to side, closed mouth; composition body; dressed; all in good condition. (See color photograph on page 300.) Some of these dolls, particularly the painted bisque ones, were used by

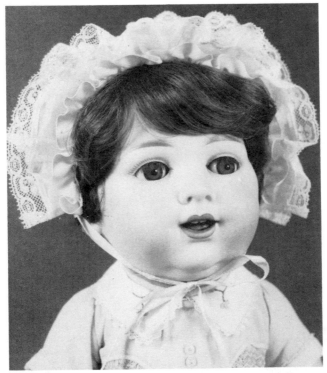

19in (48cm) 980 character baby. *Jensen's Antique Dolls.*

Armand Marseille (A.M.) continued

Vogue Doll Company in the 1930s and will be found with original Vogue labeled clothes.

Mark:

7½in (19cm)	$ 900 - 950
9in (23cm)	1100 - 1200
11in (28cm)	1400 - 1500
13in (33cm)	1800 - 2200

Painted bisque:

  7 - 8in (18 - 20cm) all original

	750 - 850

Lady: 1910 - 1930. Bisque head with mature face, mohair wig, sleep eyes, open or closed mouth; composition lady body with molded bust, long slender arms and legs; appropriate clothes; all in good condition. (For photograph see *9th Blue Book*, page 304.)

#401 and *400* (slim body):

  12 - 13in (31 - 33cm):

Open mouth	**$1000 - 1100**
Closed mouth	**1800 - 2000**

#300 (M.H.):

9in (23cm)	**850 - 950****

**Not enough price samples to compute a reliable range.

8in (20cm) 341 infant. *H & J Foulke, Inc.*

Mascotte

Maker: May Freres Cie, 1890 - 1897; Jules Nicholas Steiner, 1898—on. Paris, France
Date: 1890 - 1902
Material: Bisque head, composition and wood jointed body
Mark:
> "BÉBÉ MASCOTTE
> PARIS"

Bébé Mascotte: Bisque socket head, good wig, closed mouth, paperweight eyes, pierced ears; jointed composition and wood body; appropriate clothes; all in good condition.

17 - 19in (43 - 48cm)	**$4500 - 4800**
24 - 26in (61 - 66cm)	**5750 - 6250**

See color photograph on page 301.

Mattel — Barbie®

Maker: Mattel, Inc., Hawthorne, Calif., U.S.A.
Date: 1959 to present
Material: Hard plastic and vinyl
Size: 11½ - 12in (29 - 31cm)
Mark: 1959 - 1962: Barbie TM/Pats. Pend./© MCMLVIII/by/Mattel, Inc.
   1963 - 1968: Midge TM/© 1962/Barbie®/© 1958/by/Mattel, Inc.
   1964 - 1966: © 1958/Mattel, Inc./U.S. Patented/U.S. Pat. Pend.
   1966 - 1969: © 1966/Mattel, Inc./U.S. Patented/U.S. Pat. Pend./Made in Japan

---

First Barbie®: 1959. Vinyl; very light complexion, white irises, pointed eyebrows, ponytail, black and white striped bathing suit, holes in feet to fit stand, gold hoop earrings; mint condition.

11½in (29cm) boxed	**$3000 - 3500***
Doll only, no box or accessories	
Mint	**2000**
Very good	**1600**
Stand	**200**
Shoes	**20**
Hoop earrings	**45**

Second Barbie: 1959 - 1960. Vinyl; very light complexion, same as above, but no holes in feet, some wore pearl earrings; mint condition. Made 3 months only.

11½in (29cm) boxed	**$2500 - 3200***
Doll only, no box or accessories, very good	**1800**

*Brunette harder to find than blonde.

Third Barbie: 1960. Vinyl; very light complexion, same as above, but with blue irises and curved eyebrows; no holes in feet; mint condition.

11½in (29cm) boxed	**$600 - 700**
Doll only	**400**

Mattel — Barbie continued

Fourth Barbie: 1960. Vinyl; same as #3; but with solid body of flesh-toned vinyl; mint condition.

11½in (29cm) boxed   **$375**

Doll only   **225**

Fifth Barbie: 1961. Vinyl; same as #4; ponytail hairdo of firm Saran; mint condition.

11½in (29cm) boxed   **$275 up**

Doll only   **125 up**

#1 ***Barbie*** in "Gay Parisienne" outfit and "pink dressed doll box," very rare. *Anne Helm Collection.*

Dolls:
Black Francie:
1967, mint-in-package
$ 500 - 700
Doll only **400**
Ken #1, mint-in-box
125
Ken, bendable knees,
mint-in-box
200
Side-Part Barbie, 1965,
bendable knees, mint-
in-box **1500 - 2000**
Hair Happenin's Barbie,
1971, mint-in-box
400
**Hair Happenin's
Francie**, 1970,
mint-in-box
150
Truly Scrumptious,
1969, mint-in-box
350
Doll only **175**
Supersize Barbie,
bride, mint-in-box
125
swimsuit, mint-in-box
95

1964 Side-part Titian bubble **Barbie** with **Barbie**® box. *Anne Helm Collection.*

Twiggy, 1967, mint-in-box	150
Midge, bendable knee, mint-in-box	275
Bubble Cut Barbie, 1961 - on, mint-in-box	150 - 200
Doll only	75
Gift Sets	350 - 600 up

Black **Francie** and rare version of white **Francie** without bangs. *David Simpson Collection.*

Mattel — Barbie continued

Allen, bendable knee, mint-in-box
$ 200

Swirl Ponytail Barbie,
1964 mint-in-box **300 - 400**
Doll only **175**

Side-Part Bubble Cut Barbie,
1964 mint in box **800**
Doll only **400**

Francie without Bangs,
1964 mint in box **900**
Doll only **400**

Outfits:*
Roman Holiday **1000 up**
Gay Parisienne **1000 - 1500**
Easter Parade **1000 up**
Shimmering Magic **500 up**
Here Comes the Bride **500 up**
American Stewardess **1000 up**
Barbie Baby Sits **100**
Dogs & Duds **100**
1600 Series Outfits and Jacqueline
  Kennedy-style clothes
  250 up
Enchanted Evening **150**
*All mint-in-package.

Color *Magic Barbie,*
1966 mint-in-box **$800**
Doll only **300**

1965 Bendable leg,
side-part *Barbie.*
*David Simpson
Collection.*

American Girl Barbie, 1965 & 1966 cen-
ter part, bendable legs, mint-in-box
400 - 500
Doll only **200**
Early (1967 - 1970):
  Tutti, mint-in-box **95**
  Chris, mint-in-box **95**
  Todd, mint-in-box **95**
Black *Julia,* mint-in-box:
  one-piece suit **75**
  two-piece suit **95**
Fashion Queen Barbie **225**

Barbie® is a registered trademark of Mattel, Inc.

Metal Dolls

Maker: Various U.S. companies, such as Atlas Doll & Toy Co. and Giebeler-Falk, N.Y. U.S.A.
Date: Ca. 1917 - on
Material: All-metal, or metal head with cloth body (may have composition lower limbs)

Metal Child: All metal, body fully jointed at neck, shoulders, elbows, wrists, hips, knees and ankles; sleep eyes, open/closed mouth with painted teeth; dressed; all in good condition. (Body may be jointed composition with metal hands and feet.)
16 - 20in (41 - 51cm)
$325 - 425

Metal Baby: All-metal (with bent limbs) jointed at shoulders and hips with metal springs; molded and painted hair and facial features, painted or sleep eyes, closed or open mouth; appropriate clothes; all in good condition.
11 - 13in (28 - 33cm)
$ 85 - 95
18 - 20in (46 - 51cm) metal head, cloth body with composition lower limbs
165 - 185

12in (31cm) American all-metal baby. *H & J Foulke, Inc.*

Metal Heads

Maker: Buschow & Beck, Germany (Minerva); Karl Standfuss, Germany (Juno); Alfred Heller, Germany (Diana)
Date: Ca. 1888 - on
Material: Metal shoulder head, kid or cloth body
Mark:

Mark may often be found on front of shoulder plate.

Marked Metal Head Child: Metal shoulder head on cloth or kid body, bisque or composition hands; dressed; very good condition, not repainted. See color photographs on pages 302 and 360.

Molded hair, painted eyes, 12 - 14in (31 - 36cm)	**$110 - 135**
Molded hair, glass eyes, 12 - 14in (31 - 36cm)	**150 - 175**
20 - 22in (51 - 56cm)	**225 - 250**
Wig and glass eyes, 14 - 16in (36 - 41cm)	**225 - 250**
20 - 22in (51 - 56cm)	**275 - 325**

16½in (42cm) German metal head, cloth body. *H & J Foulke, Inc.*

Missionary Ragbabies

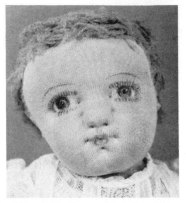

Maker: Julia Beecher, Elmira, N.Y., U.S.A.
Date: 1893 - 1910
Material: All-cloth
Size: 16 - 23in (41 - 58cm)
Designer: Julia Jones Beecher
Mark: None

Beecher Baby: Handmade stuffed stock-inette doll with looped wool hair, painted eyes and mouth, needle-sculpted face; appropriately dressed; all in good condition.

20 - 23in (51 - 59cm)   **$6000 up****
Fair condition, 18in (46cm)   **2500****
Mint condition, at auction,   **10,000**
**Not enough price samples to compute a reliable range.

22in (56cm) Missionary Ragbaby. *Nancy A. Smith Collection.*

Molly-'es

Maker: International Doll Co., Philadelphia, Pa., U.S.A. Made clothing only. Purchased undressed dolls from various manufacturers.
Date: 1920s - on
Material: All-cloth or all-composition, later hard plastic and vinyl
Clothes Designer: Mollye Goldman
Mark: Usually a cardboard tag, dolls unmarked except for vinyl

Molly-'es Composition Dolls: All-composition, jointed at neck, shoulders and hips; molded hair or wigs, sleep eyes; beautiful original outfits; all in good condition.

Babies, 12 - 15in (31 - 38cm)
         $150 - 175
Toddlers, 14 - 16in (36 - 41cm)
         200 - 225
Ladies, 18 - 21in (46 - 53cm) **450 - 500**
Sabu, (For photograph see page 3.)
   15in (38cm)   **450 - 500**
Sultan, 19in (48cm)   **600**

Internationals: All-cloth with mask faces, mohair wigs (sometimes yarn), painted features; variety of costumes, all original clothes; in excellent condition with wrist tag.
13in (33cm)   **$75 - 95**

13in (33cm) Dutch Girl, all original. *H & J Foulke, Inc.*

Mothereau

Maker: Alexandre Mothereau, Paris, France
Date: 1880 - 1895
Material: Bisque head, wood and composition body
Trademark: Bébé Mothereau
Mark: B.M.

Bébé Mothereau: Perfect bisque head, beautiful blown glass eyes, closed mouth, good wig, pierced ears; wood and composition jointed body; beautifully dressed; all in good condition.
26 - 28in (66 - 71cm)
$30,000**

**Not enough price samples to compute a reliable range.

28in (71cm) B 10 M. See color photograph on page 303. *Private Collection.*

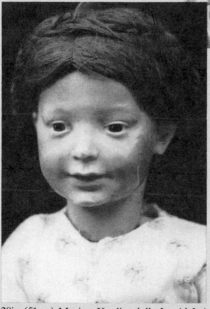

20in (51cm) Marion Kaulitz doll. *Ingrid Leibers Collection. Photograph by Norman Hurford.*

Munich Art Dolls

Maker: Marion Kaulitz
Date: 1908 - 1912
Material: All-composition, fully-jointed bodies
Size: Various
Designer: Paul Vogelsanger, and others
Mark: Sometimes signed on doll's neck

Munich Art Dolls: Molded composition character heads with hand-painted features; fully-jointed composition bodies; dressed; all in good condition.
13in (33cm)   **$2200 - 2500**
18 - 19in (46 - 48cm)   **3000 - 4000****

**Not enough price samples to compute a reliable range.

12in (31cm) fair condition   **$1100 - 1300**

Nancy Ann

Maker: Nancy Ann Storybook
Dolls Co., South San
Francisco, Calif.,
U.S.A.
Date: Mid 1930s - on
Material: Painted bisque, later
plastic
Mark: Painted Bisque:
1939 - 1948
"Story
Book
Doll
U.S.A."
Mark: Hard Plastic:
1948 - on
"STORYBOOK
DOLLS
U.S.A.
TRADEMARK
REG."
Also a gold foil wrist tag
identifying particular model

Nancy Ann Storybook *Topsy*, painted bisque, all original.
Nancy A. Smith Collection.

Marked Storybook Doll: Painted bisque,
mohair wig, painted eyes; one-piece
body, head and legs, jointed arms;
original clothes; excellent condition
with wrist tag and box.

Painted Bisque	
5 - 7½in (13 - 19cm)	**$ 50 up**
Jointed legs,	**70 up**
Swivel neck,	**80 up**
Hard Plastic	
5 - 7½in (13 - 19cm)	**45 up**
Bent-limb baby:	
Painted bisque	**100 up**
Hard plastic	**75 up**
Judy Ann	**300 up**
In storybook box with extra outfits	
	450 up
Early painted bisque with white	
painted socks	**150 up**
Glow-in-Dark with bisque	
socket head	**100 up**

Special Series Dolls:

Masquerade, bisque (jointed legs)	
	125 up
Around the World, bisque	**125 up**
Sports, bisque	**125 up**
Baby, early bisque model with closed	
fist and open mouth	**135 up**
Powder and Crinoline, bisque (jointed	
legs) 7in (18cm)	**150 up**
Operetta, bisque	**100 up**
All Time Hit Parade, bisque	
	100 up
Dolls in old "Sunburst" boxes,	
bisque	**150 up**
Dolls in boxes with special inserts	
for holidays, bisque	**150 up**
plastic	**100 up**
Nancy Ann Style Show, hard plastic	
17in (43cm)	**425 - 475**
Muffie, hard plastic	
8in (20cm)	**125 - 150**

Ohlhaver

Maker: Gebrüder Ohlhaver, doll factory, Sonneberg, Thüringia, Germany. Heads made by Gebrüder Heubach, Ernst Heubach and Porzellanfabrik Mengersgereuth.
Date: 1912 - on
Material: Bisque socket head, ball-jointed composition body
Trademarks: Revalo   Revalo
Mark: Germany
                                    3

Revalo Character Baby or Toddler: Perfect bisque socket head, good wig, sleep eyes, hair eyelashes, painted lower eyelashes, open mouth; ball-jointed toddler or baby bent-limb body; dressed; all in good condition. (For photograph see *7th Blue Book*, page 296.)
#22:
14 - 16in (36 - 41cm)   **$475 - 550**
20 - 22in (51 - 56cm)   **700 - 800**

*Allow $150 extra for toddler body.

Revalo Character Doll: Bisque head with molded hair, painted eyes, open/closed mouth; composition body; dressed; all in good condition.
Coquette,
    10 - 12in (25 - 31cm)
                           $650 - 700

Revalo Child Doll: Bisque socket head, good wig, sleep eyes, hair eyelashes, painted lower eyelashes, open mouth; ball-jointed composition body; dressed; all in good condition. Mold *#150* or *#10727*. See color photograph on page 302.
15 - 16in (38 - 41cm)
                  $500 - 550
22in (56cm)   **675 - 725**
25 - 27in (64 - 69cm)
                  800 - 900

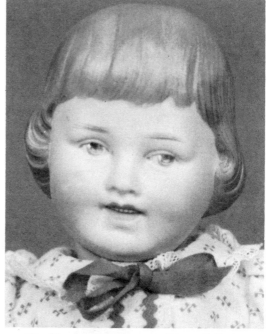

12in (31cm) Revalo character. *Private Collection.*

Old Cottage Dolls

Maker: Old Cottage Toys, Allargate, Rustington, Littlehampton, Sussex, Great Britain

Date: 1948

Designers: Greta Fleischmann and her daughter Susi

Material: Composition or hard plastic heads, stuffed cloth bodies

Size: 8 - 9in (20 - 23cm) usually

Mark: Paper label - Old Cottage Toys, handmade in Great Britain

Old Cottage Doll: Hard plastic face with hand painted features, wig, stuffed cloth body; original clothing; excellent condition.

8 - 9in (20 - 23cm) **$125 up***
12 - 13in (31 - 33cm),
   mint-in-box   **300****

*Depending upon rarity.
**Not enough price samples to compute a reliable range.

9in (23cm) Scots boy, all original. *Esther Schwartz Collection.*

Oriental Dolls

Japanese Traditional Children:
1850 - on. Papier-mâché
swivel head on shoulder
plate, hips, lower legs and
feet (early ones have jointed
wrists and ankles); cloth midsection, cloth (floating) upper arms and legs; hair wig,
dark glass eyes, pierced ears
and nostrils; original or appropriate clothes; all in good
condition.
12 - 14in (31 - 36cm)
$ 275 - 325
18 - 20in (46 - 51cm)
425 - 525
Boy, 18 - 20in (46 - 51cm)
500 - 600
Three-bend body, 11in (28cm),
at auction **2800**
Ca. 1920s, 13 - 15in (33 - 38cm)
125 - 150
17 - 18in (43 - 46cm)
185 - 225
Ca. 1940s, 12 - 14in (31 - 36cm)
85 - 95
Traditional Lady, 1920s,
10 - 12in (25 - 31cm)
150 - 175
16in (41cm) **235 - 265**
1940s, 12 - 14in (31 - 36cm)
85 - 95
Traditional Warrior, 1880s,
16 - 18in (41 - 46cm)
600 up
1920s; 11 - 12in (28 - 31cm)
250 up
Royal Personnages,
1920s & 1930s,
4 - 6in (10 - 15cm)
100 - 125
12in (31cm) **250 up**
Baby with bent limbs, Ca. 1920s:
8 - 10in (20 - 25cm)
65 - 85

12in (31cm) Japanese traditional
play doll, all original. *H & J Foulke,
Inc.*

Oriental Bisque Dolls: Ca. 1900
- on. Made by German firms
such as Simon & Halbig, Armand Marseille, J. D. Kestner and others. Bisque head
tinted yellow; matching ball-
jointed or baby body. (See
previous *Blue Books* for photographs of mold numbers
not shown here.)
S&H 1329 girl, See color photograph on page 304.
    13 - 14in (33 - 36cm)
          $1800 - 2200
    18 - 19in (46 - 48cm)
          2700 - 3000
A.M. 353 baby,
    12 - 14in (31 - 36cm)
          1150 - 1250
    10in (25cm) cloth body
          875
J.D.K. 243 baby, See color photograph on page 305.
    13 - 14in (33 - 36cm)
          4500 - 4900

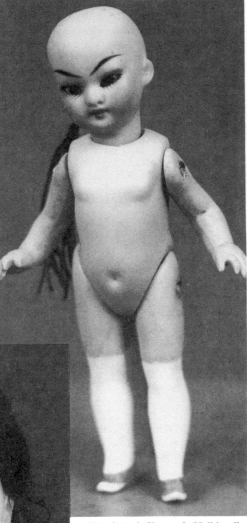

5½in (14cm) Simon & Halbig all-
bisque child. *H & J Foulke, Inc.*

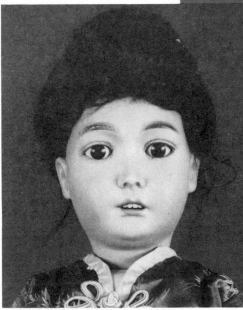

23in (58cm) 164 Oriental lady. *Private Collection.*

Oriental Dolls continued

S&H 1099, 1129, and 1199 girl, See color photograph on page 304.

15 - 17in (38 - 43cm)	**$2700 - 3200**
#220, 16 - 17in (41 - 43cm)	**3200 - 3500**
A.M. girl, 8 - 9in (20 - 23cm)	**600 - 700**
#164, 16 - 17in (41 - 43cm)	**2300 - 2500**
JDK molded hair baby, 14in (36cm)	
	6500
All-bisque S&H, 5½ (14cm)	**650**
7in (18cm)	**850 - 950**
All-bisque JDK baby:	
5½in (14cm)	**1250**
BSW #500, 14 - 15in (36 - 38cm)	
	1900 - 2200
Unmarked 4½in (12cm) painted eyes	
	150 - 175
6in (15cm) glass eyes	**425 - 450**
11 - 12in (28 - 31cm)	**825 - 875**

Baby Butterfly: 1911 - 1913. Made by E. I. Horsman. Composition head and hands, cloth body; painted black hair, painted features.

13in (33cm)   **$250****

**Not enough price samples to compute a reliable average.

Ming Ming Baby: Quan-Quan Co., Los Angeles and San Francisco, Calif., U.S.A. Ca. 1930. All-composition baby, jointed at shoulders and hips; painted facial features; sometimes with black yarn hair, original costume of colorful taffeta with braid trim; feet painted black or white for shoes. See color photograph on page 305.

10 - 12in (25 - 31cm)   **$165 - 175**

6in (15cm) A.M. 351 and 9in (23cm) A.M. 353 Oriental character babies. *Jimmy & Fay Rodolfos Collection.*

Papier-mâché
(So-Called French-Type)

Maker: Heads by German firms such as Johann Müller of Sonneberg and Andreas Voit of Hildburghausen, were sold to French and other doll makers
Date: 1816 - 1860
Material: Papier-mâché shoulder head, pink kid body
Mark: None

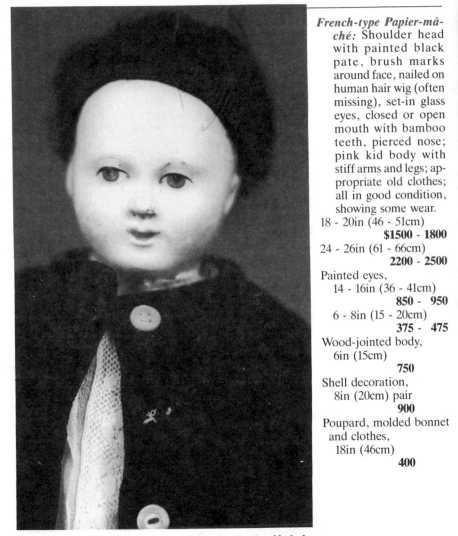

French-type Papier-mâché: Shoulder head with painted black pate, brush marks around face, nailed on human hair wig (often missing), set-in glass eyes, closed or open mouth with bamboo teeth, pierced nose; pink kid body with stiff arms and legs; appropriate old clothes; all in good condition, showing some wear.

18 - 20in (46 - 51cm)
$1500 - 1800
24 - 26in (61 - 66cm)
2200 - 2500
Painted eyes,
14 - 16in (36 - 41cm)
850 - 950
6 - 8in (15 - 20cm)
375 - 475
Wood-jointed body,
6in (15cm)
750
Shell decoration,
8in (20cm) pair
900
Poupard, molded bonnet and clothes,
18in (46cm)
400

16in (41cm) French papier-mâché with original wig. *H & J Foulke, Inc.*

Papier-mâché
(German)

Maker: Various German firms of Sonneberg such as Johann Müller, Müller & Strasburger, F. M. Schilling, Heinrich Stier, A. Wislizenus, and Cuno & Otto Dressel

Date: 1816 - on

Material: Papier-mâché shoulder head, cloth body, sometimes leather arms or kid body with wood limbs

---

Papier-mâché Shoulder Head: Ca. 1820s to 1850s. Unretouched shoulder head, molded hair, painted eyes; cloth or kid body; original or appropriate old clothing; entire doll in fair condition.

16 - 18in (41 - 46cm)
  $ 800 - 900
22 - 24in (56 - 61cm)
  1100 - 1300
32in (81cm) **1900 - 2000**
Glass eyes: 19in (48cm)
  short hair **1500 - 1800**
Flirty eyes: 23in (58cm)
  long hair **2700 - 3000**

See color photograph on page 359.

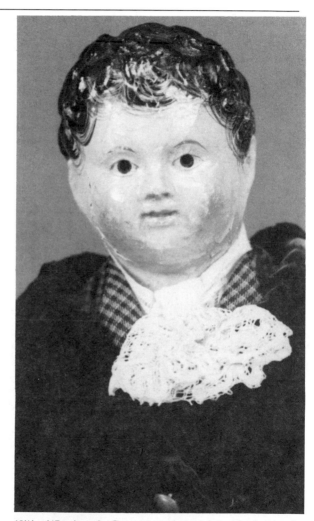

18½in (47cm) early German papier-mâché with short curly hairdo. *Private Collection.*

Papier-Mâché (German) continued

Molded Hair Papier-mâché: (so-called Milliners' models.) 1820s - 1860s. Unretouched shoulder head, various molded hairdos, eyes blue, black or brown, painted features; original kid body, wooden arms and legs; original or very old handmade clothing; entire doll in fair condition. See color photographs on pages 306.

Long curls:
9in (23cm)	$ 550
13in (33cm)	675 - 725

Covered wagon hairdo:
7in (18cm)	275 - 325
11in (28cm)	450 - 500
15in (38cm)	675

Side curls with braided bun,
9 - 10in (23 - 25cm)	650 - 750
13 - 15in (31 - 38cm)	1100 - 1300

Center part with molded bun,
7in (18cm)	525
12in (28cm)	950
Wood-jointed body	1200

Side curls with high beehive, (apollo knot)
11in (28cm)	950
18in (46cm)	1900

Coiled braids at ears, braided bun,
20in (51cm)	2000

12in (31cm) papier-mâché lady with long molded curls. *H & J Foulke, Inc.*

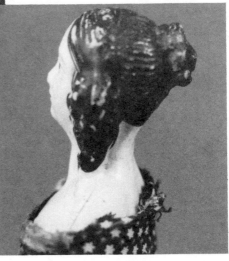

9in (23cm) papier-mâché lady with fancy hairdo. *H & J Foulke, Inc.*

Papier-Mâché (German) continued

Sonneberg-type Papier-mâché: Ca. 1880 - 1910. Shoulder head with molded and painted black or blonde hair, painted eyes, closed mouth; cloth body sometimes with leather arms; old or appropriate clothes; all in good condition, showing some wear.
Mark: Usually unmarked. Some marked:

13 - 15in (33 - 38cm)	**$250 - 300***
18 - 19in (46 - 48cm)	**350 - 400***
23 - 25in (58 - 64cm)	**500 - 550***
Glass eyes:	
13in (33cm)	**475**

*Allow extra for an unusual hairdo.

Patent Washable-type: 1880s to 1914.
See page 171.

26in (66cm) Sonneberg papier-mâché lady. *H & J Foulke, Inc.*

Parian-Type
(Untinted Bisque)

Maker: Various German firms
Date: Ca. 1860s through 1870s
Material: Untinted bisque shoulder head, cloth or kid body, leather, wood, china or combination extremities
Mark: Usually none, sometimes numbers

Unmarked Parian: Pale or untinted shoulder head, sometimes with molded blouse, beautifully molded hairdo, (may have ribbons, beads, comb or other decoration), painted eyes, closed mouth; cloth body; lovely clothes; entire doll in fine condition.

Common, plain style, 8 - 10in (20 - 25cm)	$ 125 - 165
16in (41cm)	300
24in (61cm)	475
Very fancy hairdo and/or elaborately decorated blouse	800 - 2500
Very fancy with glass eyes	1500 - 3250
Pretty hairdo, simple ribbon or comb	
14in (36cm)	375 - 425
18 - 20in (46 - 51cm)	500 - 600
Simple hairdo with applied flowers, 20in (51cm)	700
Man, molded collar and tie, 16 - 17in (41 - 43cm)	600 - 700
Boy, 19in (48cm) short black hair	1800
"Augusta Victoria," 17in (43cm)	1200
Molded plate, blonde curls, ribbon, glass eyes 14in (36cm)	1300
Alice hairdo, 21in (53cm)	750 - 800
"Countess Dagmar," 19in (48cm)	950
Molded blonde hair, blue ribbon, glass eyes, fashion face, swivel neck, 21in (53cm)	3500 - 4000
Blonde hair, blue glass eyes, 21in (53cm)	750
Irish Queen, Limbach 8552, 16in (41cm)	500
Black hair, snood, decorated plate, 16in (41cm)	700
Brown hair, snood, 24in (61cm)	1200
Pink lustre hat or snood, 17in (43cm)	1700 - 1800
Molded gray bonnet, 5in (13cm)	1100
Molded yellow bonnet, 4½in (12cm)	850
All-Parian, pink lustre boots, 5½in (14cm)	165 - 185

See color photographs on pages 306, 307 and 308.

P. D.

Maker: Probably Petit & Dumontier, Paris, France. Some heads made by François Gaultier.
Date: 1878 - 1890
Material: Bisque head, composition body
Size: Various
Mark:

P. 2 . D

P. D. Bébé: Perfect bisque head with paperweight eyes, closed mouth, pierced ears, good wig; jointed composition body (some have metal hands); appropriate clothes; all in good condition.

16 - 18in (41 - 46cm)   **$18,000 - 20,000**
26in (66cm)   **30,000**

16½ (42cm) P.1.D Bébé. *Private Collection.*

Philadelphia Baby

Maker: J. B. Sheppard & Co., Philadelphia, Pa., U.S.A.
Date: Ca. 1900
Material: All-cloth
Size: 18 - 22in (46 - 56cm)
Mark: None

Philadelphia Baby: All-cloth with treated shoulder-type head, lower arms and legs; painted hair, well-molded facial features, ears; stocking body; very good condition.

18 - 22in (46 - 56cm)   **$3500 - 4000**
Fair condition, showing wear **2500**
Very worn   **1500**

See color photograph on page 309.

Piano Baby

10in (25cm) Heubach piano baby. *H & J Foulke, Inc.*

Maker: Gebrüder Heubach, Kestner, Kling and other German makers
Date: 1880 - on
Material: All-bisque
Size: Usually under 12in (31cm), some larger
Mark: Many unsigned; some with maker's particular mark

Piano Baby: All-bisque immobile with molded clothes and painted features; made in various sitting and lying positions. Heubach quality.
4½ - 5in (12 - 13cm)
    $ 175 - 225
7 - 8in (18 - 20cm)   **375 - 475**
11 - 12in (28 - 31cm)
    750 - 850
Black, 3 - 4in (8 - 10cm)
    325 - 375
11in (28cm) two Heubach boys   **1650**
Dutch Costumes (Heubach)
10in (25cm) pair **1100**
5 - 6in (13 - 15cm)
    300 - 350
Boy and Girl Busts (Heubach)
7in (18cm) pair   **1200**
Baby in Shoe,
6in (15cm)   **350**
Walking in Father's shoes,
8in (20cm)   **350**

20½in (52cm) S.F.B.J. 235 character child with molded hair. For further information see page 370. *Private Collection.*

19in (48cm) S.F.B.J. 227 character boy. For further information see page 370, *Private Collection.*

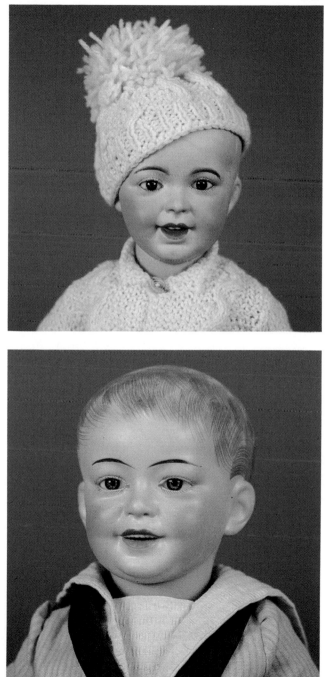

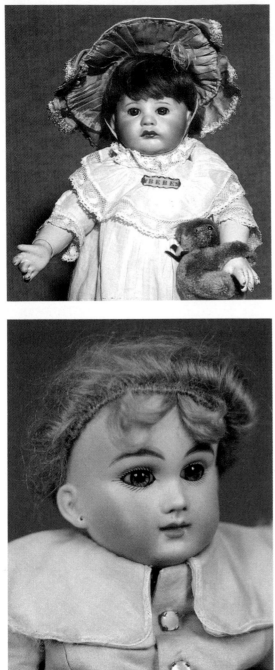

LEFT: 13in (33cm) S.F.B.J. 252 character toddler. For further information see page 370. *Private Collection.*

BELOW LEFT: 17in (43cm) Bébé Schmitt incised "1" over "A," on marked Schmitt body. For further information see page 375. *Lesley Hurford Collection.*

BELOW: 10in (25cm) German composition head doll, probably by Schilling. For further information see page 372. *H & J Foulke, Inc.*

347

19in (48cm) Schoenhut #308 pouty character girl. For further information see page 378. *H & J Foulke, Inc.*

14in (36cm) Schoenhut #308 character girl. For further information see page 378. *Ruth West Antique Dolls.*

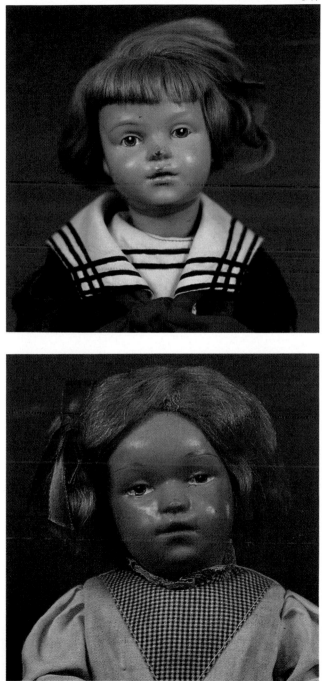
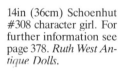

THE WORLD'S DARLING

SHIRLEY TEMPLE

12in (31cm) Ideal vinyl *Shirley Temple*, all original. For further information see page 381. *H & J Foulke, Inc.*

18in (46cm) Simon & Halbig 929 child. For further information see page 382. *Jackie Kaner.*

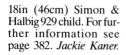

LEFT: 13in (33cm) Ideal composition *Shirley Temple*, all original. For further information see page 380. *H & J Foulke, Inc.*

24in (61cm) Simon & Halbig 1009 child. For further information see page 384. *H & J Foulke, Inc.*

9in (23cm) Simon & Halbig 1309 character children, all original. For further information see page 386. *H & J Foulke, Inc.*

9in (23cm) Simon & Halbig 603 character girl, all original. For further information see page 386. *Jackie Kaner.*

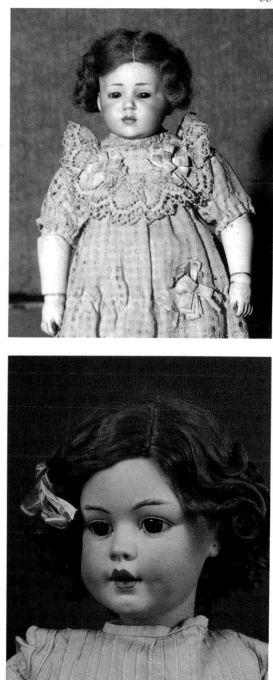

ABOVE: 8¼in (21cm) unmarked Simon & Halbig child with closed mouth. For further information see page 383. *Kay & Wayne Jensen Collection.*

RIGHT: 33in (84cm) Simon & Halbig 1279 character girl. For further information see page 386. *H & J Foulke, Inc.*

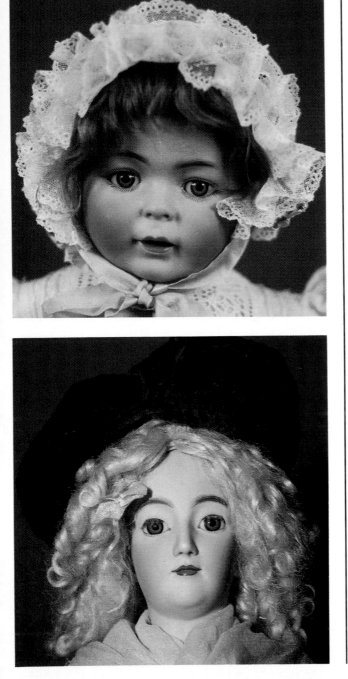

24in (61cm) Simon & Halbig *Erika* character. For further information see page 386. *Mary Barnes Kelley Collection.*

19in (48cm) Simon & Halbig 1307 lady. For further information see page 386. *Jackie Kaner.*

16in (41cm) Simon & Halbig 172-36 PIII baby with naughty eyes for Kämmer & Reinhardt. For further information see page 386. *Lesley Hurford Collection.*

Pair of Steiff felt children, all original. For further information see page 389. *Private Collection.*

354

LEFT: 16in (41cm) Jules Steiner Figure C Bébé. For further information see page 393. *Private Collection.*

BELOW LEFT: C Series Bourgoin Steiner Bébé, size 4. For further information see page 392. *Kay & Wayne Jensen Collection.*

BELOW: 6¾in (17cm) Herm Steiner pouty character. For further information see page 391. *H & J Foulke, Inc.*

28in (71cm) Jules Steiner Le Parisien Bébé A-19. For further information see page 394. *Mary Barnes Kelley Collection.*

13in (33cm) Swaine & Co. D1 character baby. For further information see page 395. *H & J Foulke, Inc.*

16in (41cm) *Terri Lee* with unusual hairdo, all original. For further information see page 396. *H & J Foulke, Inc.*

RIGHT: 18in (46cm) Izannah Walker. For further information see page 402. *Elizabeth McIntrye.*

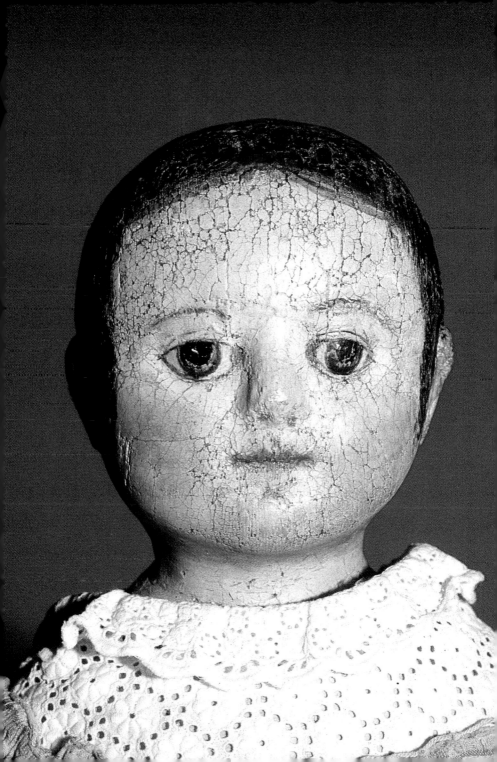

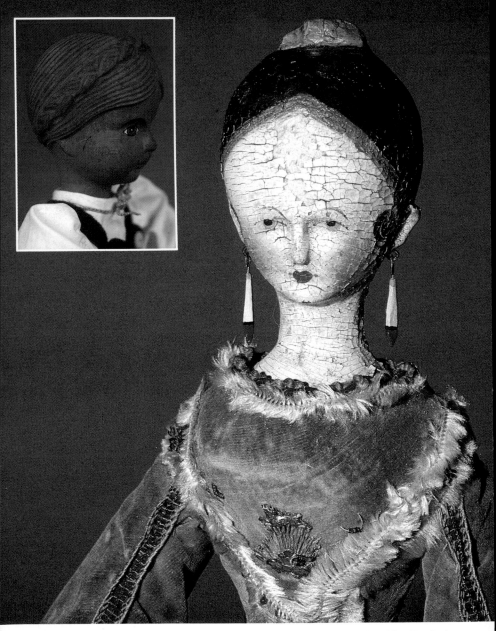

German wood doll with yellow tuck comb and earrings with fortune-telling skirt. For further information see page 410. *Elizabeth McIntyre.*

INSET: 12in (31cm) Swiss wood doll with carved braid. For further information see page 411. *H & J Foulke, Inc.*

RIGHT: 21in (53cm) German papier-mâché with flirting eyes. For further information see page 339. *Nancy A. Smith Collection.*

BELOW RIGHT: Amberg's *Mibs*, all original. For further information see page 68. *Nancy A. Smith Collection.*

BELOW: 15in (38cm) Famous Artists Syndicate *Orphan Annie*, composition shoulder head, cloth body, original dress. For further information see page 169. *H & J Foulke, Inc.*

2in (5cm) all-bisque German animal nodders. For further information see page 61. *H & J Foulke, Inc.*

18in (46cm) (unmarked metal shoulder head dolls, sleeping eyes. For further information see page 329. *H & J Foulke, Inc.*

Pincushion Dolls*
(Half Dolls)

Maker: Various German firms, such as William Goebel, Dressel, Kister & Co., J. D. Kestner, Simon & Halbig, Limbach, Hertwig & Co., Gebrüder Heubach
Date: 1900 - on
Material: China, sometimes bisque
Size: Up to about 9in (23cm)
Mark: "Germany" and numbers; a few with Goebel (see page 213), D&K or Karl Schneider marks.

Pincushions: China half figures with molded hair and painted features; usually with molded clothes, hats, lovely modeling and painting.

Arms close	**$ 30 - 40**
Arms extending but hands coming back to figure	**45 up**
Hands extended	**75 up**
Bisque child, glass eyes, 2in (5cm)	**175**
Painted eyes, 3in (8cm)	**125**
Flapper with molded dress and cloche, 4in (10cm)	**65 up**
French-style ladies	**400**
Bisque lady, wig, movable arms 4½ - 5½in (12 - 14cm)	**200 - 250**
Lady with large molded hat, 7in (18cm)	**850**
Art Deco lady, 5in (13cm)	**350**
Fancy colonial-style lady 5in (13cm)	**600**
Flapper holding mirror, 5in (13cm)	**250**
Young girl w/wide brimmed hat, carrying purple bag, 4in (10cm)	**600**
Dressel & Kister:	
Blue bandana, 5in (13cm)	**550**
Holding apple, 5½in (14cm)	**1000**
Gold and lavender helmet 4½in (12cm)	**225**
Molded hat, flying hair 4¼in (11cm)	**650**
Medieval headdress, 4¼in (11cm)	**600**

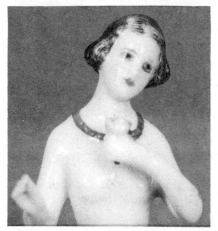

4in (10cm) pincushion lady. *H & J Foulke, Inc.*

1¾in (5cm) pincushion lady. *H & J Foulke, Inc.*

See color photograph on page 309.

Pintel & Godchaux

Maker: Pintel & Godchaux, Montreuil, France

Date: 1890 - 1899

Material: Bisque head, jointed composition body

Trademark: Bébé Charmant

Mark:

B	A
P 9 G	P 7 G

Marked P.G. Doll: Perfect bisque head, paperweight eyes, closed mouth, good wig; jointed composition and wood body; appropriate clothing; all in good condition.

20 - 24in (51 - 61cm)	**$2700 - 3200**
Open mouth, 20in (51cm)	**1900 - 2000**

18in (46cm) P. G. Bébé. See color photograph on page 309. *H & J Foulke, Inc.*

Pre-Greiner
(So-called)

Maker: Unknown and various

Date: Ca. 1850

Material: Papier-mâché shoulder head, stuffed cloth body, mostly homemade, wood, leather or cloth extremities

Mark: None

Unmarked Pre-Greiner: Papier-mâché shoulder head; molded and painted black hair, pupil-less black glass eyes; cloth (sometimes kid) stuffed body, leather extremities; dressed in good old or original clothes; all in good condition.

18 - 22in (46 - 56cm)	**$ 900 - 1200**
28 - 32in (71 - 81cm)	**1800 - 2100**
Fair condition, much wear,	
20 - 24in (51 - 61cm)	**700 - 800**
Flirty eye, 30in (76cm)	**3000**

See color photograph on page 310.

Rabery & Delphieu

Maker: Rabery & Delphieu of Paris, France
Date: 1856 (founded) - 1899 - then with S. F. B. J.
Material: Bisque head, composition body
Mark: "R. D." (from 1890)
Mark: On back of head:
Body mark:
(Please note last two lines illegible)

Marked R. D. Bébé: Ca. 1880s. Bisque head, lovely wig, paperweight eyes, closed mouth; jointed composition body; beautifully dressed; entire doll in good condition. Very good quality bisque.

12in (31cm) **$2600 - 2700**
19 - 21in (48 - 53cm) **3500 - 3700**
24in (61cm) **4200 - 4700**
28in (71cm) **5200 - 5500**
28in (71cm) stunning face and clothes, at auction **6500**
Lesser quality bisque (uneven coloring or much speckling)
16 - 18in (41 - 46cm) **2250 - 2350**
Open mouth, 19 - 22in (48 - 56cm) **2200 - 2500**

24in (61cm) R 3 D Bébé. *Kay & Wayne Jensen Collection.*

Raggedy Ann and Andy

Maker: Various
Date: 1915 to present
Material: All-cloth
Size: 4½ - 39in (12 - 99cm)
Creator: Johnny B. Gruelle

Early Raggedy Ann or Andy: All-cloth with movable arms and legs; brown yarn hair, button eyes, painted features; legs or striped fabric for hose and black for shoes; original clothes; all in fair condition. (See *Doll Classics*, page 173.)

Mark: "PATENTED SEPT. 7, 1915"

16in (41cm)	**$750 - 850**
Much wear	**500 - 550**

Molly-'es Raggedy Ann or Andy: 1935 - 1938, manufactured by Molly-'es Doll Outfitters. Same as above, but with red hair and printed features; original clothes; all in good condition. (For photograph see *8th Blue Book*, page 195.)

Mark:
"Raggedy Ann and Raggedy Andy Dolls Manufactured by Molly'es Doll Outfitters" (printed writing in black on front torso)

18 - 22in (46 - 56cm)	**$500 - 600**

Georgene Raggedy Ann or Andy: 1938-1963, manufactured by Georgene Novelties. Same as above, but with red hair and printed features; original clothes; all in good condition. See color photograph on page 310.

Mark: Cloth label sewn in side seam of body.

15 - 18in (38 - 46cm)	**$125 - 150 each**
Fair condition	**225 pair**
Asleep/Awake, 13in (33cm)	
	550 pair
Black Outlined Nose,	
19in (48cm)	**350 - 400 each**
Pair, mint condition with individual name labels and tags	**950**
Beloved Belindy	**900 - 1200**

Knickerbocker Toy Co. Raggedy Ann or Andy: 1963 to 1982. Excellent condition.

12in (31cm)	**$ 25**
24in (61cm)	**85 - 95**
36in (91cm)	**125 - 150**
Beloved Belindy (For photograph see *9th Blue Book*, page 336.)	**350 up**

13in (33cm) Georgene *Raggedy Ann & Andy* with black outlined noses. The awake side of an asleep/awake pair. *H & J Foulke, Inc.*

Raleigh

Maker: Jessie McCutcheon Raleigh, Chicago, Ill., U.S.A.
Date: 1916 - 1920
Material: All-composition or composition heads and cloth bodies
Designer: Jessie McCutcheon Raleigh
Mark: None

Raleigh Doll: Composition head, molded hair or wig, sleep or painted eyes; composition or cloth body; appropriate clothes; all in good condition. Child and baby styles.
11in (28cm) wigged   **$375 - 425**
13in (33cm) molded haiɾ   **450 - 475**

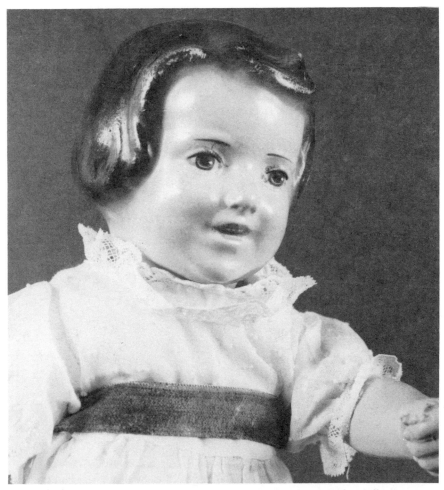

13in (33cm) Raleigh girl with molded hair and barette. *Pearl Morley Collection.*

Ravca

Maker: Bernard Ravca, Paris, France.
After 1939, New York, N.Y.,
U.S.A.
Date: 1924 - on
Material: Cloth with stockinette faces
Size: Various
Mark: Paper label: "Original Ravca Fab-
rication Francaise"

Ravca Doll: Stockinette face individually
needle sculpted; cloth body and limbs;
original clothes; all in excellent condition.
10in (25cm)   **$ 90 - 100**
Ravca-type fine quality peasant man or
lady 17in (43cm)   **210 - 235 each**

*The dolls shown in the *9th Blue Book*, page
338 and the *7th Blue Book*, page 256 should
have been captioned as Ravca-type dolls.
These dolls were not made by Mr. Ravca.

10in (25cm) Ravca stockinette lady, all original. *H & J Foulke, Inc.*

17in (43cm) Ravca-type stockinette dolls, some found with "Made in Italy" stamped on wooden
shoe. *H & J Foulke, Inc.*

Recknagel

Maker: Th. Recknagel, porcelain factory,
Alexandrienthal, Thüringia,
Germany
Date: 1886 - on
Material: Bisque head, composition or
wood-jointed body
Size: Usually small
Mark:

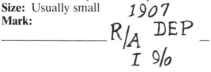

8½in (22cm) R.A. infant, composition body.
H & J Foulke, Inc.

R. A. Child: Ca. 1890s-World War I. Perfect marked bisque head, jointed composition or wooden body; good wig, set or sleep eyes, open mouth; some dolls with molded painted shoes and socks; all in good condition.

1907, 1909, 1914:
8 - 9in (20 - 23cm)   **$160 - 185**
16 - 18in (41 - 46cm)   **325 - 350**

*Fine quality bisque only.

R. A. Character Baby: 1909-World War I.
Perfect bisque socket head; cloth baby body or composition bent-limb baby body; painted or glass eyes; nicely dressed; all in good condition.
#127, 1924 and other infants,
8 - 9in (20 - 23cm) long **$225 - 275**
Character babies, *#23* and others,
7 - 8in (18 - 20cm)   **275 - 325**
Bonnet babies, *#22 & 28:*
10in (25cm)   **450 - 500**

R.A. Character #31 Max: molded hair; painted features.
8in (20cm)   **$500 - 600**

R.A. Googlies #45 and *46:*
7in (18cm)   **$250 - 300**

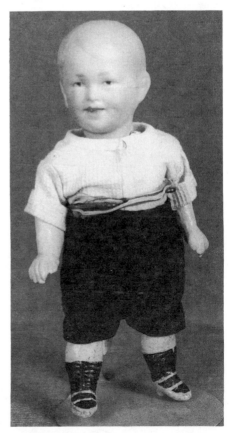

7in (18cm) R.A. 23 character boy. *H & J Foulke, Inc.*

Rohmer Fashion

Maker: Madame Marie Rohmer, Paris, France
Date: 1857 - 1880
Material: China or bisque shoulder head, jointed kid body
Mark:

Rohmer Fashion: China or bisque swivel or shoulder head, jointed kid body, bisque or china arms, kid or china legs; lovely wig, set glass eyes, closed mouth, some ears pierced; fine costuming; entire doll in good condition.

16 - 18in (41 - 46cm)   **$4500 - 5500***
Child Fashion, 20in (51cm), at auction   **7350**

See color photograph on page 311.

*Allow extra for original clothes.

Rollinson Doll

Maker: Utley Doll Co., Holyoke, Mass., U.S.A.
Date: 1916 - on
Material: All-cloth
Size: 14 - 28in (36 - 71cm)
Designer: Gertrude F. Rollinson
Mark: Stamp in shape of a diamond with a doll in center, around border "Rollinson Doll Holyoke, Mass."

Marked Rollinson doll: All molded cloth with painted head and limbs; painted hair or human hair wig, painted features (sometimes teeth also); dressed; all in good condition.

Chase-type Baby with molded hair, 18 - 22in (46 - 51cm)
          $1200 - 1500
Child with wig. (For photograph see *8th Blue Book*, page 346.)
     26in (66cm)   **2500 - 2750****
Toddler with wig. (See color photograph on page 311.
     16in (41cm)   **1750**

**Not enough price samples to compute a reliable range.

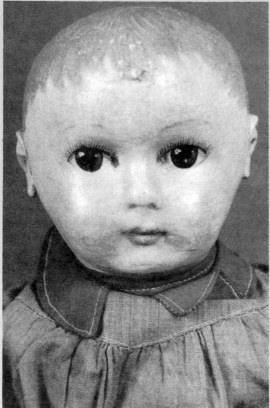

19in (48cm) Rollinson boy. *Betty Harms Collection.*

S.F.B.J.

Maker: Société Française de Fabrication de Bébés & Jouets, Paris, France
Date: 1899 -
Material: Bisque head, composition body
Mark:

DÉPOSÉ
S.F.B.J. — *S.F.B.J / 301 PARIS*

Child Doll: 1899 - on. Perfect bisque head, good French wig, set or sleep eyes, open mouth, pierced ears; jointed composition body; nicely dressed; all in good condition.

Jumeau-type, paperweight eyes (no mold number):

14 - 16in (36 - 41cm)	**$1000 - 1100**
21 - 23in (53 - 58cm)	**1650 - 1750**
25 - 27in (64 - 69cm)	**2200 - 2400**

#301: See color photograph on page 312.

12 - 14in (31 - 36cm)	**650 - 750**
20 - 23in (51 - 58cm)	**950 - 1050**
28 - 30in (71 - 76cm)	**1600 - 1700**

Lady Body,

22in (56cm)	**1200 - 1400**

#60:

12 - 14in (31 - 36cm)	**550 - 600**
19 - 21in (48 - 53cm)	**750 - 800**
28in (71cm)	**1200**

Bleuette #301, (For photograph see *8th Blue Book,* page 347.)

10in (25cm)	**725 - 775**

Walking, Kissing and Flirting:

22in (56cm)	**1700 - 1800**

Papier-mâché head *#60,* fully-jointed body:

17in (43cm)	**325 - 375**

22in (56cm) 230 character child. See color photograph on page 312. *H & J Foulke, Inc.*

S.F.B.J. continued

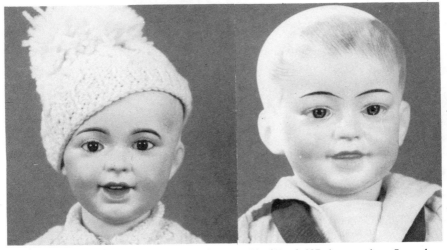

20½in (52cm) 235 character boy. See color photo-graph on page 345. *Private Collection.*

19in (48cm) 227 character boy. See color photograph on page 345. *Private Collection.*

Character Dolls: 1910 - on. Perfect bisque head, wig, molded, sometimes flocked hair on mold numbers *237, 266, 227* and*235,* sleep eyes, composition body; nicely dressed; all in good condition. (See previous *Blue Books* for illustrations of mold numbers not shown here.)

Mark:

S.F. B. J.
• 230 •
PARIS

S.F. B. J.
2 36
PARIS

#226, 235: 15 - 17in (38 - 43cm)
$ **1650 - 1850**

#227, 237: 17in (43cm)   **2200 - 2300**
21in (53cm)   **2600 - 2700**

#230, (sometimes Jumeau):
14 - 16in (36 - 41cm)   **1400 - 1500**
20 - 23in (51 - 58cm)   **1800 - 2100**

#233: Screamer, 20in (51cm)
2400**

#234: Baby, 15in (38cm)   **2600****

#236: Baby, 15 - 17in (38 - 43cm)
1000 - 1200
20 - 22in (51 - 56cm)   **1700 - 1800**
Toddler, 14 - 15in (36 - 38cm)
1600 - 1700
?7 - 28in (69 - 71cm)   **2600 - 2800**

#238, 229: Child,
15 - 16in (38 - 41cm)
Lady 23in (58cm)   **4000**

#239: Five-piece crude body, not original clothes,
13in (33cm)   **4000 - 4500**
With original wig, clothes and tags,
pristine condition   **20,000 pair**

#242: Nursing Baby 13in (33cm)
2600**

#245: Googly. See page 215.

#247: Toddler,
15 - 17in (38 - 43cm)   **2300 - 2600**
25 - 27in (64 - 69cm)   **3000 - 3500**

#251: Toddler,
14 - 15in (36 - 38cm)   **1500 - 1600**
20in (51cm)   **1900 - 2000**
27 - 28in (69 - 71cm)   **2600 - 2800**

#252: Toddler, For color photograph see page 346.
13 - 15in (33 - 38cm0   **5500 - 6000**
20in (51cm)   **7500**
27 - 28in (69 - 71cm)   **8500 - 9500**

Black papier-mâché *#247* head baby,
25in (64cm)   **550**

**Not enough price samples to compute a reliable range.

Sasha

Maker: Trendon Toys, Ltd., Reddish, Stockport, England.
Date: 1865 - 1986
Material: All-vinyl
Designer: Sasha Morgenthaler

Sasha: All-vinyl of exceptionally high
quality, long synthetic hair, painted
features, wistful, appealing expression;
original clothing, tiny circular wrist
tag; excellent condition.

16in (41cm) **$ 150 - 175**
Boxed **200**
In cylinder package
300 - 350
Gregor (boy)
150 - 175
Boxed **200**
Cora (black girl)
225 - 275
Caleb (black boy)
225 - 275
Black Baby **175 - 200**
White Baby **125 - 150**
Sexed Baby, pre 1979
225 - 250
Limited Edition Dolls:
1982 *Pintucks Dress*
300 - 350
1983 *Kiltie*
300 - 350
1985 *Prince Gregor*
300 - 350
Gotz model 1965 - 69
800
Boxed **1000**
Early model 1950s
5000 - 6000
Fair condition and
naked **2500 - 2850**
Eskimo Pair, 20in (51cm),
at auction **9000**

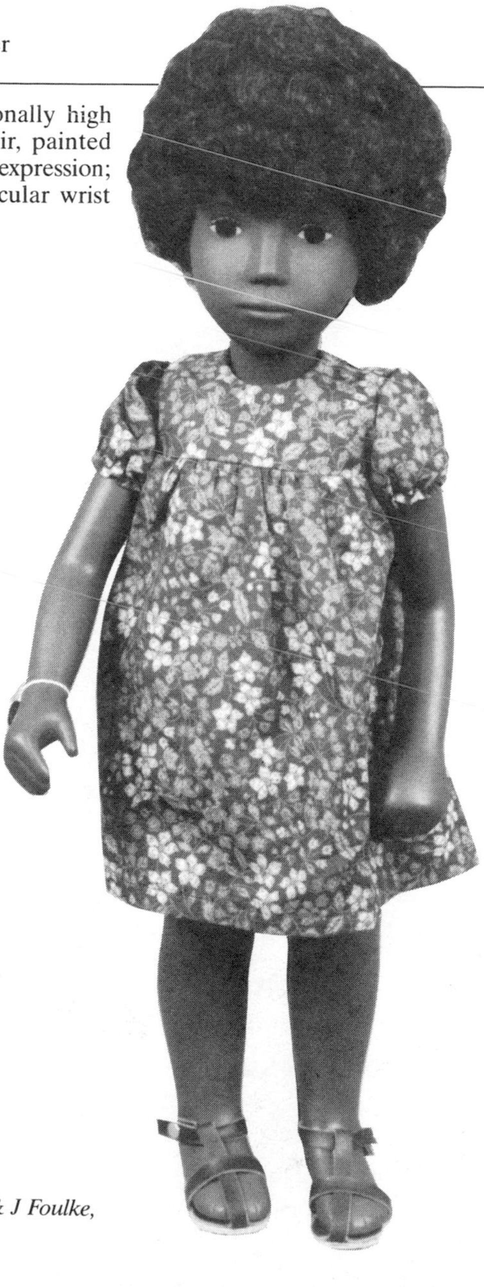

16in (41cm) *Cora*, all original. *H & J Foulke, Inc.*

F. M. Schilling

Maker: Barbara, later her son Ferdinand Max Schilling, doll factory, Sonneberg, Thüringia, Germany

Date: 1871 - on

Material: Composition head and lower limbs, cloth body; Patent Washable-type

Mark:

Size: 8 - 39in (20 - 100cm)

Schilling Täufling: Excellent quality composition head, good mohair or lamb's wool wig, paperweight eyes (sometimes sleeping eyes), closed mouth (sometimes open); cloth torso and upper limbs, composition lower limbs with molded boots or bare feet (the latter usually representing babies). See color photograph on page 346.

13 - 15in (33 - 38cm) **$325 - 375**
19 - 21in (48 - 53cm) **450 - 550**
24in (61cm) **650 - 750**
30 - 31in (76 - 79cm) **950**

20in (51cm) marked Schilling täufling, all original, intended to be a baby. *H & J Foulke, Inc.*

Bruno Schmidt

Maker: Bruno Schmidt, doll factory, Waltershausen, Thüringia, Germany. Heads by
Bähr & Pröschild, Ohrdruf, Thüringia, Germany.
Date: 1898 - on
Material: Bisque head, composition body
Mark:

2096-4

Marked B. S. W. Child Doll: Ca. 1898 -
on. Bisque head, good wig, sleep eyes,
open mouth; jointed composition
child body; dressed; all in good condition. (For photograph see *8th Blue
Book*, page 351.)

20 - 23in (51 - 58cm)	**$550 - 650**
28 - 30in (71 - 76cm)	**950 - 1100**

Marked B. S. W. Character Dolls: Bisque
socket head, glass eyes; jointed composition body; dressed; all in good condition.

#2048, 2094, 2096 (so-called *Tommy
Tucker)*, molded hair, open mouth.

13 - 14in (33 - 36cm)	**$1100 - 1200**
19 - 21in (48 - 53cm)	**1400 - 1500**
25 - 26in (64 - 66cm)	**1900 - 2000**

#2048 (closed mouth):
16 - 18in (41 - 46cm)
2200 - 2500

#2072:
23in (58cm) toddler
$ 4500 - 5000
17in (43cm) **3000**
(For photograph see *7th Blue
Book*, page 335.)

#2033 (so-called **Wendy**) **(537)**,
(For photograph see *9th Blue
Book*, page 347.)
14 - 16in (36 - 41cm)
16,000 - 23,000

#2025 (529) closed mouth,
wigged:
22in (56cm) **4500 - 5000****

#2026 (538)
22in (56cm), at auction
3850

#2097, character baby open
mouth, (For photograph see
9th Blue Book, page 347.)

13 - 14in (33 - 36cm)		
	475 -	**525**
18in (46cm)	**750 -**	**800**

#425 all-bisque baby:
6½in (17cm)
250 - 275

**Not enough price samples to
compute a reliable range.

25in (64cm) 2048 character toddler. *H & J Foulke, Inc.*

Franz Schmidt

Maker: Franz Schmidt & Co., doll factory, Georgenthal near Waltershausen, Thüringia, Germany. Heads by Simon & Halbig, Grafenhain, Thüringia, Germany.

Date: 1890 - on

Material: Bisque socket head, jointed bent-limb or toddler body of composition

---

Marked F.S. & Co. Character Baby: Ca. 1910. Perfect bisque character head, good wig, sleep eyes, open mouth, may have open nostrils; jointed bent-limb body; suitably dressed; all in good condition.

#1272, 1295, 1296, 1297, 1310:

Baby,	
12 - 14in (31 - 36cm)	$ 475 - 575
20 - 21in (51 - 53cm)	750 - 800
26 - 27in (66 - 69cm)	1400 - 1600
Toddler,	
7in (18cm)	600 - 650
13 - 15in (33 - 38cm)	675 - 775
19 - 21in (48 - 53cm)	1000 - 1100

#1286, molded hair with blue ribbon, glass eyes, open smiling mouth,
16in (41cm) toddler
$4000**

Mark:

1295
F. S. & Co.
Made in
Germany
30

Marked S & C Child Doll: Ca. 1890 - on. Perfect bisque socket head, good wig, sleep eyes, open mouth; jointed composition child body; dressed; all in good condition. Some are Mold *#293*.

6in (15cm)	$ 275 - 325
16 - 18in (41 - 46cm)	500 - 550
22 - 24in (56 - 61cm)	650 - 750
29 - 30in (74 - 76cm)	950 - 1100
42in (107cm)	3000

Mark:

S & C
SIMON & HALBIG
28

**Not enough price samples to compute a reliable range.

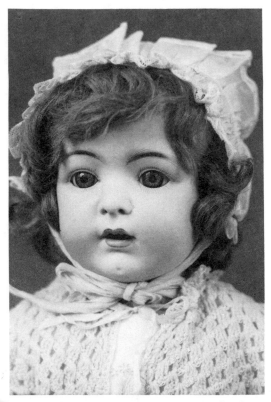

27in (69cm) 1295 character baby. *H & J Foulke, Inc.*

Schmitt

Maker: Schmitt & Fils, Paris, France
Date: 1854 - 1891
Material: Bisque socket head, composition jointed body
Size: Various
Mark: On both head and body:

Marked Schmitt Bébé: Ca. 1879. Perfect bisque socket head with skin or good wig, large paperweight eyes, closed mouth, pierced ears; Schmitt-jointed composition body; appropriate clothes; all in good condition.
Long face (as shown):
16 - 18in (41 - 46cm)
                   $12,000 - 14,000
23 - 25in (58 - 64cm) **19,000 - 21,000**
Short face. See color photograph on page 346.

16 - 18in (41 - 46cm)	**16,000 - 18,000***
22in (56cm)	**21,000 - 22,000***
Oval/Round face:	
10 - 11in (25 - 28cm)	**8500 - 9500***
17 - 19in (43 - 48cm)	**16,000 - 18,000***
23 - 24in (58 - 61cm)	**20,000 - 22,000***
Wax-Over Head,	
19in (48cm)	**1600****

*Allow one-third less for dolls which do not have strongly molded faces.
**Not enough price samples to compute a reliable range.

24in (61cm) Schmitt 4•5 Bébé with long style face. *Private Collection.*

Schoenau & Hoffmeister

Maker: Schoenau & Hoffmeister, Porzellanfabrik Burggrub, Burggrub, Bavaria, Germany. Arthur Schoenau also owned a doll factory.

Date: 1884 - on dolls; 1901 - on porcelain

Material: Bisque head, composition body

Trademarks: Hanna, Burggrub Baby, Bébé Carmencita, Viola, Kunstlerkopf, Das Lachende Baby.

Mark:

A S

S ⭐PB H
4600
Germany

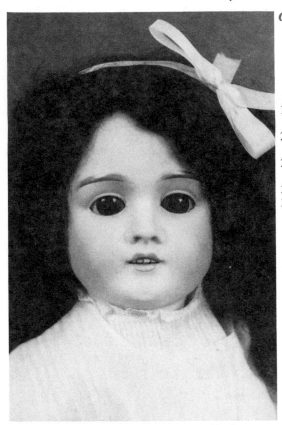

30in (76cm) 1906 child. *H & J Foulke, Inc.*

Child Doll: 1901 - on. Perfect bisque head; original or good wig, sleep eyes, open mouth; ball-jointed body; original or good clothes; all in nice condition. *#1906, 1909, 5500, 5700, 5800.*

14 - 16in (36 - 41cm)
$ 285 - 325

21 - 23in (53 - 58cm)
450 - 550

28 - 30in (71 - 76cm)
700 - 800

33in (84cm) 1000 - 1100

39in (99cm) 1800 - 1900

Schoenau & Hoffmeister continued

Character Baby: 1910 - on. Perfect bisque socket head, good wig, sleep eyes, open mouth; composition bent-limb baby body; all in good condition. *#169, 769,* "Burggrub Baby" or "Porzellanfabrik Burggrub." (For photograph see *8th Blue Book*, page 355.)

13 - 15in (33 - 38cm)	**$ 375 - 425**
18 - 20in (46 - 51cm)	**500 - 550**
23 - 24in (58 - 61cm)	**700 - 800**
28in (71cm)	**1000 - 1100**

Princess Elizabeth, 1932. (For photograph see *9th Blue Book*, page 351.)
Chubby five-piece body.

17in (43cm)	**$1900 - 2100**
20 - 23in (51 - 58cm)	**2400 - 2700**

Pouty Baby: Ca. 1925. Perfect bisque solid dome head with painted hair, tiny sleep eyes, closed pouty mouth; cloth body with composition arms and legs; dressed; all in good condition. (For photograph see *8th Blue Book*, page 355.)

11 - 12in (28 - 31cm)	**$750 - 800****

**Not enough price samples to compute a reliable range.

Hanna:

Baby, 14 - 16in (36 - 41cm)	**650 - 700**
20 - 22in (51 - 56cm)	**900 - 1000**
26in (66cm)	**1500**
Toddler, 14 - 16in (36 - 41cm)	**800 - 900**
Brown, 7½in (19cm) toddler	**275**

Das Lachende Baby, 1930. (For photograph see *8th Blue Book*, page 355.)

23 - 24in (58 - 61cm)	**2200 - 2500****

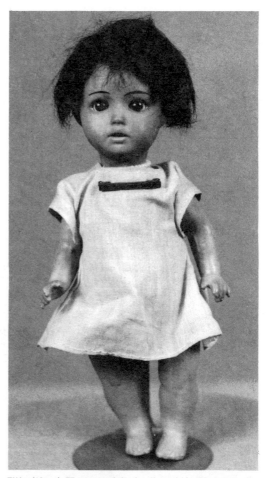

7½in (19cm) *Hanna*, original yellow shift. *H & J Foulke, Inc.*

Schoenhut

Maker: Albert Schoenhut & Co., Philadephia, Pa., U.S.A.
Date: 1872 - on
Material: Wood, spring-jointed, holes in bottom of feet to fit metal stand
Size: Various models 11 - 21in (28 - 53cm)
Designer: Early: Adolph Graziana and Mr. Leslie
Later: Harry E. Schoenhut

Mark: Paper label:

Incised:
SCHOENHUT DOLL
PAT. JAN. 17, '11, U.S.A.
& FOREIGN COUNTRIES

Character: 1911 - 1930. Wooden head and spring-jointed wooden body, marked head and/or body; original or appropriate wig, brown or blue intaglio eyes, open/closed mouth with painted teeth or closed mouth; original or suitable clothing; original paint may have light touch-up.

14 - 21in (36 - 53cm)
Excellent condition $1600 - 2100*
Good, some wear 900 - 1400*

*Allow extra for rare faces.

See color photograph on page 347.

Character with carved hair: Ca. 1911 - 1930. Wooden head with carved hair, comb marks, possibly a ribbon or bow, intaglio eyes, mouth usually closed; spring-jointed wooden body; original or suitable clothes; original paint may have light touch-up.

19in (48cm) 308 pouty character girl. See color photograph on page 347. *H & J Foulke, Inc.*

14 - 21in (36 - 53cm):
Excellent condition	$2400 - 2700
Good, some wear	1800 - 2200
Early style	3500 - 4000
20in (51cm) man	2200

Tootsie Wootsie, 15in (38cm), very bad face, at auction **975**

Baby Face: Ca. 1913 - 1930. Wooden head and fully-jointed toddler or bent-limb baby body, marked head and/or body; painted hair or mohair wig, painted eyes, open or closed mouth; suitably dressed; original paint; all in good condition, with some wear.

Mark:

Baby,
12in (31cm)	$525 - 575
15 - 16in (38 - 41cm)	700 - 775

14in (36cm) 207 carved hair boy. *H & J Foulke, Inc.*

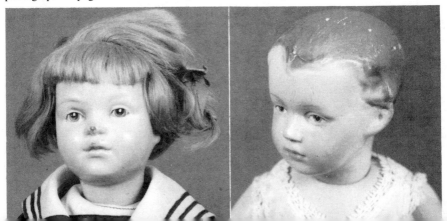

Schoenhut continued

Toddler,
11in (28cm)	**800 - 900**
14in (36cm)	**800 - 850**
16 - 17in (41 - 43cm)	**850 - 950**

Dolly Face: Ca. 1915 - 1930. Wooden head and spring-jointed wooden body; original or appropriate mohair wig, decal eyes, open/closed mouth with painted teeth; original paint; original or suitable clothes. (For photograph see *7th Blue Book*, page 343.)
14 - 21in (36 - 53cm)
Excellent condition, **$750 - 850**
Good condition, some wear,
550 - 650

Walker: Ca. 1919 - 1930. All-wood with "baby face," mohair wig, painted eyes; curved arms, straight legs with "walker" joint at hip; original or appropriate clothes; all in good condition. Original paint. No holes in bottom of feet. (For photograph see *9th Blue Book*, page 355.)
13in (33cm) **$ 800 - 850**
17in (43cm) excellent wiht original shoes **1100**

Sleep Eyes: Ca. 1920 - 1930. Used with "baby face" or "dolly face" heads. Mouths on this type were open with teeth or barely open with carved teeth. Original paint. (For photograph see *9th Blue Book*, page 354.)
14 - 21in (36 - 53cm)
Excellent condition **$1200 - 1400**
Good condition **750 - 850**

All-Composition: Ca. 1924. Jointed at neck, shoulders and hips, right arm bent, molded blonde curly hair, painted eyes, tiny closed mouth; original or appropriate clothing; in good condition. (See photograph in *8th Blue Book*, page 359.)
Paper label on back:

13in (33cm) **$500****

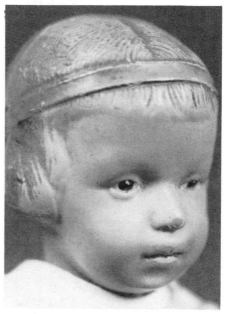
16in (41cm) 105 carved hair girl. *H & J Foulke, Inc.*

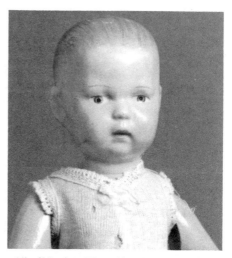
14in (36cm) toddler with painted hair. *H & J Foulke, Inc.*

**Not enough price samples to compute a reliable range.

Shirley Temple

Maker: Ideal Novelty Toy Corp., New York, N.Y., U.S.A.
Date: 1934 to present
Size: 7½ - 36in (19 - 91cm)
Designer: Bernard Lipfert

All-Composition Child: 1934 through late 1930s. Marked head and body, jointed composition body; all original including wig and clothes; entire doll in very good condition. Came in sizes 11 - 27in (28 - 69cm)

Mark: On body:

SHIRLEY TEMPLE
13

13

SHIRLEY TEMPLE

On head:

On cloth label:

Genuine SHIRLEY TEMPLE DOLL REGISTERED U.S. PAT OFF	MADE IN USA
IDEAL NOVELTY & TOY CO	

11in (28cm)	$ 675 -	725*
13in (33cm)	600 -	650*
15 - 16in (38 - 41cm)	600 -	650*
18in (46cm)	650 -	700*
20 - 22in (51 - 56cm)	800 -	850*
25in (64cm)	900 -	950*
27in (69cm)	1100 -	1200*
Button	85	
Dress, tagged	100 up	
Trunk	125	

*Allow 50% more for mint-in-box doll.
*Allow extra for a doll with unusual outfit.

See color photograph on page 348.

27in (69cm) composition *Shirley Temple* with flirty eyes, all original with button. *H & J Foulke, Inc.*

Shirley Temple continued

Baby Shirley: (For photograph see *7th Blue Book*, page 346.)
   16 - 18in (41 - 46cm) **$900 - 1000**
Made in Japan Composition Shirley: (For photograph see *8th Blue Book*, page 362.)
   7½in (19cm)   **250**
Hawaiian Shirley:
   18in (46cm)   **800 - 850****

**Not enough price samples to compute a reliable range.

Vinyl and Plastic: 1957.
   Mark: "Ideal Doll ST—12"
                 (number denotes size)

12in (31cm)	**$ 165 - 175**
15in (38cm)	**250 - 275**
17in (43cm)	**325 - 350**
19in (48cm)	**375 - 400**
36in (91cm)	**1400 - 1500**
Script name pin	**20 - 25**
Name purse	**15 - 20**

See color photograph on page 349.

Vinyl and Plastic: 1973.
16in (41cm) size only	**$100 - 110**
Boxed	**135 - 150**
Boxed dress	**35**

15in (38cm) vinyl 1957 ***Shirley Temple***, all original with script pin. *H & J Foulke, Inc.*

Simon & Halbig

Maker: Simon & Halbig, porcelain factory, Gräfenhain, Thüringia, Germany; purchased by Kämmer & Reinhardt in 1920
Date: 1869 - on
Material: Bisque head, kid (sometimes cloth) or composition body
Mark:

S 13 H _ 1079-2
949 _ DEP
S H
Germany

Child doll with closed mouth: Ca. 1879. Perfect bisque socket head on ball-jointed wood and composition body; good wig, glass set or sleep eyes, closed mouth, pierced ears; dressed; all in good condition. See *Simon & Halbig Dolls - The Artful Aspect* for photographs of mold numbers not shown here.

#719:
  19 - 21in (48 - 53cm) **$2900 - 3200**
#905, 908:
  14 - 17in (36 - 43cm) **2500 - 3000**

13in (33cm) 939 child. *H & J Foulke, Inc.*

#929: See color photograph on page 349.
  18 - 21in (46 - 53cm) **3500 - 4500****
#939:
  14in (36cm) **2500**
  17 - 20in (43 - 51cm) **2800 - 3200**
  24in (61cm) **4000 - 4100**
#949:
  15 - 16in (38 - 41cm) **1800 - 2200**

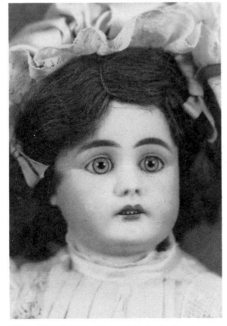

20in (51cm) 949 child. *H & J Foulke, Inc.*

**Not enough price samples to compute a reliable range.

16in (41cm) 1039 child. *H & J Foulke, Inc.*

22 - 23in (56 - 58cm)   **2600 - 2800**
28in (71cm)   **3500 - 3800**
31in (79cm) exceptionally beautiful,
   at auction   **5500**
#979:
   14 - 17in (36 - 43cm)   **2700 - 3200**
Kid Body:
#720, 740, 940, 950:
   9 - 10in (23 - 25cm)   **500 - 600**
   16 - 18in (41 - 46cm) **1300 - 1500**
   22in (56cm)   **1800**
#949:
   18 - 21in (46 - 53cm) **1600 - 2000**
S.H. (no mold number)
   13 - 15in (33 - 38cm) **1300 - 1500**
   19in (48cm) Fashion-type
                          2500 - 3000
Young lady. Composition body. See color
   photograph on page 351.
   8 - 9in (20 - 23cm)   **2700****
   Twill covered body
   9in (23cm)   **2700****

**Not enough price samples to compute a
reliable range.

All-Bisque Child: 1880 - on. All-bisque
child with swivel neck, pegged shoulders and hips; appropriate mohair wig,
glass eyes, open or closed mouth;
molded stockings and shoes.
#886 & 890:
Over-the-knee black stockings.
   5½ - 6in (14 - 15cm)   **$ 625 - 675***
   7 - 7½in (18 - 19cm)   **750 - 800***
   8½in (22cm)   **1000 - 1100***
Early model with five-strap bootines,
closed mouth:
   7 - 8in (18 - 20cm)   **1250 - 1500**
#887, Black
   7in (18cm)   **1200 - 1300**

*Allow extra for original clothes and/or blue
stockings.

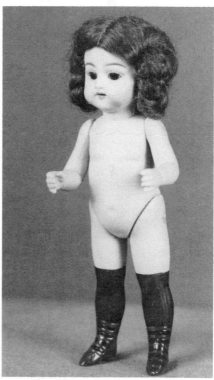

7in (18cm) 886 all-bisque child with long black
hose and brown multi-strap boots. *H & J
Foulke, Inc.*

Simon & Halbig continued

24in (61cm) 1009 child. See color photograph on page 350. *H & J Foulke, Inc.*

Child doll with open mouth and composition body: Ca. 1889 to 1930s. Perfect bisque head, good wig, sleep or paperweight eyes, open mouth, pierced ears; original ball-jointed composition body; very pretty clothes; all in nice condition. See *Simon & Halbig Dolls - The Artful Aspect* for photographs of mold numbers not shown here.

#719, 739, 749, 939:

12 - 14in (31 - 36cm)	**$1200 - 1400**
19 - 22in (48 - 56cm)	**2000 - 2400**
29 - 30in (74 - 76cm)	**3000 - 3500**

#949:

19 - 21in (48 - 53cm)	**1500 - 1900**
25in (64cm)	**2300**

#1039:

23 - 25in (58 - 64cm)	**950 - 1050**

#1078, 1079:

10 - 12in (25 - 31cm)	**550 - 600**
14 - 15in (36 - 38cm)	**600 - 650**
17 - 19in (43 - 48cm)	**650 - 700**
22 - 24in (56 - 61cm)	**725 - 800**

28 - 30in (71 - 76cm)	**1100 - 1300**
34 - 35in (86 - 89cm)	**1800 - 2100**
42in (107cm)	**3500 - 3800**

#1009:

15 - 16in (38 - 41cm)	**900 - 1000**
19 - 21in (48 - 53cm)	**1200 - 1500**
24in (61cm)	**1800**

#1248, 1249, Santa: (For photograph see page 9.)

13 - 15in (33 - 38cm)	**850 - 900**
21 - 24in (53 - 61cm)	**1200 - 1400**
26 - 28in (66 - 71cm)	**1600 - 1800**
32in (81cm)	**2200**
38in (96cm)	**3100**

#1039 key-wind walking body:

16 - 17in (41 - 43cm)	**1700 - 1800**

#1039 walking, kissing:

20 - 22in (51 - 56cm)	**900 - 1100**

#540, 550, 570, Baby Blanche:

22 - 24in (56 - 61cm)	**625 - 675**

#600:

14in (36cm)	**850**

Simon & Halbig continued

Child doll with open mouth and kid body:
Ca. 1889 to 1930s. Perfect bisque swivel head on shoulder plate or shoulder head with stationary neck, sleep eyes, open mouth, pierced ears; kid body, bisque arms, cloth lower legs; well costumed; all in good condition.

#1010, 1040, 1080:

9½in (24cm) cloth body	**$ 325**
14 - 16in (36 - 41cm)	**450 - 500**
21 - 23in (53 - 58cm)	**650 - 700**

#1009: See color photograph on page 350.

17 - 19in (43 - 48cm)	**800 - 900**

#1250, 1260:

14 - 16in (36 - 41cm)	**475 - 525**
22 - 24in (56 - 61cm)	**775 - 825**
29in (74cm)	**1000**

#949:

19 - 21in (48 - 53cm)	**1250 - 1350**

Tiny Child doll: Ca. 1889 to 1930s. Usually mold number *1079* or *1078*. Perfect bisque head, nice wig, sleep eyes, open mouth; composition body with molded shoes and socks; appropriate clothes; all in good condition.

7 - 8in (18 - 20cm)	**$ 375 - 400**
10in (25cm) walker, five-piece body	**600 - 625**

Fully-jointed:

8 - 10in (20 - 25cm)	**550 - 600**

7in (18cm) in trunk with trousseau, all original gift set	**1000**

So-called Little Women type: Ca. 1900. Mold number *1160*. Shoulder head with fancy mohair wig, glass set eyes, closed mouth; cloth body with bisque limbs, molded boots; dressed; all in good condition. (For photograph see *9th Blue Book*, page 365.)

5½ - 7in (14 - 18cm)	**$325 - 375**
10 - 11in (25 - 28cm)	**425 - 475**
Head only: 1½ - 2½in (4 - 6cm)	**60 - 80**
2½ - 3in (6 - 8cm)	**130**

Character Child: Ca. 1909. Perfect bisque socket head with wig or molded hair, painted or glass eyes, open or closed mouth, character face, jointed composition body; dressed; all in good condition. (See *Simon & Halbig Dolls - The Artful Aspect* for photographs of mold numbers not shown here.)

#120: 28 - 30in (71 - 76cm)	**$ 3000 - 4000**
#150: 17in (43cm)	**16,000 - 20,000****
#151: 12 - 15in (31 - 38cm)	**4400 - 4600**
18 - 19in (46 - 48cm)	**6500**

**Not enough price samples to compute a reliable range.

9in (23cm) 1309 character children, all original. See color photograph on page 350. *H & J Foulke, Inc.*

#153: 13in (33cm)   **22,000****
#1279: See color photograph on page 351.

12 - 14in (31 - 36cm)	**1700 - 1800**
22 - 25in (56 - 64cm)	**3200 - 3700**
32 - 34in (81 - 86cm)	**7000 - 7500**

#1299:   **1000 - 1100**
#1339: 18in (46cm)   **1000 - 1100**
   28 - 32in (71 - 81cm)   **1900 - 2100**
#1388: 23in (58cm)   **18,000****
#1398: 23in (58cm)   **18,000****
IV, #1448: 18in (46cm)
   20,000**
#1309: See color photograph on page 350.
   9in (23cm)   **2200 pair****
#603: See color photograph on page 351.
   9in (23cm)   **5500****

Character Baby: Ca. 1909 to 1930s. Perfect bisque head, molded hair or wig, sleep or painted eyes, open or open/closed mouth; composition bent-limb baby or toddler body; nicely dressed; all in good condition. (See *Simon & Halbig Dolls - The Artful Aspect* for photographs of mold numbers not shown here.)
#1294:
Baby, 17 - 19in (43 - 48cm)
   $ 675 - 750

23 - 25in (58 - 64cm)	**1100 - 1300**
Toddler, 20in (51cm)	**1100 - 1200**

#1428:

Baby, 12 - 13in (31 - 33cm)	**1000 - 1100**
Toddler 18in (46cm)	**1800 - 1900**
25in (64cm)	**2500 - 2800**

#1488:
Toddler, 14 - 15in (36 - 38cm)
   3000 - 3200
   22 - 24in (56 - 61cm)   **3800 - 4000**
#1489, Erika: See color photograph on page 352.
   Baby, 21 - 22in (53 - 56cm) **3300 - 3700**
#1498:
   Toddler, 17in (43cm)   **3000 - 3200**
#172 Baby: See color photograph on page 353.
   3400 - 3500

Lady doll: Ca. 1910. Perfect bisque socket head, good wig, sleep eyes, pierced ears; lady body, molded bust, slim arms and legs; dressed; all in good condition.
#1159:

12in (31cm)	**$ 850 - 950**
16 - 18in (41 - 46cm)	**1350 - 1650**
22in (56cm)	**2300 - 2400**
26 - 27in (66 - 69cm)	**2600 - 2800**

#1468, 1469:
   13 - 15in (33 - 38cm) Naked
   2000 - 2200
   Original clothes   **3000 - 4200**
#1303 Lady:
   15 - 16in (38 - 41cm) **10,000 - 12,000****
#152:

18in (46cm)	**15,000 up****
25in (64cm)	**25,000****

#1308 Man:
   13in (33cm)   **5500****
#1307: See color photograph on page 352.
   21in (53cm)   **20,000****
#1303 Indian: 21in (53cm)
   7000

**Not enough price samples to compute a reliable range.

S&H 1469 lady, all original. *Courtesy of Rosalie Whyel.*

Snow Babies

Maker: Various German firms including Hertwig & Co. and Bähr & Pröschild after 1910.
Date: Ca. 1890 until World War II
Material: All-bisque
Size: 1 - 3in (3 - 8cm) usually
Mark: Sometimes "Germany"

Snow Babies: All-bisque with snowsuits and caps of pebbly-textured bisque; painted features; various standing, lying or sitting positions.

1½in (4cm)	**$ 40**
2½in (6cm)	**100 - 125**
3in (9cm) huskies pulling sled with snow baby	**200**
2½in (6cm) snowman	**95**
3in (8cm) baby riding snow bear	**200**
2½in (6cm) tumbling snow baby	**125 - 140**
2in (5cm) musical snow baby	**85**
2in (5cm) baby on sled	**90**
3in (8cm) baby on sled	**175**
2in (5cm) reindeer pulling snow baby	**200**
2in (5cm) early fine quality babies with high hoods	**125 - 140**
3 small babies on sled	**150**
Santa on snow bear	**350**
2½in (6cm) babies sliding on cellar door	**200**
2in (5cm) snow dog and snow man on sled	**200**
Santa going down chimney	**250**
Snow bears	**40 - 75**
Snow boy or girl on sled	**125 - 135**

Girl rolling large snowball. *H & J Foulke, Inc.*

Snow baby riding sled. *H & J Foulke, Inc.*

Sonneberg Taüfling
(So-called Motschmann Baby)

Maker: Various Sonneberg factories such as Heinrich Stier; many handled by exporter Louis Lindner & Söhn, Sonneberg, Thüringia, Germany
Date: 1851 - 1880s
Material: Papier-mâché, wood and cloth
Size: 8in (20cm) to about 28in (71cm)
Mark: None

Sonneberg Täufling: Papier-mâché or wax-over-composition head with painted hair or wig, glass eyes, closed mouth or open mouth with bamboo teeth; composition lower torso; composition arms and legs jointed at ankles and wrists, cloth covered midsection with voice box, upper arms and legs cloth covered, called floating joints; dressed in shirt and bonnet.

Very good condition:

12 - 14in (31 - 36cm)	$ 600 -	650
18 - 20in (46 - 51cm)	900 -	1100
24in (61cm)	1450 -	1650

Fair condition, with wear:

12 - 14in (31 - 36cm)	400 -	450
18 - 20in (46 - 51cm)	650 -	750
24in (61cm)	850 -	950

NOTE: For many years it was thought that these dolls were made by Ch. Motschmann, since some were found stamped with his name; hence, they were called *Motschmann Babies* by collectors. However, research has shown that they were made by various factories and that Motschmann was the holder of the patent for the voice boxes, not the manufacturer of the dolls.

21in (53cm) Sonneberg Täufling. *H & J Foulke, Inc.*

Steiff

Maker: Fraulein Margarete Steiff, Würtemberg, Germany
Date: 1894 - on
Material: Felt, plush or velvet
Size: Various
Mark: Metal button in ear

Steiff Doll: Felt, plush or velvet, jointed; seam down middle of face, button eyes, painted features; original clothes; most are character dolls, many have large shoes to enable them to stand; all in good condition; some wear acceptable.

Children (Character Dolls):
  11 - 12in (28 - 31cm)
    $ 900
  16 - 17in (41 - 43cm)
    1300 - 1500
Caricature or Comic
  Dolls: **1400 - 4000***
  12in (31cm) *Gnome*
    1400
  18in (46cm) Soldiers
    3000 - 4000
  9in (23cm) *Mickey Mouse* **1000**
  Minnie Mouse
    1750
17in (43cm) clown
    2200
Moritz on wheel toy
    3300

*Depending upon rarity, condition and accessories.

See color photograph on page 353.

16in (41cm) Steiff man with button in ear. *Nancy A. Smith Collection.*

E.U. Steiner

Maker: Edmund Ulrich Steiner, doll factory, Sonneberg, Thüringia, Germany
Date: 1864 - on
Material: Bisque heads, kid, cloth or composition body
Trademark: Magestic
Mark:

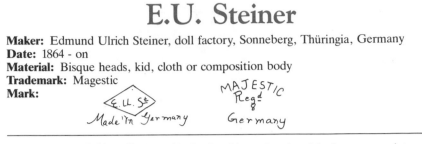

E.U. Steiner Child Doll: Ca. 1902. Perfect bisque head, original or appropriate wig, sleep or set glass eyes, open mouth; ball-jointed composition body or kid body; appropriately dressed; entire doll in good condition.

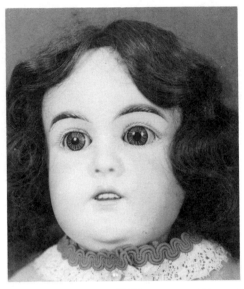

Kid body:
    14 - 16in (36 - 41cm)
        $250 - 275
    22 - 24in (56 - 61cm)
        375 - 425
Composition body:
    15 - 17in (38 - 43cm)
        325 - 375
    23 - 25in (58 - 64cm)
        450 - 500

28in (71cm) Magestic girl. *H & J Foulke, Inc.*

Herm Steiner

Maker: Hermann Steiner of Sonneberg, Thüringia, Germany
Date: 1921 - on
Material: Bisque head, cloth or composition body
Size: Various, usually small
Mark:

15
HS
Germany
240

Herm Steiner
HS
Germany

Herm Steiner continued

Herm Steiner Child: Perfect bisque head, wig, sleep eyes, open mouth; jointed composition body; dressed; in good condition.
7 - 8in (18 - 20cm)
    $150 - 175
14 - 16in (36 - 41cm)
    300 - 325
#128 with special eye movement
14in (36cm)   **350 - 375****

Herm Steiner Character Child: Perfect bisque head, molded hair and features; five-piece composition body; dressed, all in good condition.
7in (18cm)   **$250**

6¾in (17cm) Herm Steiner character child. See color photograph on page 354. *H & J Foulke, Inc.*

12in (31cm) Herm Steiner character baby, unusual model with open mouth and two lower teeth. *Richard Wright Antiques.*

Herm Steiner Infant: Perfect bisque head, molded hair, sleep eyes, closed mouth; cloth or composition bent-limb body; dressed; in good condition.
Head circumference:
    7 - 8in (18 - 20in)   **$225**
    10 - 11in (25 - 28cm)   **275**

Herm Steiner Character Baby: Perfect bisque socket head, good wig, sleep eyes, open mouth with teeth; composition jointed baby body; dressed; all in good condition.
9 - 11in (23 - 28cm)
    $250 - 285

**Not enough price samples to compute a reliable range.

Jules Steiner

Maker: Jules Nicolas Steiner and Successors, Paris, France
Date: 1855 - 1908
Material: Bisque head, jointed papier-mâché body

Marked C or A Series Steiner Bébé: 1880s.
Perfect socket head, cardboard pate, appropriate wig, sleep eyes with wire mechanism, bulgy paperweight eyes with tinting on upper eyelids, closed mouth, round face, pierced ears with tinted tips; jointed composition body with straight wrists and stubby fingers (sometimes with bisque hands); dressed; all in good condition. Sometimes with wire-operated sleep eyes. Sizes 4/0 (8in) to 8 (38in). Series "C" more easily found than "A." See color photograph on page 354.

Mark: (incised)

$S^{IE} \ A \ O$

(red script)

(incised)

$S^{IE} \ C \ 4$

(red stamp)

J. STEINER B. S. G.D.G.

8in (20cm)	**$3200 - 3500**
10in (25cm)	**3200 - 3500**
15 - 16in (38 - 41cm)	**4400 - 4900**
21 - 24in (53 - 61cm)	**6300 - 7300**
28in (71cm)	**8000 - 9000**
Motschmann-type body, 9½in (24cm) with wardrobe	**8500****

**Not enough price samples to compute a reliable range.

J Steiner. Bte Sg. Bg. J Bourgoin Se.

22½in (57cm) Series A, size 4 Bourgoin Steiner. *Kay & Wayne Jensen Collection.*

Jules Steiner continued

Round face with open mouth:
Ca. 1870s. Perfect very pale
bisque socket head, appropriate wig, bulgy paper-
weight eyes, open mouth
with pointed teeth, round
face, pierced ears; jointed
composition body; dressed;
all in good condition.

Mark: None, but some-
times body has a label

Two rows of teeth, (For photograph see *8th Blue Book*, page
378.)

18 - 20in (46 - 51cm)
$3000**

Kicking, crying bébé, mechani-
cal key-wind body with composition arms and lower legs. (For
photograph see *9th Blue Book*,
page 374.)

2100 - 2300

Motschmann-type body with
bisque shoulders, hips and
lower arms and legs. (For photograph see *7th Blue Book*,
page 361 and color photograph
on page 220.)

18 - 21in (46 - 53cm)
6500**

**Not enough price samples to
compute a reliable range.

Figure A or C Bébé: Ca. 1887 -
on. Perfect bisque socket
head, cardboard pate, ap-
propriate wig, paperweight
eyes, closed mouth, pierced
ears; jointed composition
body; dressed; all in good
condition. Figure "A" more
easily found than "C."

Mark: (incised)

J. STEINER
B^TE S.G.D.G.
PARIS
FIRE A 15

28in (71cm) Figure A, size 19 Steiner. *Private Collection.*

16in (41cm) Figure C Steiner. See color photograph on
page 354. *Private Collection.*

Jules Steiner continued

Body and/or head may be stamped:
"Le Petit Parisien
BEBE STEINER
MEDAILLE d'OR
PARIS 1889"
or paper label of doll carrying flag

8in (20cm)	**$ 2600 - 3000**
10in (25cm)	**3000 - 3300**
15 - 16in (38 - 41cm)	**4200 - 4700**
22 - 25in (56 - 64cm)	**6300 - 7300**
28in (71cm)	**7700 - 8000**
34in (86cm), at auction	**11,000**
17in (43cm) lovely face, all original, at auction	**6000**
Open mouth, 17in (43cm)	**2500**

*Allow slightly more for Figure C.

14in (36cm) Le Parisien Bébé, A-7. *Private Collection.*

Bébé Le Parisien: 1892 - on. Perfect bisque socket head, cardboard pate, appropriate wig, paperweight eyes, closed or open mouth, pierced ears; jointed composition body; dressed; all in good condition. See color photograph on page 355.
Mark: head (incised):

A -19
PARIS

(red stamp):
"LE PARISIEN"
body (purple stamp):
"BEBE 'LE PARISIEN'
MEDAILLE D'OR
PARIS"

Closed mouth:

13 - 15in (33 - 38cm)	**$3500 - 4000**
18 - 20in (46 - 51cm)	**5000 - 5500**
23 - 25in (58 - 64cm)	**6000 - 7000**

Open mouth:

20 - 22in (51 - 56cm)	**2600 - 2800**

Figure B Bébé:
Open mouth:

24in (61cm)	**5000****
33in (84cm)	**7200****

**Not enough price samples to compute a reliable range.

Swaine & Co.

Maker: Swaine & Co., porcelain factory, Hüttensteinach, Sonneberg, Thüringia, Germany
Date: Ca. 1910 - on for doll heads
Material: Bisque socket head, composition baby body
Mark: Stamped in green:

Swaine Character Babies: Ca. 1910 - on. Perfect bisque head; composition baby body with bent limbs; dressed; all in good condition.

Incised Lori: (molded hair, glass eyes, open/closed mouth)
  22 - 24in (56 - 61cm)   **$2800 - 3200**
#232: (open-mouth *Lori*):
  20 - 22in (51 - 56cm)   **1600 - 1800**
DIP: (wig, glass eyes, closed mouth):
  9 - 10in (23 - 25cm)   **650 - 750**
  15in (38cm)   **1200 - 1300**
  17in (43cm) toddler   **1800**
DV: (molded hair, glass eyes open/closed mouth):
  12 - 14in (31 - 36cm)   **1300 - 1500**
DI: (molded hair, intaglio eyes, open/closed mouth):
  12 - 13in (31 - 33cm)   **825 - 875**
B.P., B.O.: (smiling character):
  16 - 18in (41 - 46cm)   **4000****
F.P.:
  9in (23cm)   **1600****

**Not enough price samples to compute a reliable range.

For photographs see **Doll Reader®**, April 1989, pages 156 to 159.

13in (33cm) D 1 character baby. See color photograph on page 356. *H & J Foulke, Inc.*

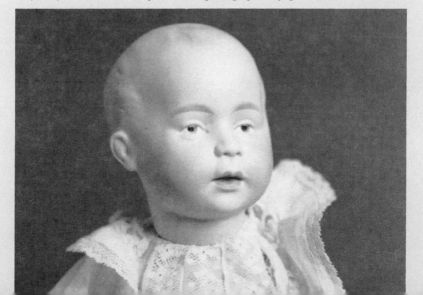

Terri Lee

Maker: TERRI LEE Sales Corp., V. Gradwohl, Pres., U.S.A.
Date: 1946-Lincoln, Neb.,; then Apple Valley, Calif., from 1952-Ca. 1962
Material: First dolls, rubbery plastic composition; later, hard plastic
Size: 16in (41cm) and 10in (25cm)
Mark: embossed across shoulders
   First dolls:

> "TERRI LEE
> PAT. PENDING"

   raised letters
   Later dolls: "TERRI LEE"

Terri Lee Child Doll: Original wig, painted eyes; jointed at neck, shoulders and hips; all original clothing and accessories; very good condition. 16in (41cm): See color photograph on page 356. **$ 225 - 275***

Patty-Jo (black),	**450 - 475**
Jerri Lee,	
16in (41cm)	**225 - 275**
Benjie (black),	**500**
Tiny Terri Lee, inset eyes, (For photograph see *8th Blue Book*, page 381.)	
10in (25cm)	**135 - 150**
Tiny Jerri Lee, inset eyes,	
10in (25cm)	**185**
Connie Lynn,	**350 - 400**
Gene Autry,	**1500****
Linda Baby, (For photograph see *8th Blue Book*, page 381.)	
Ginger Girl Scout,	
8in (20cm)	**100 - 110**

*Allow extra for special outfits and gowns.
**Not enough price samples to compute a reliable range.

16in (41cm) *Terri Lee*, all original with wrist flower. *H & J Foulke, Inc.*

Thuillier

Maker: A. Thuillier, Paris, France. Some heads by F. Gaultier.
Date: 1875 - 1893
Material: Bisque socket head on wood, kid or composition body $A.8.T.$
Mark:

AT·N° 8

Marked A. T. Child: Perfect bisque head, cork pate, good wig, paperweight eyes, pierced ears, closed mouth; body of wood, kid or composition in good condition; appropriate old wig and clothes, excellent quality.

12 - 13in (31 - 33cm)	**$38,000 - 45,000**
16 - 18in (41 - 46cm)	**52,000 - 58,000**
22 - 24in (56 - 61cm)	**63,000 - 68,000**
23in (58cm) all original, at auction	**75,000**

See color photograph on page 17.

Approximate size chart:
1 = 9in (23cm)
3 = 12in (31cm)
7 = 15½in (39cm)
9 = 18in (46cm)
12 = 22 - 23in (56 - 58cm)

12in (31cm) A 3 T Bébé. *Private Collection.*

Unis

Maker: Société Française de Fabrication de Bébés et Jouets.
(S. F. B. J.) of Paris and Montruil-sous-Bois, France
Date: 1922 - on
Material: Bisque head, composition body
Size: 5in (13cm) up
Mark: 71 ⟨UNIS FRANCE⟩ 142
301

13in (33cm) Unis 60 child, all original. *Esther Schwartz Collection.*

Unis Child Doll: Perfect bisque head, wood and composition jointed body; good wig, sleep eyes, open mouth; pretty clothes; all in nice condition.

#301 or 60 (fully-jointed body):

8 - 10in (20 - 25cm)	**$ 400 -**	**450**
15 - 17in (38 - 43cm)	**550 -**	**600**
23 - 25in (58 - 64cm)	**850 -**	**950**
28in (71cm) original box	**1300**	

Five-piece body:

5in (13cm) painted eyes	**135 -**	**165**
6½in (17cm) glass eyes	**190 -**	**210**
11 - 13in (28 - 33cm)	**300 -**	**325**
Black or brown bisque,		
11 - 13in (28 - 33cm)	**350 -**	**375**

Princess (See page 264):
#251 character toddler:

14 - 15in (36 - 38cm)	**1300 -**	**1400**

Composition head 301 or 60:

11 - 13in (28 - 33cm)	**150 -**	**175**
20in (51cm)	**350 -**	**400**

Composition head #251 or #247 Toddler,

22in (56cm)	**650**

Vogue-Ginny_s

Maker: Vogue Dolls, Inc.
Date: 1937 - on
Material: 1937 - 1948 composition, 1948 - 1962 hard plastic
Size: 7 - 8in (18 - 20cm)
Creator: Jennie Graves
Clothes Designer: Virginia Graves Carlson
Clothes Label: "Vogue," "Vogue Dolls," or

> VOGUE DOLLS, INC.
> MEDFORD, MASS. USA
> ® REG U.S. PAT OFF

All-composition Toddles: Jointed neck, shoulders and hips; molded hair or mohair wig, painted eyes looking to side; original clothes; all in good condition.

Mark: "VOGUE" on head
"DOLL CO." on back
"TODDLES" stamped on sole
of shoe

7 - 8in (18 - 20cm)	**$200 - 225**
Mint condition	**250 - 275**

Hard Plastic Ginny: All-hard plastic, jointed at neck, shoulders and hips (some have jointed knees and some walk); nice wig, sleep eyes (early ones have painted eyes, later dolls have molded eyelashes); original clothes; all in excellent condition with perfect hair and pretty coloring.

Mark: On strung dolls: "VOGUE DOLLS"
On walking dolls: "GINNY// VOGUE DOLLS"

Willie with caracul wig, all original. *H & J Foulke, Inc.*

Toddles boy, all original. *H & J Foulke, Inc.*

Vogue-Ginny continued

Tyrolean pair, strung, all original. *H & J Foulke, Inc.*

7 - 8in (18 - 20cm):
  1948 - 1949:
    Painted eyes   **$225 - 325***
    Separate outfits   **50 - 65**
  1950 - 1953:
    Painted eyelashes, strung, **225 - 275***
    Caracul wig   **325 - 350**
    Separate outfits   **50 - 65**
  1954:
    Painted eyelashes, walks   **175 - 225***
    Separate outfits   **45 - 55**
  1955 - 1957:
    Molded eyelashes, walks   **125 - 150***
    Separate outfits   **40 - 50**
  1957 - 1962:
    Molded eyelashes, walks, jointed knees
                             100 - 125*
    Separate outfits   **30 - 40**
  Black Ginny   **700 up**
  Crib Crowd Baby, 1950   **600***

*Allow extra for mint-in-box dolls.

Ginny Bunny, all original. *H & J Foulke, Inc.*

Vogue-Ginny continued

Accessories:

Ginny's Pup	**$150**
Cardboard Suitcase with contents	**40**
Parasol	**15**
Gym Set	**250 - 275**
Dresser, Bed, Rocking Chair, Wardrobe,	**55 each**
Shoe Bag with shoes	**35 - 40**
Luggage Set	**100**
School Bag	**75 - 85**
"Hi I'm Ginny" Pin	**50**
Ginny's First Secret Book	**125**

Ginny walker, painted lashes, all original. *H & J Foulke, Inc.*

Ginny's Pup, all original and boxed. *H & J Foulke, Inc.*

Wagner & Zetzsche

Maker: Wagner & Zetzsche, doll factory, Ilmenau, Thüringia, Germany. Bisque heads by porcelain factories including Gebrüder Heubach and Alt, Beck & Gottschalck
Date: 1875 - on
Material: Bisque head, cloth, kid or composition body, celluloid-type heads

---

Closed-mouth Child: Ca. 1880s. Perfect turned bisque shoulder head with solid dome (mold *639*) or open crown (mold *698*), sometimes with plaster dome, mohair wig, paperweight eyes (a few with sleep eyes), flat eyebrows, closed mouth, small ears; kid or cloth body with bisque hands; appropriate clothes; all in good condition.
   Mark: Blue paper body label with "W Z" initials entwined in fancy scroll.

15 - 17in (38 - 43cm)	$ 700 - 800
20 - 22in (51 - 56cm)	950 - 1150
26in (66cm)	1400

Character Baby or Child: Ca. 1910. Perfect bisque socket head, wig, sleep eyes, open mouth with upper teeth; dressed; all in good condition.
Mark:

#10586 made by Gebrüder Heubach.
Baby body,
16 - 18in (41 - 46cm)
$650 - 750
Kid and composition body,
14 - 16in (36 - 41cm)
500 - 600
#10585 (shoulder head, kid body):
16 - 18in (41 - 46cm)
375 - 425

17in (43cm) 698 1/2 head by Alt, Beck & Gottschalck for Wagner & Zetzsche. *Dolly Valk Collection.*

Wagner & Zetzsche continued

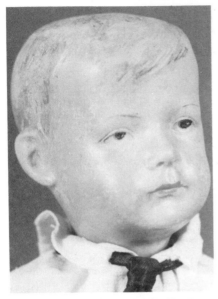

14in (36cm) *Harald. H & J Foulke, Inc.*

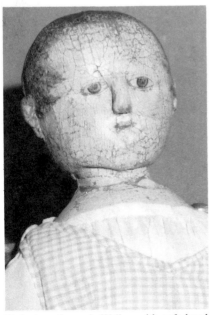

Early type Izannah Walker with soft head. *Elizabeth McIntyre.*

Portrait Children: 1915 - on. Celluloid-type head (*Haralit*) with molded hair, painted eyes. Portraits of the children of Max Zetzsche: *Harold, Hansi,* and *Inge.*

Mark: "Harald
W.Z."
(or name of child)

14in (36cm) *Harald.*
Fair condition   **$250 - 275****
8in (20cm) *Hansi*   **125 - 150**
Inge, 1924, 14in (36cm). For photograph see *8th Blue Book*, page 279.
Excellent   **500 - 550****

**Not enough price samples to compute a reliable range.

Izannah Walker

Maker: Izannah Walker, Central Falls, R.I., U.S.A.
Date: 1873, but probably made as early as 1840s
Material: All-cloth
Size: 15 - 30in (38 - 76cm)
Mark: Later dolls are marked:

" *Patented Nov. 4ᵗʰ 1873* "

Izannah Walker Doll: Stockinette, pressed head, features and hair painted with oils, applied ears, treated limbs; muslin body; appropriate clothes; in good condition.
17 - 19in (43 - 48cm)   **$18,000 - 22,000**
Fair condition,   **8000 - 12,000**
Poor condition,   **3000 - 4000**

See color photograph on page 357.

Wax Doll, Poured

Maker: Various firms in London, England, such as Montanari, Pierotti, Peck, Meech, Marsh, Morrell, Cremer and Edwards
Date: 1850s through the early 1900s
Material: Wax head, arms and legs, cloth body
Mark: Sometimes stamped on body with maker or store

Poured Wax Child: Head, lower arms and legs of wax; cloth body; set-in hair, glass eyes; original clothes or very well dressed; all in good condition. For photograph see *9th Blue Book*, page 385.

17 - 19in (43 - 48cm)	**$1350 - 1650***
24 - 26in (61 - 66cm)	**1900 - 2300***
Lady, 22 - 24in (56 - 61cm)	
	2500 - 3500

Man, 18in (46cm) inset mustache	
	1650 - 1750**
Pierotti, incised on shoulder	
17 - 21in (43 - 53cm)	**1600 - 1800**
Morrell, 18in (46cm) child	
	1800
Montanari, all original and boxed,	
12in (31cm), at auction	**2800**
Lackluster ordinary face	
20 - 22in (51 - 56cm)	**800 - 1000**

*Greatly depending upon appeal of face.

Wax (Reinforced)

Maker: Various firms in Germany
Date: 1860 to 1890
Material: Poured wax shoulder head lined on the inside with plaster composition to give strength and durability, (not to be confused with wax-over-composition which simply has a wax coating), muslin body usually with wax-over-composition lower arms and legs.
Mark: None

Reinforced Poured Wax Doll: Poured wax shoulder head lined on the inside with plaster composition, glass eyes (may sleep), closed mouth, open crown, pate, curly mohair or human hair wig nailed on (may be partially inset into the wax around the face); muslin body with wax-over-composition lower limbs (feet may have molded boots); appropriate clothes; all in good condition, but showing some knicks and scrapes.

16in (41cm) reinforced wax child. *H & J Foulke, Inc.*

11in (28cm)	**$ 250 - 300**
14 - 16in (36 - 41cm)	**375 - 425**
19 - 21in (48 - 53cm)	**550 - 650**
Lady, 23in (58cm)	**1000**
with molded shoulder plate	
	2500**
Socket head on ball-jointed composition body (Kestner-type)	
9in (23cm)	**700****

**Not enough price samples to compute a reliable range.

Wax-Over-Composition

Maker: Numerous firms in England, Germany or France
Date: During the 1800s
Material: Wax-over-shoulder head of some type of composition or papier-mâché, cloth
body, wax-over-composition or wooden limbs
Mark: None

English Slit-head Wax: Ca. 1830 - 1860. Wax-over-shoulder head with round face, not
rewaxed; human hair wig, glass eyes (may open and close by a wire), faintly smiling;
original cloth body with leather arms; original or suitable old clothing; all in fair
condition, showing wear.

14 - 15in (36 - 38cm)	$ 600 - 700
18 - 22in (46 - 56cm)	850 - 950
26in (66cm) all original and excellent	2000
30in (76cm) all original and boxed, cracked face	1100
17in (43cm) case doll, all original	850

Molded Hair Doll: Ca.
1860 - on. German
wax-over-shoulder
head, not rewaxed;
molded hair some-
times with bow, glass
sleep or set eyes; origi-
nal cloth body; wax-
over or wooden ex-
tremities with molded
boots or bare feet; nice
old clothes; all in good
condition, good qual-
ity.

14 - 16in (36 - 41cm)
$275 - 325
22 - 25in (56 - 64cm)
475 - 525
Alice hairdo, 16in (41cm)
Early model, squeaker
torso   550 - 650

21in (53cm) wax-over-composition child. *H & J Foulke, Inc.*

Wax-Over-Composition continued

15in (38cm) Bartenstein baby. *H & J Foulke, Inc.*

Wax Doll With Wig: Ca. 1860s to 1900. German. Wax-over-shoulder head, not rewaxed; blonde or brown human hair or mohair wig, blue, brown or black glass eyes, sleep or set, open or closed mouth; original cloth body, any combination of extremities mentioned above, also arms may be made of china; original clothing or suitably dressed; entire doll in nice condition.

Standard quality:

11 - 12in (28 - 31cm)	**$125 - 150**
16 - 18in (41 - 46cm)	**300 - 325**
22 - 24in (56 - 61cm)	**400 - 450**

Superior quality (heavily waxed):

11 - 12in (28 - 31cm)	**225 - 250**
16 - 18in (41 - 46cm)	**400 - 450**
22 - 24in (56 - 61cm)	**600 - 650**
30in (76cm)	**750**
25in (64cm) lovely, all original	**950**

Bonnet Wax Doll: Ca. 1860 to 1880. Wax-over-shoulder head, with molded bonnet; molded hair may have some mohair or human hair attached, blue, brown or black set eyes; original cloth body and wooden extremities; nice old clothes; all in good condition.

16 - 17in (41 - 43cm) common model	**$ 350 - 450**
20in (51cm) boy with cap	**550 - 600**
21in (53cm) early round face with molded poke bonnet	**2300****
16in (41cm) molded hat perched on forehead	**2500****
24in (61cm) molded blue derby-type hat	**2000****

Double-Faced Doll: 1880 - on. Fritz Bartenstein. One face crying, one laughing, rotating on a vertical axis by pulling a string, one face hidden by a hood. Body stamped "Bartenstein."

15 - 16in (38 - 41cm)	**$850**

**Not enough price samples to compute a reliable range.

Norah Wellings

Maker: Victoria Toy Works, Wellington, Shropshire, England, for Norah Wellings
Date: 1926 - Ca. 1960
Material: Fabric: Felt, velvet and velour, and other material, stuffed
Designer: Norah Wellings
Mark: On tag on foot: "Made in England by Norah Wellings"

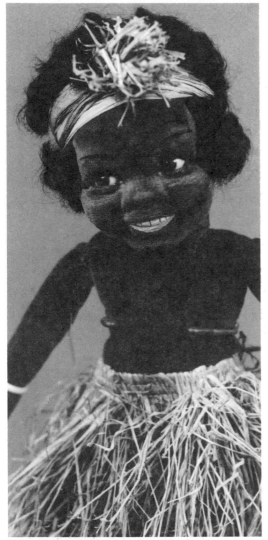

Wellings Doll: All-fabric, stitch-jointed shoulders and hips; molded fabric face (also of papier-mâché, sometimes stockinette covered), painted features; all in excellent condition. Most commonly found are sailors, Canadian Mounties, Scots and Black Islanders.

Characters (floppy limbs):
8 - 10in (20 - 25cm)
$ 50 - 85
13 - 14in (33 - 36cm)
135 - 165

Glass eyes,
14in (36cm) Black
175 - 200

Old Couple,
26in (66cm)   **1200 pair**
Children:
12 - 13in (31 - 33cm)
400 - 500
16 - 18in (41 - 46cm)
600 - 700
23in (58cm)   **1000 - 1200**
Glass eyes,
16 - 18in (41 - 46cm)
700 - 800

14in (36cm) Wellings black girl with glass eyes. *H & J Foulke, Inc.*

Wellington

Maker: Martha L. Wellington, Brookline, Mass., U.S.A.
Date: 1883 - on
Material: Stockinette
Size: 22 - 24in (56 - 61cm)
Mark: Cloth label on back

Wellington Baby: All stockinette with oil painted head and lower limbs, needlesculpted features, painted eyes and hair, distinctive buttocks with rounded cheeks; appropriate old clothes.
Excellent condition
$13,000 up**
Poor to fair condition
4000 - 5000

**Not enough price samples to compute a reliable range.

Wislizenus

Maker: Adolf Wislizenus, doll factory, Waltershausen, Thüringia, Germany. Heads made by Bähr & Pröschild, Simon & Halbig and Ernst Heubach.
Date: 1851 - on
Material: Bisque head, composition ball-jointed body
Trademarks: Old Glory, Special, Queen Quality
Mark:

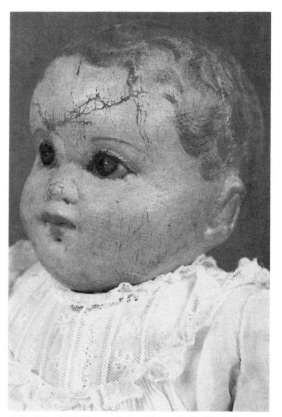

24in (61cm) Wellington baby. *Nancy A. Smith Collection.*

Papier-mâché Shoulder Head: Molded and painted black or blonde hair, painted eyes, closed mouth; cloth body sometimes with leather arms; old or appropriate clothes; all in good condition, showing some wear. (For photograph see *7th Blue Book*, page 303.)

Wislizenus continued

Mark:

A. W.
Serial 3

13 - 15in (33 - 38cm) $250 - 300*
18 - 19in (46 - 48cm)   350 - 400*
23 - 25in (58 - 64cm)   500 - 550*
28in (71cm)   650*
Glass eyes, 18in (46cm)   475

*Allow extra for an unusual hairdo.

Wislizenus Child Doll: Ca. 1890 - on. Perfect bisque head, composition ball-jointed body; good wig; blue or brown sleep eyes, open mouth; dressed; all in good condition.

17 - 19in (43 - 48cm)   **$375 - 425**
23 - 25in (58 - 64cm)   **525 - 575**

Wislizenus Character Doll: Ca. 1910. Perfect bisque socket head, molded hair, painted or glass eyes, open/closed mouth with molded teeth; composition toddler body; dressed; all in good condition. (For photograph see *8th Blue Book*, page 394.)

#110 or *115:*
16 - 18in (41 - 46cm)   **$1000 - 1200**
#110 glass eyes,
14in (36cm), at auction   **4500****

Marked A.W. Character: Ca. 1910. Perfect bisque socket head, good wig, sleep eyes, open/closed mouth with molded tongue and two separated porcelain teeth; bent-limb baby body. (For photograph see *7th Blue Book*, page 379.)
26in (66cm)
$1800 - 2000**

**Not enough price samples to compute available range.

22in (56cm) Special. *H & J Foulke, Inc.*

Wood, English

Maker: English craftsmen
Date: Late 17th to mid 19th century
Material: All-wood or with leather or cloth arms
Mark: None

William & Mary Period: Ca. 1690. Carved wooden face, painted eyes, tiny lines comprising eyebrows and eyelashes, rouged cheeks, flax or hair wig; wood body, cloth arms, carved wood hands (fork shaped), wood-jointed legs. Appropriate clothes; all in fair condition.

12 - 17in (31 - 43cm)	**$50,000 up**

Queen Anne Period: Ca. early 1700s. Carved wooden face, dark glass eyes (sometimes painted), dotted eyebrows and eyelashes; jointed wood body, cloth upper arms; appropriate clothes; all in fair condition.

24in (61cm)	**$25,000 up**
29in (74cm) all original with box, at auction	**69,800**

Georgian Period: Mid to late 1700s. Round wooden head with gesso covering, inset glass eyes (later sometimes blue), dotted eyelashes and eyebrows, flax or hair wig; jointed wood body with pointed torso; appropriate clothes; all in fair condition.

12 - 13in (31 - 33cm)	**$2500 - 3000**
16 - 18in (41 - 46cm)	**4500 - 5000**
24in (61cm)	**6000 - 6500**

Early 19th Century: Wooden head, gessoed, painted eyes, pointed torso, flax or hair wig; old clothes (dress usually longer than legs); all in fair condition.

13in (33cm)	**$1300 - 1600**
16 - 21in (41 - 53cm)	**2000 - 3000**

For additional photographs see *9th Blue Book*, pages 222 and 223.

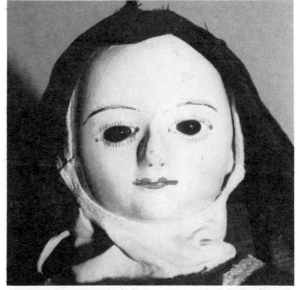

15in (38cm) English wood, Queen Anne period. *Richard Wright Antiques.*

Wood German
(Early)

Maker: Craftsmen of the Grodner Tal, Austria, and Sonneberg, Germany, such as Insam & Prinoth (1820 - 1830) Gorden Tirol and Nürnberg verlegers of peg-wood dolls and wood doll heads.
Date: Late 18th to 20th century
Material: All-wood, pegged or ball-jointed
Mark: None

Early to Mid 19th Century: Delicately carved head, varnished, carved and painted hair and features, with a yellow tuck comb in hair, painted spit curls, sometimes earrings; mortise and tenon peg joints; old clothes; all in fair condition.

14in (36cm) early 19th century German wood; real gold used to gild comb and earrings. *Richard Wright Antiques.*

6 - 7in (15 - 18cm)**$ 650 - 750**
12 - 13in (31 - 33cm)
1350 - 1450
17 - 18in (43 - 46cm)
1800 - 2000
9in (23cm) exceptional all original condition **1700 - 1750**
Fortune Tellers
17 - 20in (43 - 51cm)
2500 - 3000

See color photograph on page 358.

Late 19th Century: Wooden head with painted hair, carving not so elaborate as previously, sometimes earrings, spit curls; dressed; all in good condition.
4in (10cm) **$125**
7 - 8in (18 - 20cm) **175 - 225**
12in (31cm) **350**
Wood shoulder head, carved bun hairdo, cloth body, wood limbs:
9in (23cm) all original
$350
17in (43cm) **500**
24in (61cm) **800**

Early 20th century: Turned wood head, carved nose, painted hair, peg-jointed, painted white lower legs, painted black shoes.
11 - 12in (28 - 31cm)
$50 - 75

Wood, German
(Later)

Maker: Various companies, such as Rudolf Schneider and Schilling, Sonneberg, Thüringia, Germany
Date: 1901 - 1914
Material: All-wood, fully jointed or wood head and limbs, cloth body
Mark: Usually none; sometimes Schilling "winged angel" trademark

---

"Bébé Tout en Bois" (Doll all of Wood): All of wood, fully jointed; wig, inset glass eyes, open mouth with teeth; appropriate clothes; all in fair to good condition.

10 - 13in (25 - 33cm)	**$350 - 425**
17 - 19in (43 - 48cm)	**600 - 700**
22 - 24in (56 - 61cm)	**850**

13in (33cm) German all-wood doll. *H & J Foulke, Inc.*

Wood, Swiss

Maker: Various Swiss firms
Date: 20th century
Material: All-wood or wood head and limbs on cloth body
Size: Various, but smaller sizes are more commonly found
Mark: Usually a paper label on wrist or clothes

Swiss Wooden Doll: Wooden head with hand-carved features and hair with good detail (males sometimes have carved hats); all carved wood jointed body; original, usually regional attire; excellent condition.

9 - 10in (23 - 25cm)	**$225 - 250**
12in (31cm)	**350**
18in (46cm)	**650 - 750**

10½in (27cm) Swiss wood girl, all original with label. *H & J Foulke, Inc.*

Glossary

Applied Ears: Ear molded independently and affixed to the head. (On most dolls the ear is included as part of the head mold.)

Bald Head: Head with no crown opening, could be covered by a wig or have painted hair.

Ball-jointed Body: Usually a body of composition or papier-mâché with wooden balls at knees, elbows, hips and shoulders to make swivel joints; some parts of the limbs may be wood.

Bébé: French child doll with "dolly face."

Belton-type: A bald head with one, two or three small holes for attaching wig.

Bent-limb Baby Body: Composition body of five pieces with chubby torso and curved arms and legs.

Biscaloid: Ceramic or composition substance for making dolls; also called imitation bisque.

Biskoline: Celluloid-type of substance for making dolls.

Bisque: Unglazed porcelain, usually flesh tinted, used for dolls' heads or all-bisque dolls.

Breather: Dolls with an actual opening in each nostril; also called open nostrils.

Breveté (or Bté): Used on French dolls to indicate that the patent is registered.

Character Doll: Dolls with bisque or composition heads, modeled to look lifelike, such as infants, young or older children, young ladies and so on.

China: Glazed porcelain used for dolls' heads and *Frozen Charlottes*.

Child Dolls: Dolls with a typical "dolly face" which represents a child.

Composition: A material used for dolls' heads and bodies, consisting of such items as wood pulp, glue, sawdust, flour, rags and sundry other substances.

Contemporary Clothes: Clothes not original to the doll, but dating from the same period when the doll would have been a plaything.

Crown Opening: The cut-away part of a doll head.

DEP: Abbreviation used on German and French dolls claiming registration.

D.R.G.M.: Abbreviation used on German dolls indicating a registered design or patent.

Dolly Face: Typical face used on bisque dolls before 1910 when the character face was developed; "dolly faces" were used also after 1910.

Embossed Mark: Raised letters, numbers or names on the backs of heads or bodies.

Feathered Eyebrows: Eyebrows composed of many tiny painted brush strokes to give a realistic look.

Fixed Eyes: Glass eyes which do not move or sleep.

Flange Neck: A doll's head with a ridge at the base of the neck which contains holes for sewing the head to a cloth body.

Flapper Dolls: Dolls of the 1920s period with bobbed wig or molded hair and slender arms and legs.

Flirting Eyes: Eyes which move from side to side as doll's head is tilted.

Frozen Charlotte: Doll molded all in one piece including arms and legs.

Ges. (Gesch.): Used on German dolls to indicate design is registered or patented.

Googly Eyes: Large, often round eyes looking to the side; also called roguish or goo goo eyes.

Hard Plastic: Hard material used for making dolls after 1948.

Incised Mark: Letters, numbers or names impressed into the bisque on the back of the head or on the shoulder plate.

Intaglio Eyes: Painted eyes with sunken pupil and iris.

JCB: Jointed composition body. See *ball-jointed body*.

Kid Body: Body of white or pink leather.

Lady Dolls: Dolls with an adult face and a body with adult proportions.

Mohair: Goat's hair widely used in making doll wigs.

Molded Hair: Curls, waves and comb marks which are actually part of the mold and not merely painted onto the head.

Motschmann-type Body: Doll body with cloth midsection and upper limbs with floating joints; hard lower torso and lower limbs.

Open-Mouth: Lips parted with an actual opening in the bisque, usually has teeth either molded in the bisque or set in separately and sometimes a tongue.

Open/Closed Mouth: A mouth molded to appear open, but having no actual slit in the bisque.

Original Clothes: Clothes belonging to a doll during the childhood of the original owner, either commercially or homemade.

Painted Bisque: Bisque covered with a layer of flesh-colored paint which has not been baked in, so will easily rub or wash off.

Paperweight Eyes: Blown glass eyes which have depth and look real, usually found in French dolls.

Papier-mâché: A material used for dolls' heads and bodies, consisting of paper pulp, sizing, glue, clay or flour.

Pate: A shaped piece of plaster, cork, cardboard or other material which covers the crown opening.

Pierced Ears: Little holes through the doll's earlobes to accommodate earrings.

Pierced-in Ears: A hole at the doll's earlobe which goes into the head to accommodate earrings.

Pink Bisque: A later bisque of about 1920 which was pre-colored pink.

Pink-toned China: China which has been given a pink tint to look more like real flesh color; also called lustered china.

Rembrandt Hair: Hair style parted in center with bangs at front, straight down sides and back and curled at ends.

S.G.D.G.: Used on French dolls to indicate that the patent is registered "without guarantee of the government."

Shoulder Head: A doll's head and shoulders all in one piece.

Shoulder Plate: The actual shoulder portion sometimes molded in one with the head, sometimes a separate piece with a socket in which a head is inserted.

Socket Head: Head and neck which fit into an opening in the shoulder plate or the body.

Solid-dome Head: Head with no crown opening, could have painted hair or be covered by wig.

Stationary Eyes: Glass eyes which do not move or sleep.

Stone Bisque: Coarse white bisque of a lesser quality.

Toddler Body: Usually a chubby ball-jointed composition body with chunky, shorter thighs and a diagonal hip joint; sometimes has curved instead of jointed arms; sometimes is of five pieces with straight chubby legs.

Topsy-Turvy: Doll with two heads, one usually concealed beneath a skirt.

Turned Shoulder Head: Head and shoulders are one piece, but the head is molded at an angle so that the doll is not looking straight ahead.

Vinyl: Soft plastic material used for making dolls after 1950s.

Watermelon Mouth: Closed line-type mouth curved up at each side in an impish expression.

Wax Over: A doll with head and/or limbs of papier-mâché or composition covered with a layer of wax to give a natural, lifelike finish.

Weighted Eyes: Eyes which can be made to sleep by means of a weight which is attached to the eyes.

Wire Eyes: Eyes which can be made to sleep by means of a wire which protrudes from doll's head.

Selected Bibliography

Anderton, Johana. *Twentieth Century Dolls*. North Kansas City, Missouri: Trojan Press, 1971.

_____. *More Twentieth Century Dolls*. North Kansas City, Missouri: Athena Publishing Co., 1974.

Angione, Genevieve. *All-Bisque & Half-Bisque Dolls*. Exton, Pennsylvania: Schiffer Publishing Ltd., 1969.

Borger, Mona. *Chinas, Dolls for Study and Admiration*. San Francisco: Borger Publications, 1983.

Cieslik, Jürgen and Marianne. *German Doll Encyclopedia 1800-1939*. Cumberland, Maryland: Hobby House Press, Inc., 1985.

Coleman, Dorothy S., Elizabeth Ann and Evelyn Jane. *The Collector's Book of Dolls' Clothes*. New York: Crown Publishers, Inc., 1975.

_____. *The Collector's Encyclopedia of Dolls, Vol. I & II*. New York: Crown Publishers, Inc., 1968 & 1986.

Foulke, Jan. *Blue Books of Dolls & Values, Vol. I-IX*. Cumberland, Maryland: Hobby House Press, Inc., 1974-1989.

_____. *Doll Classics*. Cumberland, Maryland: Hobby House Press, Inc., 1987.

_____. *Focusing on Effanbee Composition Dolls*. Riverdale, Maryland: Hobby House Press, 1978.

_____. *Focusing on Gebrüder Heubach Dolls*. Cumberland, Maryland: Hobby House Press, 1980.

_____. *Kestner, King of Dollmakers*. Cumberland, Maryland: Hobby House Press, Inc., 1982.

_____. *Simon & Halbig Dolls, The Artful Aspect*. Cumberland, Maryland: Hobby House Press, Inc., 1984.

_____. *Treasury of Madame Alexander Dolls*. Riverdale, Maryland: Hobby House Press, 1979.

Gerken, Jo Elizabeth. *Wonderful Dolls of Papier-Mâché*. Lincoln, Nebraska: Doll Research Associates, 1970.

Hillier, Mary. *Dolls and Dollmakers*. New York: G. P. Putnam's Sons, 1968.

_____. *The History of Wax Dolls*. Cumberland, Maryland: Hobby House Press, Inc.; London: Justin Knowles, 1985.

King, Constance Eileen. *The Collector's History of Dolls*. London: Robert Hale, 1977; New York: St. Martin's Press, 1978.

Mathes, Ruth E. and Robert C. *Dolls, Toys and Childhood*. Cumberland, Maryland: Hobby House Press, Inc., 1987.

McGonagle, Dorothy A. *The Dolls of Jules Nicolas Steiner*. Cumberland, Maryland: Hobby House Press, Inc., 1988.

Merrill, Madeline O. *The Art of Dolls, 1700-1940*. Cumberland, Maryland: Hobby House Press, Inc., 1985.

Noble, John. *Treasury of Beautiful Dolls*. New York: Hawthorn Books, 1971.

Schoonmaker, Patricia N. *Effanbee Dolls: The Formative Years 1910-1929*. Cumberland, Maryland: Hobby House Press, Inc., 1984.

Shoemaker, Rhoda. *Compo Dolls, Cute and Collectible, Vol. I-III*. Menlo Park, California: 1971, 1971 & 1979.

Tarnowska, Maree. *Fashion Dolls*. Cumberland, Maryland: Hobby House Press, Inc., 1986.

About the Author

The name Jan Foulke is synonymous with accurate information. As the author of the *Blue Book of Dolls & Values*®, she is the most quoted source on doll information and the most respected and recognized authority on dolls and doll prices in the world.

Born in Burlington, New Jersey, Jan Foulke has always had a fondness for dolls. She recalls, "Many happy hours of my childhood were spent with dolls as companions, since we lived on a quiet country road, and until I was ten, I was an only child." Jan received a B.A. from Columbia Union College, where she was named to the *Who's Who in American Colleges & Universities* and was graduated with high honors. Jan taught for twelve years in the Montgomery County school system in Maryland, and also supervised student teachers in English for the University of Maryland, where she did graduate work.

Jan and her husband, Howard, who photographs the dolls presented in the *Blue Book*, were both fond of antiquing as a hobby, and in 1972 they decided to open a small antique shop of their own. The interest of their daughter, Beth, in dolls sparked their curiosity about the history of old dolls — an interest that quite naturally grew out of their love of heirlooms. The stock in their antique shop gradually changed and evolved into an antique doll shop.

Early in the development of their antique doll shop, Jan and Howard realized that there was a critical need for an accurate and reliable doll identification and price guide resource. In the early 1970s, the Foulkes teamed up with Hobby House Press (publishers of *Doll Reader*® Magazine) to produce (along with Thelma Bateman) the first *Blue Book of Dolls & Values*, originally published in 1974. Since that time, the Foulkes have exclusively authored and illustrated the nine successive editions, and today the *Blue Book* is regarded by collectors and dealers as the definitive source for doll prices and values.

Jan and Howard Foulke now dedicate all of their professional time to the world of dolls: writing and illustrating books and articles, appraising collections, lecturing on antique dolls, acting as consultants to museums, auction houses and major collectors, and selling dolls both by mail order and through exhibits at major shows throughout the United States. Mrs. Foulke is a member of the United Federation of Doll Clubs, Doll Collectors of America, and the International Doll Academy.

Mrs. Foulke has appeared on numerous TV talk shows and is often quoted in newspaper and magazine articles as the ultimate source for doll pricing and trends in collecting. In 1985, both "USA Today" and "The Washington Post" observed that the *Blue Book of Dolls & Values* was "the bible of doll collecting."

In addition to her work on the ten editions of the *Blue Book of Dolls & Values*, Jan Foulke has also authored: *Focusing on Effanbee Composition Dolls; A Treasury of Madame Alexander Dolls; Kestner, King of Dollmakers; Simon & Halbig: The Artful Aspect; Focusing on Gebruder Heubach Dolls; Doll Classics;* and *Focusing on Dolls.*

Index

Text references are indicated in alphabetical and numerical order. Often there is a photograph to accompany the text reference. References to illustrations indicate that photographs appear on a different page.